D0122773

By the Same Author

The Monkey Puzzle: *Reshaping the Evolutionary Tree* (with John Gribbin)
Not Work Alone: *A Cross-Cultural View of Activities Superfluous to Survival* (ed. with Roger Lewin)

MAN-MADE LIFE

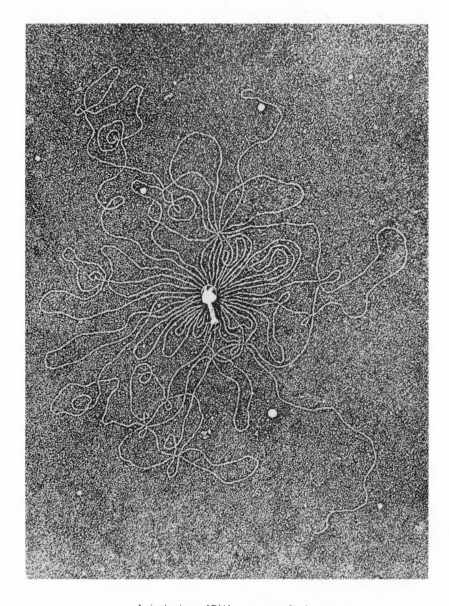

A single piece of DNA spews out of a virus.
(*Courtesy Albrecht K. Kleinschmidt and Elsevier Biomedical Press*)

MAN-MADE LIFE

AN OVERVIEW OF THE SCIENCE,
TECHNOLOGY AND COMMERCE
OF GENETIC ENGINEERING

JEREMY
CHERFAS

PANTHEON BOOKS, NEW YORK

LIBRARY

MAY 2 6 1983

UNIVERSITY OF THE PACIFIC

407116

Copyright © 1982 by Jeremy Cherfas

All rights reserved under International and Pan-American
Copyright Conventions. Published in the United States by
Pantheon Books, a division of Random House, Inc., New
York, and simultaneously in Canada by Random House of
Canada Limited, Toronto. Originally published in Great
Britain by Basil Blackwell, London.

Library of Congress Cataloging in Publication Data

Cherfas, Jeremy.
  Man-made life.

  Bibliography: p.
  Includes index.
  1. Genetic engineering. 2. Genetic engineering—
Industrial applications. I. Title.
QH442.C46   1983   660'.6   82-14379
ISBN 0-394-52926-X
ISBN 0-394-71312-5 (pbk.)

Manufactured in the United States of America
First American Edition

CONTENTS

PREFACE

The instructions needed to construct and maintain a living organism are written in a four-letter code. The letters are grouped into words three letters long. Behind that absurdly simple account lies a great research effort by a diverse body of scientists, a century-long enterprise that came to fruition towards the end of the 1960s when the final words of the code were deciphered. In the few years since, molecular biologists have gone way beyond those achievements. They can now read the code with ease, manufacture new bits of code that will do things as instructed, and shuffle instructions between utterly different types of organism. They can engineer genes to suit almost any purpose. This book is about the tools the genetic engineers use and the tasks they tackle with them.

The tools and the knowledge to use them have emerged from basic research, and while they will undoubtedly serve the community at large in the future, they have already made extremely important contributions to our understanding of the processes of life. Much information has been uncovered that simply could not have been known just ten years ago. The most mind-boggling of these concerns a virus called ΦX174. It multiplies within bacteria, and carries its instructions as a string of 5386 letters. ΦX174 was the first organism to have its genetic message read in its entirety. When Frederick Sanger and his colleagues in Cambridge scrutinized that 'message', they were amazed to find overlapping instructions. The three-letter words that specify one protein contain, within them, an entirely distinct message for a different protein. By shifting the starting position, so that the same letters are grouped into words differently, the virus specifies two proteins in the space for one. I do not consider it hyperbole to call this superb piece of packaging a wonder of evolution, and without the techniques of genetic engineering it would not have been discovered.

The revelations of genetic engineering are awesome and fascinating, but one cannot expect them to affect everyone in the same way. The practical benefits are closer to hand. In February 1982 an issue of the journal *Science* contained some unremarkable looking photographs. One showed a collection of bacteria, the sort of picture that is now fairly commonplace. The bacteria seemed a bit lumpy, but otherwise quite ordinary (see page 166 below). They were, in fact, insulin factories. The lumps were packages of insulin, manufactured by the bacteria in response to instructions from a human insulin gene, deliberately placed in the bacteria by genetic engineers. The other photograph showed a collection of needle-shaped crystals (see page 179). They too looked quite ordinary, until one read that they were crystals of pure interferon. This wonder drug, scourge of viruses and possibly of cancer too, is so hard to obtain that its effects have not yet been properly evaluated. It has always been too impure and too scarce to crystallize. Now here were crystals of pure interferon, and like the insulin they too were made in bacteria according to instructions from a human. In this book you will find the details of how these, and other, marvels were achieved.

The ability to create living organisms to order – 'man-made life' is no exaggeration – brings with it responsibilities. The furore that surrounded the birth of genetic engineering is testimony to the strong passions that this sort of power arouses. Many of us have a deep fear of genetic meddling, a fear that Mary Shelley, for example, capitalized upon in her novel *Frankenstein*. The public response to the scientists' new abilities reflected that fear and uncertainty, and the scientists' own concern was indicated in their decision to halt experimentation while they assessed the completely unknown risks. Now, almost ten years on, genetic engineering is seen as no more dangerous than other forms of microbiology. But the issues of safety and responsibility, and the effects that the commercial aspects of genetic engineering are having on the old academic freedoms, are still cause for concern. Those worries too are discussed in this book. With the knowledge we have today there can no longer be any excuse for the uninformed debate that characterized the early stages. Back in 1977 Alfred Velluci, mayor of Cambridge, Massachusetts, asked the president of the National Academy of Sciences to investigate reports of a hairy, nine-foot creature with orange eyes. Velluci felt that the animal might be connected in some way to genetic engineering work; how, he didn't specify. That sort of thing should not happen now that we know so much more about molecular biology.

This book is about a science, the applications of that science, and the morality of those applications. It is not complete, nor is it definitive, but I hope it is informative. In the nature of things the writing is at times technical, although I have tried to ensure that the detail is understandable. Chapter 4 in particular may seem somewhat daunting, but it describes the basic processes that the genetic engineers use; persevere, and the rest will be that much clearer.

I must acknowledge the help and support given to me by several people. John Clark rekindled my enthusiasm. John Davey was a kind, thoughtful and patient editor. An unknown reader made several suggestions that improved the final product; as is customary, the errors that remain are mine alone. Colleagues at Oxford, notably Marian Dawkins, Alan Grafen and Mark Ridley, were kind enough to listen to me talking about genes when I should perhaps have been talking about behaviour. Roger Lewin is all one could want as a friend and mentor.

Acknowledgement must also be made to the following sources on which some of the figures have been based: figs. 1.2, 1.3, 4.3, 4.7 from Watson, J. D. and Tooze, J., *The DNA Story*, W. H. Freeman and Company, 1981, pp. 539, 565, 567; fig. 2.1 from Campbell, A. M., How viruses insert their DNA into the DNA of the host cell, copyright © 1976 by Scientific American, Inc., all rights reserved; fig. 1.4 from Kornberg, A., The synthesis of DNA, copyright © 1968 by Scientific American, Inc., all rights reserved; figs. 4.1, 4.2 from Cohen, S. N., The manipulation of genes, copyright © 1975 by Scientific American, Inc., all rights reserved; figs. 1.5, 5.1 from Grobstein, C., The recombinant-DNA debate, copyright © 1977 by Scientific American, Inc., all rights reserved; figs. 4.6, 4.8 from Gilbert, W. and Villa-Komaroff, L., Useful proteins from recombinant bacteria, copyright © 1980 by Scientific American Inc., all rights reserved.

London
April 1982

For Sylvia

1

BEGINNINGS

The early history and blossoming of molecular biology

It starts with a thin soup of bacteria cells, about a thousand million individuals suspended in a broth of nutrient chemicals and doubling in number every half hour or so. The soup is cloudy because the cells reflect light, and it is warm because the cells grow best at blood temperature. This culture is to be used as a source of DNA, the most vital of the many chemicals found in living cells.

The first step is to concentrate the cells a bit, remove them from the nourishing broth; the instrument to do this is a centrifuge. The test tube full of cloudy soup is whirled round at about 8000 revolutions per minute. The cells, normally kept suspended in the liquid by the random motion of the molecules around them, are forced down to the bottom of the test tube by centrifugal force, and after 30 minutes or so of this treatment the broth has separated into an absolutely clear liquid above a small pellet, dingy and greyish yellow. The pellet is made up of the compacted mass of cells, and most of the liquid can now be poured away. Now the pellet must be broken up again, the cells resuspended in a small amount of liquid, by vibrating the test tube with a mechanical shaker. Once again we have a cloudy broth, but now it is much thicker than before.

Each bacterial cell has a wall that keeps its insides inside and protected from the environment. To get at the DNA we have to destroy the cell walls and release the cytoplasm within. There are many ways to do this, but the method of choice in most laboratories involves two chemicals. The first is EDTA – ethylenediamine tetra-acetate – which removes magnesium ions (charged atoms) from the cell walls. Without the magnesium, the walls become very weak. The second chemical is SDS – sodium dodecyl sulphate. It is a detergent, and just as washing-up liquid dissolves grease, SDS dissolves the long fatty molecules that make up the cell wall. The combination of EDTA and SDS is an effective mixture, breaking open the cell walls and releasing the chemicals inside. As the cells are dissolved they no longer reflect the light and the mixture becomes transparent once again. After half an hour at body temperature the test tube is clear.

It is also very viscous; where before the broth acted essentially like water, now it is more like egg white. The reason is that the DNA, formerly neatly packaged within the cells, has been released from its confines. It is a long thin molecule, and the swirling DNA strings intertwine to make the liquid sticky. Of course, there is a lot more inside the average bacterial cell than DNA, and the next step is to get rid of some of those other chemicals. The detergent has dealt with the fats; the major remaining impurity is protein, which accounts for about 15 per cent of the average bacterial cell. To get rid of it we add phenol – carbolic acid – though chloroform will do just as well. Carbolic acid found a use as one of the first antiseptics precisely because it does attack proteins, thereby killing the cells. It causes proteins to precipitate out of the solution, and because it is heavier than the liquid the phenol sinks to the bottom and takes the protein with it. Shaking the mixture at this stage would break the delicate DNA strands into small pieces, so we rock the test tube gently back and forth to mix the phenol with the broth. Immediately the mixture becomes even thicker, and grey. Once again, half an hour in the centrifuge separates the protein and phenol from the DNA. At the bottom of the tube is a small clear layer, phenol, and on top of that a thick and faintly repellant white band of coagulated proteins. Above the protein is another layer of clear liquid, and that is the layer that contains the DNA.

Getting the DNA-rich layer out of the tube and away from the protein and phenol is a problem, because any attempt to suck it out is thwarted by the viscosity of the liquid; it pulls itself back out of the end of the pipette. The answer is to use a pipette with a bent tip, and to remove the sticky liquid one drop at a time. That done, you have a test tube full of DNA in solution. What now? The most spectacular trick is to pull the DNA out of the solution and make it into a fibre. Alcohol – ordinary alcohol but absolutely pure – can be poured into the tube where, unlike phenol, it floats above the DNA. A glass rod, dipped through the alcohol and into the DNA, picks up some of the long fibres. As the rod is pulled back through the alcohol the fibres precipitate, and we can draw out of the test tube a long glistening filament, gossamer fine but quite strong, of almost pure DNA.

Suspended from the tip of a glass rod we now have hundreds of thousands of individual DNA strands, lying side by side and making up a fine thread, just as the individual hairs of a sheep are spun to make a thread of wool. What we do with it now is limited only by our imagination.

DNA discovered

DNA – deoxyribonucleic acid – is something of a miracle molecule. The word DNA is far and away the most common single word in the titles of scientific papers, so well known that I was content to launch straight in to its extraction without any further ado, confident that you would be aware of its importance, if not the reasons behind that importance.

But why is DNA so special? Because it contains, coded along its length, all the information needed to construct and maintain the complex machinery of the living cell. It also contains the information needed to reproduce itself, so that, in a very real sense, DNA is a living molecule. Living things are able to reproduce themselves, and DNA can reproduce itself; it really is fundamental to life. Indeed, there are many biologists who view the entire panoply of life, from the precise biochemical reactions guided by enzymes to societies and even ethical behaviour, simply as devices used by DNA to ensure its own survival. These considerations do not concern us here; what is important is that DNA is the primary determining force of every living thing. The information that it contains ultimately directs the manifold complexity of life.

Despite its central importance, DNA spent a long time unrecognized. Johann Friedrich Miescher, a young Swiss of 25 studying in the German town of Tubingen, first found the substance in 1869. Miescher was interested in the chemistry of the cell nucleus, a small body found within the cells of all living things except bacteria. His source of nuclei was the white blood cells that constitute the pus that oozes from surgical wounds, and he plundered the local surgical clinic for discarded dressings. White blood cells have relatively large nuclei, which Miescher diligently separated from their surrounding cytoplasm. His analyses revealed the presence of a hitherto unknown compound, which was acidic and rich in phosphorus, and was apparently organized into very large molecules. He called the compound 'nuclein', and when he moved back to his

native Basle was able to exploit a less unpleasant source of nuclei –
sperm cells from the salmon that thrived then in the Rhine – to
continue his studies of this fascinating compound.

Richard Altmann, a student of Miescher's, coined the phrase
'nucleic acid', and within a few years the essential chemistry of the
compound had been quite thoroughly worked out. There is a sugar
– a ribose – that contains five carbon atoms in a ring, and a
phosphorus atom surrounded by four oxygen atoms to make a
phosphate group. It is the phosphate group that makes nucleic
acids acidic, and it also links the sugars together in an unending
alternation of sugar and phosphate. Attached to each sugar in this
chain is a third type of compound called a base; the triptych of
sugar, base and linking phosphate group is called a nucleotide. But
while sugar and phosphate alternated predictably along the nucleic
acid molecule, the bases were altogether more perplexing. They
came in five varieties, known as guanine, adenine, cytosine,
thymine and uracil (usually designated simply by their initials: G,
A, C, T and U); and although all forms of life contain nucleic acids,
the precise ratios of the five bases vary from one to the other.

Later, by the 1920s, two different nucleic acids had been
distinguished. One, found primarily inside the cell nucleus, was
DNA. The other, more common in the cytoplasm around the
nucleus, contained a very slightly different sugar: ribose instead of
DNA's deoxyribose, which lacks a single atom of oxygen. This was
called ribonucleic acid, RNA. The two nucleic acid molecules are
alike in many respects, both consisting of a long chain of alternating sugar and phosphate with a base attached to each sugar. RNA
and DNA both contain adenine, guanine and cytosine, but
whereas in DNA the fourth base is thymine, in RNA it is the
chemically similar uracil (see figure 1.1).

Quite apart from discovering DNA, Miescher also displayed
great insight into the problems posed by the biochemicals of living
things. And in addition to insight he showed great foresight. Three
years before he died of tuberculosis at the age of 55, he wrote a
letter to his uncle, in which he pointed out that large biochemical
molecules often consist of a repetition of similar, but not identical,
subunits. This, Miescher said, gave these molecules the potential
to harbour the hereditary message, 'just as the words and concepts
of all languages can find expression in twenty-four to thirty letters
of the alphabet'.[1] Alas, as Horace Freeland Judson points out,

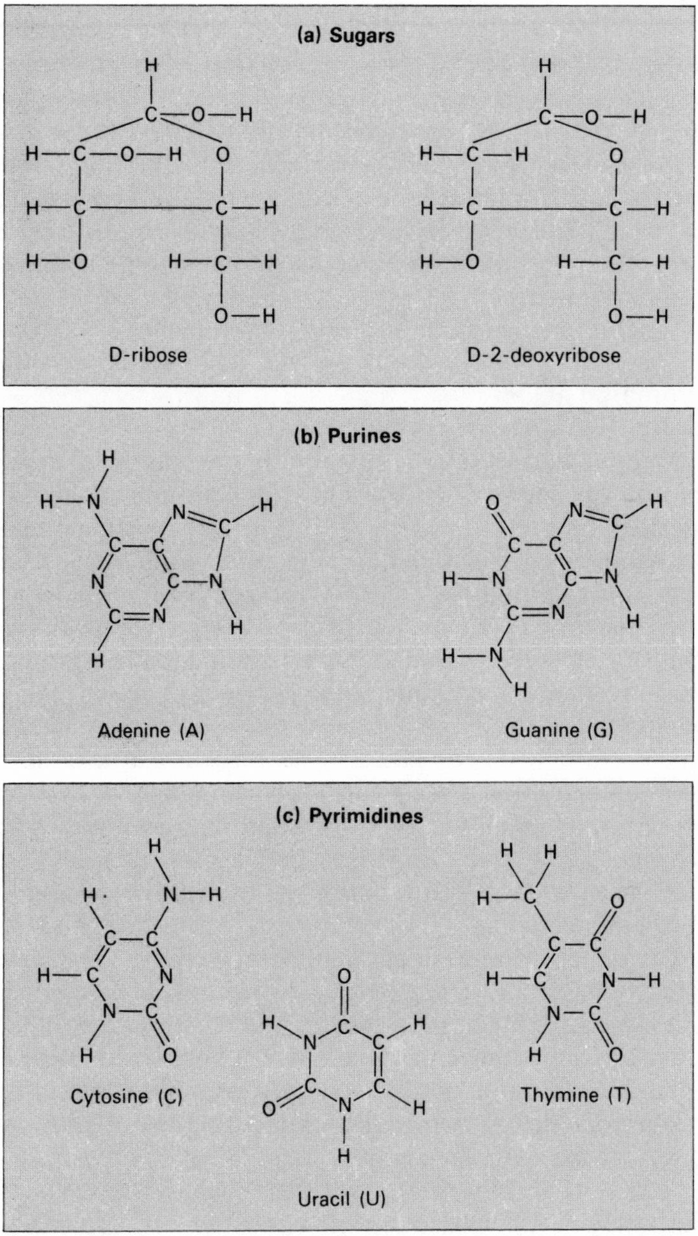

Figure 1.1
The components of nucleic acids (H = hydrogen, C = carbon, N = nitrogen, O = oxygen). Sugars are strung together with phosphate groups, and a base is attached to each sugar. DNA uses D-2-deoxyribose sugar and RNA D-ribose. Both nucleic acids use the same two purines, but thymine in DNA is replaced by uracil in RNA.

'Miescher's notion was fatally imprecise. The molecules he offered as examples were albumin and haemoglobin, both proteins.'[2]

Indeed, the central importance of DNA to heredity was a long time in the recognizing, and most biochemists saw things much as Miescher had. Proteins were the interesting molecules; nucleic acids, which had been located tightly bound to proteins in the chromosomes that divided so neatly whenever the cell divided, were an irrelevancy.

Incriminated at last

In 1928, biologists were astounded by an experiment of deceptive simplicity, an experiment that eventually incriminated DNA as the molecule of heredity. Frederick Griffith, a doctor doing research at the Ministry of Health's Pathological Laboratory in London, injected mice with two different preparations of the disease-causing bacteria *Streptococcus pneumoniae*, also known as pneumococcus. One preparation contained a mutant form of the bacterium that did not, alone, have any harmful effects. The other contained the usual, virulent and lethal, form of pneumococcus, but the bacteria had been killed by heating the culture; this preparation too had no ill-effects when injected alone. The mice that received the double injection of two harmless preparations died, and from their blood Griffith collected and cultured live and virulent pneumococci indistinguishable from those that had been dead when injected.

Nobody knew what to think of this strange phenomenon, which apparently made nonsense of what was known of genetics and inheritance. But 'bacterial transformation', as it was called, was real enough, and the experiment was quickly and successfully repeated in laboratories around the world. One laboratory in particular took up the challenge of transformation, that of Oswald T. Avery at the Rockefeller Institute in New York. Avery's colleagues first of all discovered that they could do the experiment without the mice. The two forms of pneumococcus, virulent and non-virulent, can easily be grown on artificial media, and they look very different. The virulent sort forms a smooth glistening colony, the result of a mucus coat that surrounds each cell and protects it from the defences of the hapless host. The non-virulent mutant grows into rough crinkled colonies; it lacks the protective mucus coat and so is successfully repulsed when it tries to invade a host. Cultures of rough pneumococci, grown in the presence of heat-killed smooth pneumococci, gave rise to smooth colonies. Late in 1931 James Alloway, also a member of Avery's laboratory, went further. He ground up the virulent smooth bacteria and passed the mixture through a sieve so fine that the empty cell walls, other debris and any unbroken cells could not pass through. Even this filtered extract had the power to transform rough mutants. What is more, when Alloway added alcohol to the filtered extract, he ended up with a viscous, 'thick syrupy precipitate'.[3]

Over the next dozen or so years Avery and his team single-mindedly pursued the 'transforming factor', as it came to be known. At first, like everyone else, they thought it might be a protein. But after many years of unremitting effort the evidence was overwhelming. The transforming principle – and it took 20 gallons (75 litres) of pneumococcus culture to produce less than a hundredth of an ounce (25 milligrams) of the stuff – behaved in every respect like a nucleic acid and not a bit like a protein. It was not affected by the enzymes that digest proteins, nor did it show up in chemical tests for proteins. Enzymes known to attack DNA destroyed the transforming principle utterly, but it was not touched by those that worked only on RNA. It had to be DNA that carried the hereditary message down the generations, but how?

A second classic experiment clinched the vital role of nucleic acids in heredity. Alfred Hershey and Martha Chase, at the Cold Spring Harbor Laboratory on Long Island, were trying to unravel the reproduction of the minute viruses known as 'bacteriophages' (because they infect bacteria). These viruses consist of a protein coat surrounding a strand of nucleic acid. A single virus can infect a bacterium, which bursts open some 30 minutes later to release a shower of hundreds of new viruses, each a replica of the infecting phage. The question was whether the protein coat had anything to do with the infective process, or whether only the nucleic acid was involved. Hershey and Chase made use of the fact that DNA does not contain sulphur, which protein does, while protein does not contain the phosphorus that DNA does. They grew phage and bacteria in a culture that contained radioactive phosphorus, thus tagging the nucleic acid; or they used 'hot' (that is, radioactive) sulphur in the culture, thereby attaching the radioactive label to the proteins. Then they infected unlabelled bacteria with the hot phage, separated the empty protein coat from the bacteria, and tried to see where the label had gone.

The difficult part was separating phage from bacterium; all sorts of grinding arrangements failed to do the trick, and the final breakthrough came with the loan of a liquidizer or blender. A few moments in the liquidizer easily broke the phage coats away from the cells, as revealed by electron micrographs, and a centrifuge separated the bacterial cells from the culture liquid and discarded viral protein coats. Labelled protein always stayed in the liquid; none came down with the cells. Labelled DNA, by contrast, stayed with the cells, which eventually released fully infective newly made viruses. It was not as rigorous as Avery's series of studies, but the work of Hershey and Chase – remembered today as the 'Waring

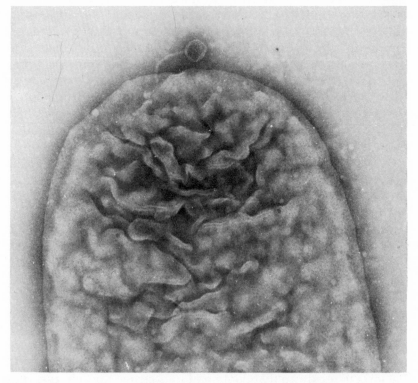

Plate 1.1
An empty lambda bacteriophage, which has just inserted its DNA into the *Escherichia coli* it is attached to. (*Photograph by Maria Schnoss, supplied by Jack D. Griffith*)

blender experiment' – confirmed that the transforming principle, the source of hereditary information, was DNA. But it got no nearer to the tantalizing problem: what was it about DNA that enabled it to fulfil the functions of a memory bank?

Two gloved hands: the golden helix

The story of the delicious solution to the problem of DNA's structure needs no retelling here.[4] James Watson and Francis Crick devised their model in a flurry of activity in the spring of 1953. They introduced it to the world with an opening paragraph remarkable for its understatement: 'We wish to suggest a structure for the salt of deoxyribose nucleic acid (DNA). This structure has novel features which are of considerable biological interest.'[5] The structure was the renowned double helix, and it permitted DNA to fulfil its assigned role with great simplicity.

The key to the double helix is the jigsaw-like fit of the the bases. Guanine and adenine, two of the bases, are composed of two linked rings of carbon and nitrogen. They are members of the class of compounds known as 'purines'. Cytosine and thymine have but a single carbon–nitrogen ring; they are called 'pyrimidines'. What Watson and Crick realized was that guanine could join with cytosine, by means of links called 'hydrogen bonds', to form a double structure that had a shape exactly that of adenine linked to thymine. The only difference is that guanine and cytosine join at three places while adenine and thymine link at only two places; aside from this, the joined purine–pyrimidine pairs are all but identical (see figure 1.2). And because of the difference in the number of available links, guanine will link only with cytosine and adenine will link only with thymine. (Occasionally the 'wrong' linkages will occur, but not often; joining thymine to guanine is like trying to put a two-pin plug into a three pin socket – it can be done, but it isn't easy.)

Watson and Crick's notion of linking purine to pyrimidine made sense of an observation that had been around, more or less unheeded, for five years or more. Erwin Chargaff had measured the amount of each base in DNAs from several different sources: bacteria, man, ox, pig, sheep and yeast. He discovered that these various DNAs differed in the overall composition of their bases,

Beginnings

but that the ratio of thymine to adenine, like the ratio of cytosine to guanine, was always very close to one. In other words, while the relative proportions of the bases varied from species to species, the amount of purine was always the same as the amount of pyrimidine and, furthermore, the amount of adenine matched the amount of thymine while the amount of guanine matched the amount of

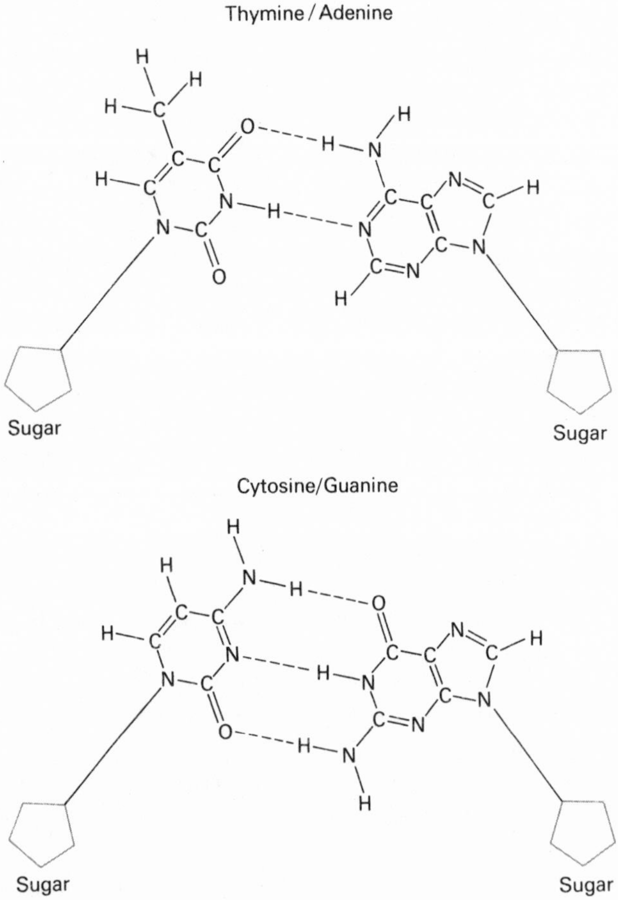

Figure 1.2
Bonding between bases. The purine–pyrimidine pairs on opposite strands are held together by so-called hydrogen bonds (dashed lines). The shape of the TA pair exactly matches the CG pair, which is why the order of the bases along the DNA does not affect the molecule's shape.

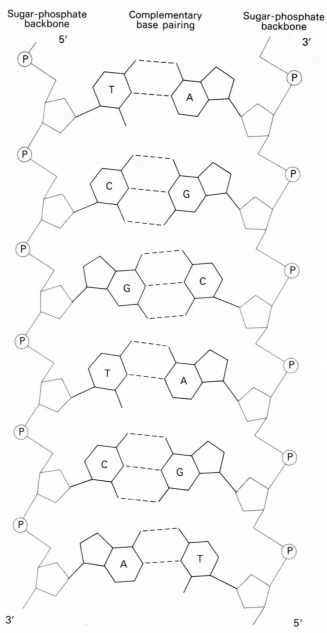

Figure 1.3
Complementary base-pairing. The two DNA strands run in opposite directions, with hydrogen bonds between complementary pairs holding them together.

cytosine. Base-pairing, as envisaged by Watson and Crick, made Chargaff's ratio inevitable (see figure 1.3).

So in the double helix there are two strands of DNA that twine about one another, linked by the paired bases. The sugar–phosphate backbone has a direction, because the phosphate group joins the third carbon (numbered by agreed convention) of one ribose ring to the fifth carbon of the next. The two ends of the chain are thus labelled the 3′ and 5′ ends respectively, and in the double helix the chains run in opposite directions. The 3′ end of one chain is opposite the 5′ end of the other. The familiar analogy is that of a spiral staircase, where the sugar–phosphate backbone of each strand represents a banister and the joined bases are the steps themselves (see figure 1.5).

Watson and Crick provided the key measurements of the helix, measurements that conformed to the data then available and that have since been confirmed by more precise methods. The steps of the staircase, the purine–pyrimidine pairs, are 3.4 angstroms apart (1 angstrom = one ten-millionth of a millimetre), and the helix

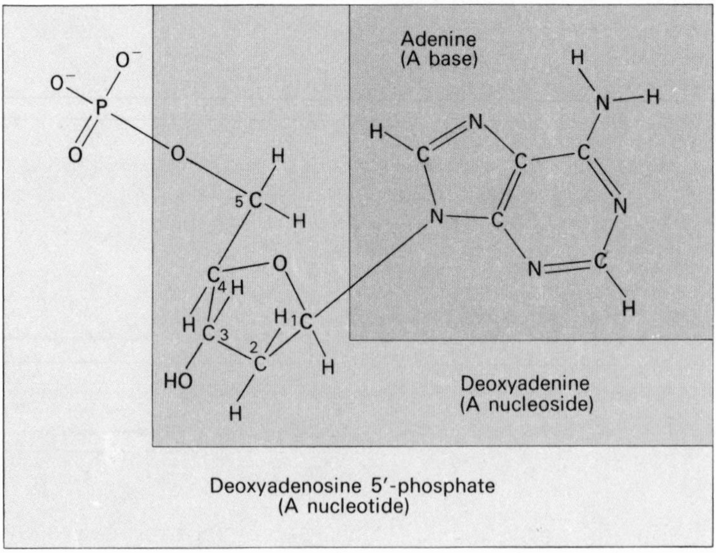

Figure 1.4
Naming of parts. A base attached to a sugar is a nucleoside. With an added phosphate group instead of one hydrogen atom, the nucleoside becomes a nucleotide. Nucleic acids are long chains of linked nucleotides. (*Copyright © 1968 by Scientific American, Inc.*)

goes through one complete turn every ten rungs, every 34 angstroms. The entire molecule is about 20 angstroms across, but may be 1 millimetre or more long. To put this into some sort of perspective, the average DNA of a bacterium has proportions equivalent to a violin string 1 millimetre across and 400 metres long. The weight of the molecule is obviously proportional to its length, but DNA is so thin that a molecule stretching the 150 million kilometres between the earth and the sun would weigh less than half a gram.[6]

So much for the physical nature of DNA; the interest of the Watson–Crick model lies not so much in what it is as in what it does. Because of the pairing of the basis, the two strands that make up a double helix are, in a sense, mirror images of one another. Where there is an A on one there will be a T on the other, and a sequence of, say, CACG will always find itself opposite a sequence of GTGC. Each strand contains all the information needed to construct a complementary strand to twin with. If the double helix unzipped, and if there were a ready supply of component nucleotides and enzymes to join them together, two double strands would be constructed from one. CACG on one strand would pair up with G, T, G and C, while on the other strand GTGC would pair with C, A, C and G. The molecule would reproduce. As Watson and Crick said, 'It has not escaped our notice that the specific pairing we have postulated immediately suggests a possible copying mechanism for the genetic material.'[7] Each strand of the double helix could act as a template for the entire duplex. Showing that this was indeed the case was again a matter for experiments, some intuitive and brilliant, others thorough and methodical but no less brilliant.

Arthur Kornberg's group at Washington University in St Louis, Missouri, extracted a complex of bacterial enzymes that would synthesize DNA from raw materials. The synthesis would work only if all four nucleotides were present at the same time, and it also required the presence of a small amount of natural DNA as a sort of primer. The suggestion was that the enzyme system made the new DNA by replicating the primer strands and not by assembling the nucleotides from scratch. Later they showed that DNA synthesized in this way was every bit as active as the natural original.

The real clincher, though, was an experiment devised by

Matthew Meselson, a young graduate student from Chicago. With Franklin Stahl at the California Institute of Technology, Meselson performed an experiment that James Watson called 'classic', and that Watson's predecessor as director of Cold Spring Harbor, John Cairns, called, without qualification, 'the most beautiful experiment in biology'.[8] The idea was to distinguish the copy DNA from the original, and the obvious approach was to try and label one, but not the other, with radioactive isotopes. Meselson and Stahl went another route. They decided to try and make the labelled DNA heavier than ordinary DNA, but they needed to devise a method of separating light from heavy DNA. The method is called 'density-gradient centrifugation', and though it sounds complex, it isn't.

The buoyancy of an object in liquid depends exactly on the mass of liquid it displaces – Archimedes' principle. Meselson and Stahl quickly discovered that the chemical caesium chloride, analogous to common salt but much heavier, can be made into a solution so dense that DNA will just float on it. The clever bit was to rotate the solution of caesium chloride in an ultracentrifuge, spinning it round at about 45 000 revolutions per minute, where a force 140 times stronger than gravity pulled at the molecules. After a few hours of this the heavy caesium ions tended to collect near the bottom of the tube, forming a gradient of density along the whirling tube. DNA placed in the tube with the caesium solution would collect at a specific point on the gradient. The molecules that started out near the bottom would find, as the caesium collected near them, that they were more buoyant than the surrounding liquid, and so would float away from the end of the tube. Those nearer the top would sink as the caesium was forced away. The migrating DNA molecules would gather at a point where the density of the solution was exactly equivalent to their own density. And if there were two sorts of DNA, of different density, they would separate out and collect at different points on the gradient.

Meselson and Stahl grew billions of bacteria in a broth that contained a heavy isotope of nitrogen in the form of ammonium chloride. After 14 generations they were confident that all the nitrogen in the bacteria's DNA was of the heavy variety. They took a sample, centrifuged the cells down, and chilled the pellet. Then they added a huge excess of ordinary ammonium chloride, made with the normal, light isotope of nitrogen, to the growing cells in the broth. At intervals over the next few generations they removed

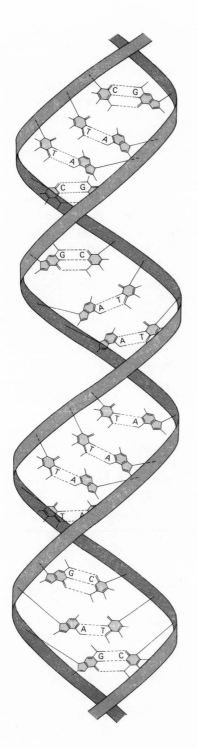

Figure 1.5
The double helix. This simplified diagram shows an idealized view of two DNA strands, their sugar–phosphate backbones forming the twin helices, which are held together by bonds between pairs of complementary bases. Adenine always pairs with thymine and guanine always pairs with cytosine. (*Copyright© 1977 by Scientific American, Inc.*)

further samples, spun the cells down, and chilled them. Finally, with the experimental samples complete, they took a reference sample of cells that had been growing on ordinary nitrogen all the time. Meselson and Stahl broke the cells open with detergent and extracted the DNA. They added each lot of DNA to a solution of caesium chloride and spun the tubes at 44 700 r.p.m. for 24 hours. A photograph taken by ultraviolet light as the tubes spun round revealed the bands of DNA (see plate 1.2).

The first sample, harvested from cells in heavy nitrogen, formed a band in the denser region near the bottom of the tube. The reference sample, of normal DNA, formed a similar band at the top. The two types, mixed together and then spun, separated cleanly into two bands, one above the other. Those were the two markers. If, as Watson and Crick suggested, each strand of DNA acted as a template for the other, the new molecules would contain one old strand and one new. At the end of the first generation of bacteria grown in ordinary nitrogen, all the DNA would contain one heavy strand and one normal strand; the density of the hybrid strand would be midway between that of pure heavy DNA and pure normal DNA, so the DNA from the first generation would collect midway between the two markers. It did. In the second generation there would be two kinds of DNA: half, constructed on the template of old, heavy DNA would be hybrid; the rest would be of normal density. In the spinning tubes, that is exactly what Meselson and Stahl saw. The evidence was incontrovertible. DNA reproduced, in the jargon, 'semi-conservatively'. The strands separated and each then accumulated a new partner. The old strands did not stay together, nor were they completely broken up; they were semi-conserved.

Meselson and Stahl provided solid support for Watson and Crick's original intuition, which Crick explained in 1957:

The two chains of the DNA, which fit together as a hand fits into a glove, are separated in some way and the hand then acts as a mold for the formation of a new glove while the glove acts as a mold for a new hand. Thus we finish up with two gloved hands where we had only one before.[9]

The code

Gloved hands are all very well, and go a long way to explain how DNA fulfils its obligations to reproduce faithfully and make new

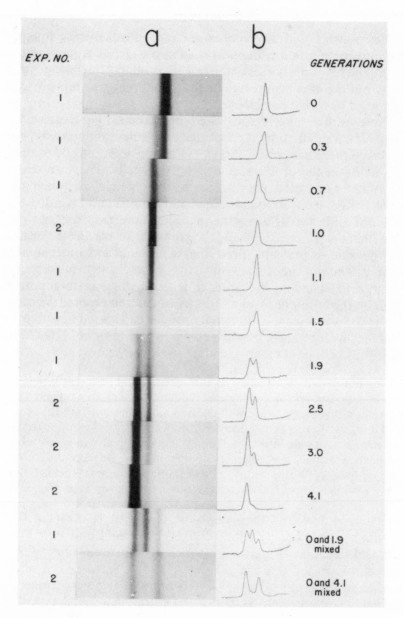

Plate 1.2
Semi-conservative replication of DNA. The dark bands show DNA of different density. (The column labelled b is a trace of the density of the dark bands, used to localize the DNA more accurately.) In the first generation, all the DNA is hybrid and lies between completely heavy and completely light DNA. This demonstrates that new double-stranded DNA is formed from one old strand and a newly synthesized complementary partner. (*Courtesy Matthew Meselson*)

copies of itself. Still the problem remains of exactly how it stores the information that it duplicates so easily. DNA is just a set of plans; the real workhorses of the cell are proteins. It is proteins that carry out the chemical reactions that sustain life, so it is proteins that must be formed by DNA.

Proteins, like nucleic acids, are biopolymers, long chains made up of repeating subunits. The subunits are called 'amino acids', and although there are scores of possible amino acids only 20 of them are found in the proteins made by living cells. They are strung together by so-called 'peptide bonds' to make chains, which may be anywhere from 50 to more than 500 amino acids long. It is the order of amino acids along the peptide chain, the primary structure, that determines the shape the protein will take and the tasks it will be able to perform. Fred Sanger, then at the Biochemistry Department of Cambridge University, began in 1945 a mammoth attempt to elucidate the primary structure of one rather small protein, the hormone insulin. This was an extremely bold decision, for it was by no means certain that proteins had a fixed structure, or that they were long polypeptide chains, as J. S. Fruton, a biochemist turned historian, makes clear:

In view of the various speculations during the period 1920–1940, Sanger's decision to embark on a long and difficult task clearly reflected the conviction that proteins are well-defined molecules in which the amino acid units are linked by peptide bonds to form long polypeptide chains. His success, not only in showing this to be true, but also in giving others confidence to attack the sequences of other proteins, marked the end of a century-long collective effort in which many eminent chemists and biologists made important discoveries but also took wrong turnings.[10]

Sanger's boldness is without question. He got his reward, too. The insulin he obtained as purified crystals from the Boots Pure Drug Co. Ltd Research Department, which of course was interested in the hormone for treating diabetics. People have talked about tonnes of pancreas being involved, but as Sanger told me, 'we probably got through 5–10 grams of this material [crystalline insulin]; this would have corresponded to 50 kilograms of pancreas'.[11] The average cow weighs about 500 kilos, and its pancreas about 400 grams, so Sanger's 10 grams of insulin required about 125 cows, 62 ½ tonnes; but he did not have to do the purification himself.

Ten years and ten grams of insulin after his bold decision, Sanger had what he sought: the precise order of the 51 amino acids, arranged in two separate chains, that go to make up the insulin of the cow. It was the amino acid sequence that gave the protein its properties, and it was the DNA that somehow specified the sequences of the amino acids (see figure 1.6).

According to the Watson–Crick model, the pairs of bases that connect the double helix are set – AT and CG – but there is nothing to specify the order of bases along a single strand. Indeed, part of the beauty of the model is that every base-pair is equivalent as far as the structure of the DNA is concerned, so that they can be strung together to make up any sequence along the strand. That being the case, it became natural to think, as Miescher had (erroneously) done 60 years earlier, in terms of some sort of equivalence between the sequence of bases along the DNA and the sequence of amino acids along the protein. At first it was thought that there might be a direct physical connection, that the different amino acids would somehow fit into the wide groove along the double helix at specific places determined by the nucleotide sequence, later to be enzymically fastened end to end into the protein chain. Then it became clear that this could not be, and that there had to be some sort of intermediary between the nucleotide sequence along the gene and the amino acid sequence along the protein specified by that gene. A code translated the message of the gene into the structure of the protein, and the goal in laboratories all over became to crack the genetic code.

Crick, as usual, saw a way to do just that: 'The genetic code could be broken easily if one could determine both the amino acid sequence of a protein and the base sequence of the piece of nucleic acid that codes it. A simple comparison of the two sequences would yield the code'.[12] At the time this approach was simply impossible. The protein could certainly be sequenced, although the effort that Sanger put into insulin was enormous, but nobody knew even how to begin a search for the insulin gene. Today it could be done, and easily; the irony is that it would be all but impossible to decipher the genetic code from the sort of Rosetta Stone comparison Crick had in mind. There are vast stretches of DNA within many genes that never show up in the protein products of those genes. Because we know the code, we recognize these silent stretches for the interlopers they are; without a knowledge of the code, they would

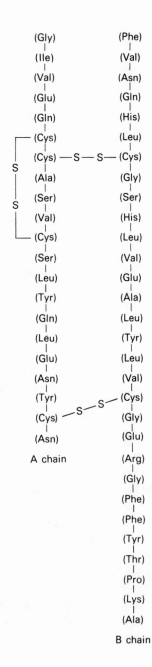

Figure 1.6
Insulin, the first protein to be deciphered. The 51 amino acids that make up insulin are strung together in two chains. The chains are held together by sulphur bridges between cysteine groups. (Full names of the amino acids are given in table 1.1.)

have made life very difficult indeed for any would-be genetic cryptologist.

As it was, indirect methods provided a very good picture of the way information was stored as DNA and translated into proteins. A number of threads came together in the early 1960s to enable molecular biologists to crack the genetic code. There was Francis Crick's formulation, in 1958, of the Central Dogma of Molecular Biology: information could be transferred only from nucleic acids to proteins, not the other way round. There was the postulation, and subsequent discovery, of an intermediary made of RNA that acts as a go-between from the gene on the DNA to the ribosomes, small organelles where proteins are made. This became known as 'messenger RNA', or mRNA. Another hypothetical molecule, called the 'adaptor' by Sydney Brenner, had the job of reading the coded message and converting the sequence of bases into the specific amino acid that was called for. These too were soon isolated, and again turned out to be made of RNA. They ferry the amino acids to the ribosomes and their correct spot in the growing protein chain, and they are called 'transfer RNA', or tRNA. The Central Dogma became 'DNA makes RNA makes protein' (see figure 1.7).

Elegant experiments showed that genes and the proteins they coded were indeed colinear; the information along the gene

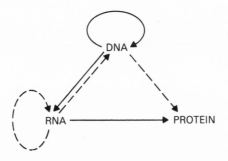

Figure 1.7
The Central Dogma. Information can pass between the two sorts of nucleic acid, and from both of these to proteins, but it cannot pass from proteins back to nucleic acids. The solid arrows represent routine transfers; the broken ones, transfer under special circumstances.

matched the information along the protein. Charles Yanofsky and his colleagues at Stanford laboriously collected variants of the bacterium *Escherichia coli* that had mutations in a particular enzyme. They found the position in the protein chain of each altered amino acid, and compared them with maps of the mutations in the genes. The order of the different amino acid changes along the protein matched exactly the order of the mutations along the gene. At the same time, Sydney Brenner at Cambridge was exploiting a class of mutant phages called 'amber mutants'. These had the peculiar property of stopping protein manufacture too soon, producing only partial fragments of the normal coat proteins. (Once the code had been cracked, it became clear that amber mutants had a stop sign misplaced in the middle of the gene.) Brenner compared the size of the fragment made by each amber mutant with the distance of the mutation from the end of the DNA (which he measured, like Yanofsky, by classical genetic mapping methods). Again, the orders matched. DNA and protein were colinear; the order of information along one specified the order of information along the other.

From all this evidence, and a great deal of their own extremely elegant work with classical genetics, Crick and Brenner deduced three fundamental properties of the code. First, the code is made up of triplets; one amino acid is represented by three nucleotides in the mRNA. The triplet is called a 'codon', and it behaves like a word in English. Three-letter words are the smallest possible units that will convey all the meaning of the DNA in a language of only four letters. Single-letter words are obviously out, and so too are two-letter words, because there are only 16 different two-letter words but 20 amino acids. It had to be triplets, which provide 64 different combinations, more than enough to specify the 20 amino acids. (Four-letter words would be an inappropriate waste.) Second, because there are 64 codons but only 20 amino acids, the code is degenerate. Any amino acid can correspond to more than one codon. Finally, the code is sequential and non-overlapping. The nucleotides are read, in groups of three, beginning at some definite starting place.

All three inferences were confirmed by experiment, except that some 20 years after the attack on the code began Fred Sanger's group in Cambridge found a partial exception to the final point. The bacteriophage ΦX174 – whose entire DNA sequence is fully known – has a couple of overlapping genes. The same single stretch of DNA codes for one protein if you start at one nucleotide, and for another entirely different protein if you start at another. This is a miracle of packaging, squeezing the most information into a short stretch of DNA, but it is not clear just how widespread overlapping genes are.

Table 1.1 The genetic code

First position (5′ end)	Second position				Third position (3′ end)
	U	C	A	G	
U	Phenylalanine	Serine	Tyrosine	Cysteine	U
	Phenylalanine	Serine	Tyrosine	Cysteine	C
	Leucine	Serine	Ochre (Stop)	(Stop)	A
	Leucine	Serine	Amber (Stop)	Tryptophan	G
C	Leucine	Proline	Histidine	Arginine	U
	Leucine	Proline	Histidine	Arginine	C
	Leucine	Proline	Glutamine	Arginine	A
	Leucine	Proline	Glutamine	Arginine	G
A	Isoleucine	Threonine	Asparagine	Serine	U
	Isoleucine	Threonine	Asparagine	Serine	C
	Isoleucine	Threonine	Lysine	Arginine	A
	Methionine	Threonine	Lysine	Arginine	G
G	Valine	Alanine	Aspartic Acid	Glycine	U
	Valine	Alanine	Aspartic Acid	Glycine	C
	Valine	Alanine	Glutamic Acid	Glycine	A
	Valine	Alanine	Glutamic Acid	Glycine	G

The details of the code were sorted out in three or four series of mutually reinforcing experiments. Marshall Nirenberg of the National Institutes of Health at Bethesda, Maryland, devised a cell-free system, like Kornberg's DNA synthesizing system, that would make proteins. He added radioactively labelled amino acids and several types of synthetic RNA, and looked to see which

amino acids were incorporated into peptide chains. The method
had its drawbacks, chiefly that it gave the composition of the codon
but not the actual order of bases, but nevertheless 35 of the 40
codons that Nirenberg had cracked by 1965 turned out to be
correct. Gobind Khorana at Wisconsin also deciphered the code,
and he and Nirenberg confirmed one another's results. Nirenberg
also took a different look at the code with his colleague Philip
Leder. They invented what has become known as the 'triplet
binding assay', a technique that allowed them to see which amino
acid was associated with which codon. Nirenberg and Leder mixed
particular known mRNA triplets with radioactive transfer RNAs
and ribosomes in a system that mimicked the living cells, and then
passed the whole lot through a filter made of nitrocellulose. The
ribosomes, with the single triplet mRNA and attached amino acid,
stuck to the paper, while all the other amino acids and their tRNAs
passed right through. Twenty sets of amino acids for each mRNA
triplet, each with a different one made artificially radioactive,
provided almost the entire code, 50 of the 64 codons. The rest,
including three 'stop' signals and the 'start' signal, came slowly
through other techniques, and by the end of 1966 the decoding of
DNA was complete. Every triplet was known and, to some people's surprise, the code was the same in all organisms. It didn't
matter whether the DNA was in a man, a microbe or a marigold;
the code was identical. It was a universal code, powerful evidence
that all life had descended from a single successful ancestor with
one working code.

The calm

Towards the end of the 1960s an outsider looking at molecular
biology might have perceived a certain sterility to it all. The big
problems – genes, DNA, the genetic code – had been solved and
the army of scientists appeared to be in that seemingly sterile phase
when they learn more and more about less and less. The broad
outlines of the picture had been delineated, and it remained only to
fill in the fine detail. DNA, the double helix, replicated itself with
the aid of enzymes. The hereditary message of the genes was
carried as triplets of nucleotides along the DNA, and these were
converted into mRNA, ferried away from the nucleus and to the

ribosomes. There they directed the synthesis of proteins, different sorts of tRNA bringing the requisite amino acids along and reading the code words. How exactly the cell regulated the active working of some genes and the suppression of others was a matter of detail. The work was routine. The excitement of the early days seemed to have resolved itself from a frantic race for knowledge into a gentle pursuit of greater understanding. This was reflected in published works. While researching this book, I looked through every issue of many journals and magazines. One, *American Scientist*, which covers all that is excellent in science, carried seven articles on molecular biology in the ten years after 1965, and none in the preceding five years.

The calm, however, was about to be shattered. Just around the corner lay discoveries that were to change the entire face of molecular biology: sequencing techniques to do in a couple of months what had once taken years; enzymes to snip DNA cleanly and at known points into manageable chunks; other enzymes to join the chunks together again in the desired order; vastly improved methods for extracting and purifying genes. The toolkit of the genetic engineer was beginning to be assembled. The long, slow relay from Miescher, through Griffith and Avery, Watson, Crick, Brenner, Nirenberg and Khorana, Sanger, Meselson and all the other pioneer participants, had begun to accelerate.

2

RESTRICTION

The development of the precision scalpels that make genetic engineering possible

Richard Roberts, a senior investigator at the Cold Spring Harbor Laboratory on Long Island, New York, is a collector. Not of stamps, or butterflies, or even beermats, but of enzymes. And the enzymes he collects are no ordinary enzymes; they are the machine tools of the genetic engineer, the precision cutters that allow the researcher to slice DNA cleanly at any known point. From time to time Roberts publishes his list in one of the learned journals; in 1978 he had about 160, and by 1980 the list had grown to 212.[1] The list is now published each year in January, and Roberts fully expects the 1982 edition to top 300.

The published list grew out of a series of informal versions that Roberts circulated, which molecular biologists all over the world found enormously useful. They now help to keep the catalogue up to date by sending Roberts the information whenever they discover a new cutting enzyme. But what are these enzymes? Where did they spring from and how do they work?

Made in *E. Coli*

Back in 1952, at the University of Illinois, Salvador Luria and his assistant Mary Human began to investigate a very interesting problem. The targets of their curiosity were bacteriophages, the so-called T phages, that infect the bacterium *Escherichia coli*.[2]

Spread on to a nutritive agar jelly and kept warm, a thin suspension of *E. coli* cells will double every 30 minutes or so, quickly forming a smooth greyish-yellow carpet over the surface of the jelly. But if the suspension is deliberately infected with bacteriophage, about one virus for every 10 000 cells, and then grown as before, the bacterial lawn looks very different. Instead of being smooth and flawless, it is pockmarked by several small round holes. Each of these is called a plaque, and represents the site where a bacterial cell that was infected by virus came to rest. The DNA of the virus, injected through the virus's tail into the cell, subverts the bacterial machinery and forces it to obey the coded instructions of the viral genetic message, producing not bacterial components but viral components. These are assembled into new viruses and some time after infection, usually about an hour, the cell bursts and releases 200 or so new viruses (see figure 2.1). These infect neighbouring cells and repeat the process. By the end of 24 hours the myriad offspring of each successful virus have radiated out in a circle, destroying the bacteria around them and creating a clear plaque in the bacterial lawn (see plate 2.1).

There are many different sorts of phage, some labelled T2, T4, T6, T7 and so on, and many different strains of *E. coli*. Some strains of *E. coli* seemed to be protected against infection by certain of the phage types. Luria and Human discovered that growing T2 phage in one host often altered its properties so that it could no longer infect strains that it was usually quite at home in. But the altered phage was able to grow in dysentery bacteria (*Shigella dysenteriae*) and, most mysteriously, the offspring after growth in *Shigella* had regained their full infective power. The change that had come over the phage, whatever it was, was completely reversible, so it was certainly not a genetic mutation. It seemed to depend more on the host machinery that the previous generation had used to create the present viruses than on any property of the phage itself. Further experiments by Guiseppe Bertani in Luria's lab, and Jean Weigle at the California Institute of Technology, confirmed this strange discovery and added more details.

Bertani worked with a different phage, called lambda, which also attacks *E. coli*. Lambda grew beautifully on *E. coli* strain C, but the daughter phages coming out of strain C could not infect strain K. At least, not usually; one in 10 000 of the daughter phages from C did produce a plaque in a lawn of K cells, and every one, rather than 1 in 10 000, of the viruses recovered from that plaque would now grow freely in strain K. They would also grow in strain C, but a single cycle of growth in C immediately changed the virus back so that it was again unable to grow properly in K.

At that stage, it looked as if there were two separate processes involved in the fight between bacteria and their virus parasites. Some strains of bacteria could successfully prevent virus attack. They were said to restrict the growth of certain types of phage. But if the phage could escape the restriction process, the survivors were somehow modified and able to infect the restrictive host freely. The infectiveness of a virus apparently depended on its most recent host.

The systematic observations of Luria, of Bertani, and of Weigle introduced a measure of regularity to the strange phenomenon that

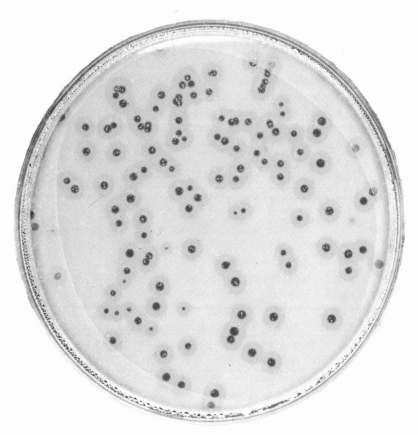

Plate 2.1
Plaques on a bacterial lawn. Each dark circle represents the spread of infection from a single bacterium infected with a bacteriophage. *(Courtesy Public Health Laboratory Service, Colindale)*

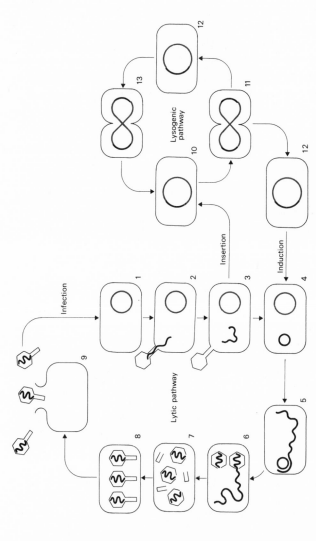

Figure 2.1
Life-cycle of bacteriophage lambda. One of two things happens after a viral particle injects its DNA into an *E. coli* cell (2 and 3). In the lytic pathway, the viral DNA forms a circle (4) and replicates to give a long string of concatenated viral genomes (5). Then the viral genes direct the synthesis of head and tail proteins and the enzymes to chop up the long string and package the new viral DNA into the heads (6 and 7). Heads and tails come together to form mature viral particles (8) and finally, about an hour after infection, the bacterium bursts to release a hundred or so new viruses (9) that can go on to infect other *E. coli* cells (1). Alternatively, the viral DNA can insert itself into the host DNA (10) and live quietly as a prophage, replicating along with the host's chromosome (11, 12, and 13) and being passed on to the daughter cells. This can go on for an indefinite period, but certain environmental events – ultraviolet light, X-rays, heat, certain chemicals – can trigger the prophage out of the host DNA and into replication. This process, called induction, takes the bacteriophage back to the lytic pathway (4). (*Copyright © 1976 by Scientific American, Inc.*)

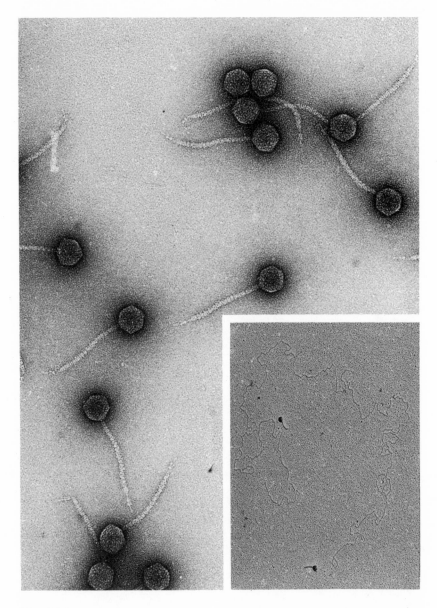

Plate 2.2
Bacteriophage λ. The 20-sided head and long tail, through which the DNA is injected into the host, are clearly visible. The inset shows the long DNA strands, normally packed within the head. (*Courtesy Erika Hartwieg and Jonathan King; inset courtesy Jack D. Griffith*)

came to be called 'host-controlled restriction'. These observations made sense, too, of other results that had been noticed, but not pursued, by earlier workers. Public health workers need to identify disease-causing bacteria quickly and accurately to prevent epidemics. Different strains of bacteria are resistant to different antibiotics, require different vaccines and so on, and a valuable advantage can be gained by knowing the exact identity of the culprit before trying to treat the disease. One of the identification methods bacteriologists use is so-called 'phage typing'. They infect a lawn of the suspect strain with a set of 25 or more different sorts of bacteriophage and see which types of phage are able to grow and which are restricted. This alone will often tell the bacteriologist what strain he is dealing with. But sometimes things go wrong.

Ephraim S. Anderson and A. Felix worked at the Public Health Service's Central Enteric Reference Laboratory and Bureau in Colindale, north London. The major part of the laboratory's work was to identify the culprits behind various gastric upsets, often in cases of food poisoning. Prompted by Luria and Bertani's revelations of the mysteries of T2 and lambda, Anderson and Felix announced that in 1947, five years earlier, they had noted a similar thing with *Salmonella typhi*, one of the bacteria that causes food poisoning.[3] Certain phages, called 'Vi-typing phages', were restricted by some strains of *S. typhi* and could grow on others. But if a phage was forced to grow on a restrictive host, it produced new phages that were no longer restricted on the original host. For Anderson and Felix this was a nuisance, because it meant that they had to keep their stocks of Vi-typing phages separate if they were to identify the *S. typhi* strains correctly; but in the light of the later work their observations made a great deal of sense. Anderson is, perhaps not unnaturally, a little bitter that he is seldom recognized as a pioneer in the field of restriction, but it is not that easy to make the connection between changing specificity – at that time thought to be a property of the virus – and restriction, a property of the host.

Some time after these events, Luria produced an explanation of the whole curious phenomenon of host-controlled restriction. He couched his account in literary terms. The genetic code, he said, was a universal language, each distinct triplet of bases along the DNA representing the same amino acid in all living things. So if one was looking at the code simply as a reader, the meaning would be the same regardless of who was doing the reading. Now suppose that, instead of regarding the code as a mere reader, one looks at it with the eye of a bibliophile. Little marks might, like the typeface or design of this book, reveal who constructed the code, who printed the book. Restricting bacteria were able to scrutinize all the DNA inside their walls, including that of the infecting phage. As a result they could tell that the phage DNA was foreign, and destroy it. To protect themselves, they would have to be able to recognize their own DNA, perhaps by modifying its structure in some way, and prevent it being destroyed. Occasionally a stretch of viral DNA would escape scrutiny and, while being replicated by the cell, would be modified and protected in the same way that the cell's own DNA is modified and protected. Instead of reading 'made in *E. coli* (not strain K)', the DNA would now read 'made in *E. coli* strain K', and the vigilant restriction enzymes would be fooled. What the printer's marks might be, and how the foreign DNA was destroyed, remained mysteries.

Protection and destruction

For roughly ten years from Luria's description of host-controlled restriction, the mechanics of restriction and modification remained unknown. Then, in 1962, Werner Arber, a Swiss biochemist at the University of Geneva, revealed what was going on.[4] Arber had been inspired by a period spent with Jean Weigle in California, and he and Daisy Dussoix, a student working for her PhD, concentrated their efforts on a variant of phage lambda and two strains of *E. coli*, K12 and KP1. Their lambda phage would grow well in K12, but hardly at all in P1; less than 2 in 10 000 K12 phage particles survive P1, but those that do will breed equally well both in K12 and in KP1. Arber and Dussoix redid the experiment carefully, allowing the phage from KP1 to infect and burst just one K12 cell each, with no continued infection by the resulting daughter phage. The result was rather a surprise. Instead of just 2 particles in 10 000 being able to infect KP1, Arber and Dussoix got 1 in every 100 or so. Because the number of daughter viruses produced in a single cell before it burst was about 100, Arber and Dussoix argued that one progeny phage in each cell literally inherited the physical modification that had protected its parent.[5]

This is complicated, so it is worth going through it again. Most phages grown on KP1 will not grow on K12, because they lack the made-in-K12 mark, but those that do grow will later grow in KP1 and K12. If you take a phage that grew first on KP1, then on K12, and allow it to infect a single KP1 cell, one in a hundred of the particles you get is able to infect K12. This may seem odd, but can be explained simply. The phage that grew in K12 picked up a 'made in K12' mark, and that mark is present when it infects KP1 again, and enables *that particular phage* to infect K12 in the future. Arber and Dussoix argued that one progeny phage in each cell inherited the physical modification that had protected the parent particle. Indeed, the infective 1 in 100 *is* the parent DNA, complete with its previously acquired 'made in K12' mark, repackaged into a new coat. On 8 December 1978, when his contribution to science was recognized by a Nobel prize, Arber explained their idea to an elegant Stockholm audience: 'We were convinced that this [modification] was transferred from the infecting parental phage particle. But was it a diffusible internal phage protein or was it perhaps carried on the parental DNA molecule?'[5]

It turned out to be on the DNA, and to be a stable alteration to the molecule, not affected by the sometimes violent chemical procedures used to purify DNA. Finding out that the modification – which, as Luria had said, affected the substance of the DNA but not the spelling of the genetic message – consisted of tacking a small chemical group, a so-called methyl group, on to specific nucleotides in the DNA, took a little longer – until the early 1970s, in fact. When Arber grew *E. coli* on a medium deficient in methionine, the amino acid that cells use as a source of methyl groups, the bacteria lost their ability to modify DNA (see figure 2.2). Indeed, other experiments suggested that cells would not survive long without methionine because their own DNA was unprotected and so, in a sort of inevitable suicide, the cell's restriction enzymes turned on the very DNA that had created them.

While Arber was working out that modification involved changes to the DNA, Dussoix and another colleague, Grete Kellenberg, tried to find out what restriction really was. They grew phages on strain K12 bacteria which had in turn grown up in a medium that contained ^{32}P, a radioactive isotope of the element phosphorus. As a result, the phage DNA contained a radioactive label and could be traced. Dussoix and Kellenberg infected various strains of *E. coli*, some restrictive and others not, with the labelled phage. After an interval of 3, 7 or 15 minutes they stopped all chemical reactions in the cells and looked to see what happened to the radioactive label. On strain K12, which of course did not restrict the growth of phage that had been grown on K12, over 90 per cent of the hot phosphorus was in the form of large insoluble molecules inside the bacteria. On P1, which did restrict phage growth, more than half the phosphorus was floating freely in solution and obviously no longer part of a DNA molecule. Even after as little as three minutes, unmodified DNA injected into restrictive cells was completely ineffectual, having been broken down into tiny bits.

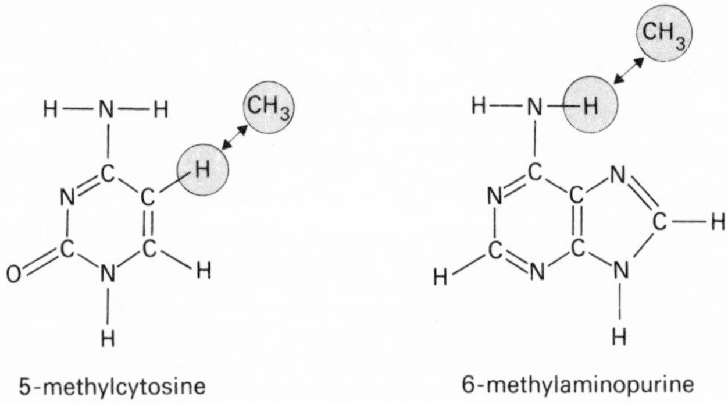

5-methylcytosine   6-methylaminopurine

Figure 2.2
Modified bases. The substitution of a methyl (CH3) group for one of the hydrogen atoms in a base marks that base out and protects the DNA from restriction enzymes.

The enzyme isolated

After Chicago and California, where he had pioneered density-gradient methods for separating large molecules, and had been part of the team that isolated messenger RNA, Matthew Meselson found himself with his own lab at Harvard. In 1966 Robert Yuan, a Fellow of the Damon Runyon Memorial Foundation, arrived as a postdoctoral fellow. Meselson offered Yuan a choice of two projects. Either he could investigate the enzymes involved in the recombination of phage T4, or he could search for the host restriction enzymes. Undaunted by previous failures, and encouraged by

Meselson, Yuan decided to make a frontal attack on restriction enzymes.[6] They chose to purify the enzymes responsible for restriction in an *E. coli* of strain K, its code number in the American Type Culture Collection being 1100. A mutant derivative, number 1100.293, lacks the genes that make the restriction enzyme and hence does not have the ability to destroy foreign DNA.

To pursue the purification, they needed a way to measure the restriction power of any extract, and Meselson adapted the density-gradient method. DNA, being a relatively heavy molecule, sinks slowly if it is centrifuged in a solution of sugar, but the compact twisted circles of lambda phage DNA sink much more quickly than DNA that has been opened out. Lambda DNA, treated with a crude extract of 1100.293 (that is, unrestricted), sank 2 cm in an hour and 48 minutes; by contrast, it sank only 1½ cm in the same time if treated with an extract of the restricting strain. Clearly, the restricting strain did have the power to open up the DNA and make it sink more slowly. The assay method was a bit tedious: labelled DNA had to be tracked through the density gradient by counting the particles emitted by each successive millimetre of sucrose solution; but it worked, and revealed when DNA had been broken up by enzymes and when it had not.

Purification began, as it almost always does, with a technique called 'dialysis'. The rag-bag mixture of proteins and everything else from the cells is put into a sack made of a special material and submerged in a mixture of solvents. The small impurities pass through the membrane and the dialysate, as it is called, that is left behind is a purer solution of the large proteins. (Dialysis, essentially, is like washing; the technique is in everyday use to clean kidney patients' blood of harmful impurities.) Unfortunately for Meselson and Yuan, the dialysate of *E. coli* K seemed to have no restriction activity. DNA was untouched by it. This stumped them for a while and caused a frustrating delay, until they discovered that two other chemicals, so-called 'co-factors', were needed for the restriction enzyme to work. One of these was ATP, the molecule that stores and transports energy in the cell. The other was S-adenosylmethionine, SAM for short. As SAM provides methyl groups, and is needed for good restriction in living cells, it was no great surprise that the cell extract also needed it. ATP and SAM provided the crude cell extract with quite a powerful destructive effect on lambda DNA.

With the requirements of the reaction all worked out, Meselson and Yuan proceeded to the business of purification. They grew *E. coli* in vast amounts, until the stock broth was a soup containing 600 million cells in every millilitre. The stock culture was spun down in a centrifuge, the spent broth thrown away, and the cells stored at –20 °C. From the frozen mass, they took 120 grams of cells and whirled them in a blender with tiny glass beads. The beads, like a miniature crushing mill, broke open the cells and released the cytoplasm. Two hours at 35 000 r.p.m. separated the empty cell walls from the cytoplasm, which tests showed was able to degrade DNA.

Cytoplasm contains a great deal more than restriction enzyme; apart from all the other enzymes, there are assorted other chemicals that are not wanted. The 300 millilitres of crude extract now had to be cleaned up. The first stage was to separate the proteins from the other chemicals. Ammonium sulphate is gentler than phenol and does this nicely, making the proteins precipitate out of solution. Meselson and Yuan collected and precipitated protein and dissolved it up in a special mixture, which they dialysed to get rid of small impurities. Then they purified the dialysate by column chromatography.

The principle of column chromatography is simple. A mixture, in this case of proteins, is poured on to the top of a column of some absorbent material. Meselson and Yuan used chemically treated cellulose. The proteins tend to stick to the cellulose, but they can be washed off again by the buffer solution they are dissolved in. Each protein has a characteristic stickiness that determines the speed at which it will travel through the column. Stickier proteins get left behind, while not so sticky ones are the first to drip out of the end of the column.

Meselson and Yuan poured the dialysate, 100 ml of it, on to a column, 6 cm across and 11 cm deep, of specially prepared cellulose. The proteins sorted themselves out, and the two researchers washed the column with a litre of buffer solution, taking care to collect separate 50 ml samples, or fractions, as they dripped through. The restriction activity was sure to have collected in one or more of those 200 samples, but to find out which one they had to go through the tiresome business of incubating some of each sample with DNA, putting the DNA on to a sucrose gradient, and seeing whether the DNA had been attacked. When it was all done the results were clear. All the activity was concentrated in just two of the fractions. The rest could be thrown away.

The two fractions were mixed together, dialysed again, and put through the chromatographic separation once more. This time the column was taller and thinner, 1 cm by 15 cm, and made of slightly different cellulose, all of which combined to enhance the separation yet further. Washing the samples out now used only 300 ml, and each fraction was only 9 ml; but again, each fraction had to be tested to see whether it had the power to restrict DNA. The restriction activity was concentrated into just three adjacent 9 ml fractions. The fractions were pooled, dialysed, and concentrated down to 7.5 ml by removing water. Chromatography now was too insensitive to separate the constituents of the mixture, because if there were several proteins they were essentially all equally sticky. But they might be of different density, so the final step was a purely physical separation using a density gradient.

The 7.5 ml was divided into three portions and each was placed on top of a test-tube containing a density gradient of glycerol. The tubes were spun at 25 000 r.p.m. for 20 hours and gingerly removed from the centrifuge. A pin-prick in the bottom of each tube allowed the glycerol and layered proteins to drip out, each millimetre of liquid in the tube collected as a separate fraction and tested. Three fractions had the power to break up DNA; they were over 5000 times more active than the crude cell extract.

Those days, Yuan recalled, formed 'one of the most exciting periods in my life'.[7] 'The long hours made the finding of open eating places an added complication.'[8] At the end of it, with 'great joy', he and Meselson published their work in *Nature*. From the 8 grams of protein in the original extract, Meselson and Yuan had obtained something like half a thousandth of a gram, but that tiny amount contained practically all the restriction activity of the 120 grams of *E. coli* cells. With pure enzyme, they could look in detail at how it worked.

Destroyer and protector

Meselson and Yuan's enzyme was technically an endonuclease. That is, it acted within a double helix of DNA to break it, rather than attacking the ends of the helix. When they attacked labelled

DNA with the enzyme, very little of the radioactive phosphorus found its way into the solution. Most of it stayed bound up in the DNA, which proved that the enzyme did not just break up the DNA molecule by chomping away at one end. Also, the enzyme worked perfectly well on the closed circles of DNA that comprise the genetic message of lambda phage. So it attacked double-stranded, whole DNA.

The product of the pure enzyme was also double-stranded DNA, though obviously in shorter lengths. Incubating a mixture of DNA and enzyme extensively and then adding more enzyme did little to alter the pattern of settling of the DNA in the sucrose gradients, a pattern that resembled the one that would be obtained if the entire lambda DNA were divided into four quarters. Another trick proved that the degraded DNA was double-stranded. Normal double helices settle at the same speed in strong and weak salt solutions, whereas single-stranded DNA curls up in strong salt solution and settles three times more quickly than in a weak solution. Meselson and Yuan found that the enzyme-treated DNA settled at the same speed regardless of salt concentration; it was double-stranded. Furthermore, there are no single-strand breaks, or nicks, in the treated DNA. Separating the two chains does not alter the settling pattern, as it would if some of the strands were nicked into shorter pieces.

It looked as if the restriction enzyme from *E. coli* K worked in two stages. It made a break in one strand and then, some 30 seconds later, the second strand broke. Meselson and Yuan couldn't tell whether the same enzyme molecule made both breaks, nor were they sure whether the enzyme was attacking a specific sequence along the DNA. The pattern of fragments that they got suggested that the enzyme might recognize just a few sites that it then attacked, but they couldn't be certain that this was so.

Perhaps the most interesting result was that a modification on just one of the two strands protected the molecule from the enzyme. DNA molecules from phages grown in K were modified and protected against the enzyme of K. Those grown in C were not. Meselson and Yuan separated the DNA strands in samples from the two types of phage and then mixed the single strands. Some of the DNA from K-grown phage came together with strands from C-grown phage to form hybrid double helices, known as heterodu-plexes, on which one strand, the K strand, was protected and the other not. The enzyme did not attack these hybrid strains, not even to make a nick in just the unmodified strand. This finding was extremely important, as Meselson and Yuan realized:

The resistance of heteroduplexes may serve to protect newly replicated bacterial DNA from attack by the cells' own restriction enzyme, allowing time for modification of the newly synthesized chain. Indeed, if restriction and modification are accomplished by the same enzyme, the choice between the two reactions may normally be governed by whether the substrate is an unmodified homoduplex or a heteroduplex, respectively.[9]

Perverse complexity

The achievements of Matthew Meselson and Robert Yuan in isolating and purifying the restriction enzyme of *E. coli* and working out how it operated were enormous. But it was only in 1979 that we gained a real understanding of how it works. The reason for the delay was, as the writers of one textbook put it, that the enzyme Meselson and Yuan chose to work with is 'perverse in the complexity of its behaviour'.[10] The final story is astounding.

The enzyme is large, and is made of three parts. One recognizes a specific sequence of bases on the DNA. The second cuts the DNA if, and only if, the recognition site contains no protective methyl groups. The third part adds methyl groups to one strand if the other strand already has one. The recognition site is 13 nucleotides long:

5' —A—A—C—N—N—N—N—N—N—G—T—G—C— 3'

3' —T—T—G—N—N—N—N—N—N—C—A—C—G— 5'

The middle section of six N's indicates that the exact identity of those nucleotides is irrelevant, but the flanking sequences of three and four are vital. How the enzyme recognizes the site is a mystery, although it looks as if the recognition part of the molecule fits inside the groove of the double helix and reads its way along. If, when it comes to a recognition site, it finds a methyl group on one strand (the exact location of the protective methyl is still unknown), it acts as a methylase and adds protection to the other strand. If it finds both strands methylated, it stops reading and falls off the helix. If it finds no methyl groups it destroys the helix.

The exact details of destruction still aren't known for the enzyme from *E. coli* K, but a very similar enzyme from strain B is better understood.[11] John Rosamond worked it out with some colleagues while he was a visiting researcher at Berkeley, using direct observa-

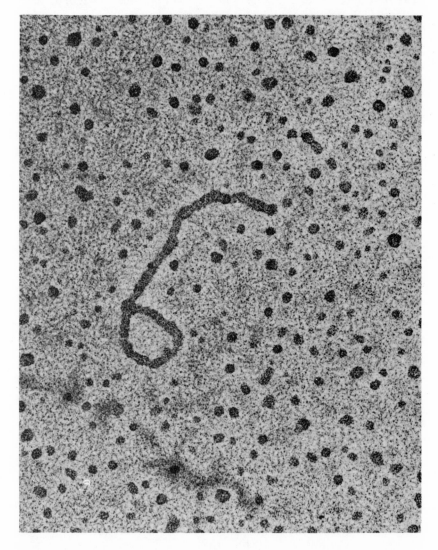

Plate 2.3
Looped DNA, held in place by the Class I restriction enzyme *Eco* B. (*Courtesy John Rosamond*)

tion, with an electron microscope, and a series of cleverly contrived stretches of DNA (manufacture of which, ironically, had to await developments in the technology of restriction enzymes). The DNA in question had target sites for the enzyme at different distances from the end of the molecule. Only if the site was more than 1000 bases from the end of the DNA did the enzyme cut it. And it never cut the DNA at the recognition site; the damage was always at least 1000 bases from the site.

The enzyme becomes bound to the recognition site and undergoes some sort of transformation, perhaps losing one of its subunits. Then, while still attached at that site, it begins to pull the DNA through itself. It always pulls in DNA from the same side of the sequence, the side with three recognition bases, holding on to the four-base site and, effectively, travelling along the DNA. Looking at the complex of DNA with enzyme in the electron microscope, Rosamond could see loops at the end of the molecules (see plate 2.3). These loops show the enzyme frozen in the act of walking along the DNA. When it has pulled in a certain amount of DNA, somewhere between 1000 and 5000 nucleotides, it stops. Nobody knows why it stops where it does; certainly, the site of the break is not fixed either with respect to the recognition site or with regard to the sequences of bases there. Perhaps it is as simple as a kink in the DNA. In any case, regardless of the reason why the enzyme stops tracking along the molecule, once it has stopped it makes a nick in one of the strands. Other enzymes come along and attack the exposed DNA in the nick, dissolving away a stretch of about 75 nucleotides before the second strand is broken. The result is two fragments of DNA that can be swiftly degraded by yet more enzymes. And long after the DNA has been severed the restriction enzyme remains bound to the recognition site, where it breaks down large amounts of ATP. Some ATP is used to power the hauling in of the DNA through the enzyme, but why the cell continues to waste energy molecules with such profligacy is not clear; it might be a man-made artefact caused by lack of some vital regulatory molecule in the test-tube cell substitute, or it may represent a specific extra function for the restriction enzyme that is at present unknown.

There are undoubtedly further twists to be unravelled in the byzantine knot of restriction enzyme activity. And all that complexity, while undoubtedly fascinating, hardly seems worth all the effort. What use is a cutting tool that, while it recognizes a specific site, nevertheless makes itself felt at some random point 5000 bases away from that site? The answer, quite simply, is that, aside from its intrinsic interest, the restriction enzyme that Meselson and Yuan purified from *E. coli* K prompted a search for other restriction enzymes, and the vast majority of these turned out to be much simpler. They recognize a sequence and, without any need for ATP or SAM, break the DNA right there and then. No tracking, no randomness, just a nice clean slice. And tools like that are very handy indeed.

A whole new class

Sharing the Nobel platform with Werner Arber in December 1978 were Hamilton Smith and Daniel Nathans. Smith and Nathans are both professors of microbiology at the prestigious Johns Hopkins University School of Medicine in Baltimore, Maryland. Where Arber had pioneered the detailed investigation of the enzymes that lay behind host-controlled restriction, Smith was honoured for discovering a whole new class of restriction enzymes, and Nathans for putting those enzymes to work in the service of fundamental molecular biology.

It began, as success stories often do in science, with a lucky chance. Smith, at the time a recently arrived member of the Johns Hopkins faculty, was working with bacteria called *Haemophilus influenzae* strain Rd. This had the useful property of being very changeable, and Smith began to investigate some of the transformations that the bacteria underwent as they swapped bits of DNA with other bacteria. With a young graduate student, Kent Wilcox, Smith used a viscometer to measure the extent to which cell extracts broke up DNA. Long strands of DNA form a very viscous solution, while smaller ones are less viscous; a decrease in viscosity mirrors the break-up of DNA. As another part of the study, Smith allowed the *H. influenzae* cells to take up radioactively labelled DNA from various sources and then tried to recover this donor DNA to see what had happened to it. One day, Smith and Wilcox offered the bacteria labelled DNA from a phage called P22, a virus that Smith had long been familiar with. To their surprise, when they came to look for the labelled DNA in the cells, they couldn't find any.

When he received his Nobel prize Smith continued the story for his audience in Stockholm, trying hard to conceal the emotion involved:

With Meselson's recent report in our minds, we immediately suspected that the phage DNA might be undergoing restriction, and our experience with viscometry told us that this would be a good assay for such an activity. The following day, two viscometers were set up, one containing P22 DNA and the other, *Haemophilus* DNA. Cell extract was added to each and we quickly began taking measurements. As the experiment progressed, we became increasingly excited as the viscosity of the *Haemophilus* DNA held steady while that of the P22 DNA fell. We were confident that we had discovered a new and highly active restriction enzyme.[12]

Their confidence, needless to say, was not misplaced, but it took a considerable amount of effort to find out what they had and how it worked.

Smith and Wilcox went through more or less the same stages that Meselson and Yuan had gone through; there is really no alternative, and the purification of almost any protein from a cell would be bound to involve many of the same procedures. The starting point was a culture of *H. influenzae*, growing in a 12 litre vat of sustaining brain and heart broth. Instead of glass beads, Smith used ultrasonic vibrations to break open the cells and release the cytoplasm. Put in the viscometer with P22 DNA, just ten-millionths of a litre of the crude cell extract was enough to start breaking up the DNA and reducing the viscosity. The crude cell extract was washed, separated chromatographically, washed again, and separated again. At the end, having left out the purification by density gradient that Meselson and Yuan had used, Smith and Wilcox had an enzyme that was 200 times more active than the raw cytoplasm.

This restriction enzyme needed neither ATP nor SAM, though it would not work unless there were magnesium ions present. It was smaller than the *E. coli* K enzyme, with a molecular weight of only about 70 000. It attacked foreign DNA with alacrity, reducing the genome of T7 from a single length of molecular weight 26 400 000 to about 40 bits with an average molecular weight of 1 450 000. The bits were all double-stranded, and no nucleotides were removed from the chain. The enzyme appeared to chop through the DNA in one go, producing nicks in the two strands at almost the same time and place. They christened the enzyme 'endonuclease R';

endonuclease because, like Meselson and Yuan's enzyme, it attacked nucleic acid molecules from within (that is, it could break the middle of a chain – exonucleases attack at the tips of the molecules), and R for restriction.

Meselson and Yuan had guessed that their enzyme recognized a specific sequence of bases. For similar reasons, namely the relatively small number of breaks produced, Smith and Wilcox felt the same way about their enzyme. But they went further and estimated the length of the recognition site. T7 DNA is about 40 000 bases long, and the *Haemophilus* enzyme broke this into 40 pieces about 1000 bases long. On a stretch of randomly organized DNA a particular unique sequence of, say, four bases would occur roughly every 256 bases; clearly, four bases is too small a site. To occur every 1000 or so bases, a site would need to be five or six bases long. At the very end of their paper announcing the new restriction enzyme, Smith and Wilcox derived this estimate and then had the satisfaction of stating: 'In the accompanying paper . . . the base sequence recognized by endonuclease R is completely identified and provides confirmation of this estimate.'[13]

Recognition

At the same time as he had been working on the properties of the *H. influenzae* restriction enzyme, Smith was also tackling the question of its recognition site. Kent Wilcox was in on the early stages of this project too, but could not continue because the army had sent him his draft notice of induction. His prime preoccupation therefore became to complete the formal requirements of his master's degree. Smith continued alone for a time, and then was joined by Thomas Kelly Jr.

All the evidence pointed to a specific recognition site. Of the 40 000 sugar–phosphate links in each chain of the viral DNA, the enzyme broke only 40. There had to be some sort of guidance mechanism to get the enzyme to cleave just there. The strategy Smith and Kelly adopted sounds simple. They would look at the ends of the fragments and identify the nucleotides there. If the site was specific, they would find a specific pattern of nucleotides ending each and every fragment. Putting it into practice required a battery of other enzyme systems, two sorts of radioactive label and a great deal of ingenuity.

The starting point was purified endonuclease R and T7 DNA labelled with ^{33}P. This is a radioactive form of phosphorus that is less energetic than the usual ^{32}P; it was used as a general label to tell them where the DNA was. Smith and Kelly attacked the single nucleotide at the 5′ end of the fragments first. An enzyme called alkaline phosphatase removes the phosphate group from the end of a fragment. This done, the fragments were incubated with ATP labelled with energetic ^{32}P and another enzyme, polynucleotide kinase. This enzyme transfers the labelled phosphorus from the ATP to the nucleoside. After an hour at blood heat the doubly labelled DNA – ^{33}P throughout and ^{32}P at the 5′ end – was extracted, purified and analysed.

Snake venom is the source of yet another enzyme, this one called snake venom phosphodiesterase. This has the useful property of breaking DNA into its component nucleotides, leaving the phosphate group attached to the 5′ carbon of the sugar. When the venom enzyme had done its work Smith and Kelly had a mixture of four different nucleotides, all radioactively labelled but some – the nucleotides that were at the 5′ end of the restriction fragment – labelled with ^{32}P while all the others carried only ^{33}P. The problem now was first to separate the four nucleotides, and then to identify the ones that had the hotter ^{32}P label. Separation was routine, using electrophoresis. Similar to chromatography, electrophoresis is a process in which an electric current frog-marches the molecules through a thin layer of cellulose. Molecules that are small, or highly charged, move faster than those that are large, or not so highly charged. Once separated, the nucleotides had to be identified. This is where the differential labelling came in. ^{33}P is not very energetic, and the particles it gives off as it decays are easily blocked. ^{32}P, on the other hand, gives off more energetic particles. Smith laid a sheet of Kodak X-ray film on either side of the cellulose gel that had been used for electrophoresis. As the phosphorus decayed it gave off particles, which collided with the silver grains in the film and left a permanent record of their position. The radioactive phosphorus essentially takes a picture of itself; hence the name autoradiography. One side of the gel was in direct contact with the film. Strong and weak particles could get to the silver, so ^{33}P and ^{32}P each made their mark. On the other side of the gel was the gel's thin supporting plastic. Flimsy though this was, it was enough to stop the weaker decay products of ^{33}P. Only the hotter label of the terminal nucleotide would show on this film (see plate 2.4).

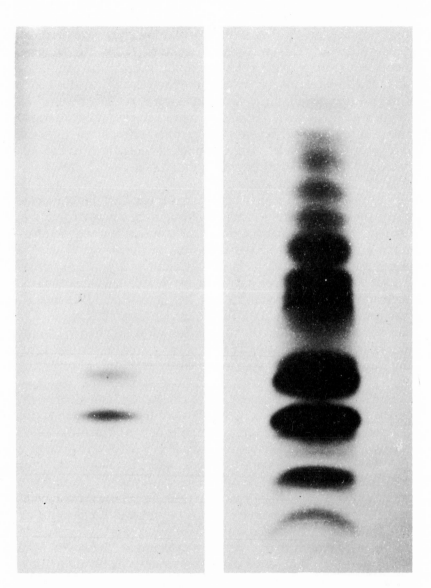

Plate 2.4
Restriction enzyme recognition site. The dark strip on the right represents the radioactivity of all the nucleotides near the 5' end of the recognition site. On the left is an autoradiograph of the same gel taken through a thin screen; only the two terminal nucleotides, labelled with the more energetic ^{32}P, leave a mark. (*Courtesy Hamilton Smith*)

Conceptually simple, this intellectual breakthrough was absolutely fundamental to the work that was to follow. But after the very first run, when they looked at the films and compared the exposed positions with the pattern they got with known nucleotides, Smith must have been a bit disappointed. The hot label was present in two nucleotides, 63 per cent attached to the adenine and the remaining 37 per cent to guanine. So the cleavage site was 'not absolutely specified'.[14] All was not lost, however, for adenine and guanine are both purines; the enzyme made a break on the 5' side of a purine, but didn't distinguish between adenine and guanine.

What was the penultimate nucleotide on the fragment? As before, the phosphorus on the end was replaced with a hot phosphorus, but instead of using snake venom, an enzyme called exonuclease I was brought in. This nibbles away at DNA fragments from the 3' end, but stops when there are just two nucleotides left. Again, the dinucleotides were separated and autoradiographed. The label was again in two places. One, with 62 per cent of the radioactivity, could have been either AA, or CG, or GC. The other was either GA or AG. Snake venom separated the first pair into single nucleotides; all the hot label was on adenine, so the pair was definately AA. The second pair's ^{32}P was also on the adenine, so this one was GA. The site was specific. The 5' base could be either A or G, but the next base along was always an adenine.

The final three bases on the 5' end of the fragment turned out to be AAC and GAC, so the specificity was holding up. What about the other side of the break, the 3' end of the fragments? Here another bit of thought enabled Smith and Kelly to take a shortcut. There were, logically, only two ways that the enzyme could work. It could either break the DNA duplex evenly, producing fragments with flush ends, or it could break unevenly, so that the fragments had one longer strand at the end. Only if the break was even, and the ends flush, would the sequence of bases at the 3' end of the fragment be exactly complementary to the sequence at the 5' end. Yet another enzyme – micrococcal nuclease – was brought in. This enzyme breaks whole DNA into single and double nucleotides, those from the 3' end being double nucleotides joined by a single phosphate. Smith and Kelly separated these out from all the other nucleotides by chromatography and found that they were of two different sorts. Breaking them up and looking at the individual nucleotides revealed that one was TC and the other TT. This was exactly what they would predict if the break is even. They had almost all the details of the recognition site: it was

$$5' \; —G—T—Py—Pu—A—C— \; 3'$$
$$3' \; —C—A—Pu—Py—T—G— \; 5'$$

with the break coming between the two unspecified bases in the middle. (Notice that the sequence is a palindrome. It reads the same on the two strands, just as the sentence 'able was I ere I saw Elba' reads the same forwards or backwards. The vast majority of subsequently identified recognition sites turned out likewise to be palindromic; the consequences of this are extremely important.) Such a sequence of six bases would occur in a random genome once every 1024 base-pairs. The fragments of T7 DNA produced by endonuclease R were about 1000 base-pairs long, while those of P22 were 1300 base-pairs long. As Kelly and Smith noted:

These facts suggest that the sequence [above] contains sufficient information to account fully for the observed degree of specificity of endonuclease R. However, since strictly speaking neither the T7 nor the P22 DNA molecule represents a truly random collection of nucleotides, the possibility remains that the recognition region for endonuclease R might be larger.[15]

They had to look at the fourth nucleotide from the end; if that too was specific, the recognition region was longer than six base-pairs. Fortunately, it was not.

The recognition site of a restriction enzyme had been fully identified, and the pace of progress was speeding up. Thirty years from the first phage-typing to Luria's experiments; ten years from Luria to Arber; eight years from Arber to Meselson and Yuan; and two years from them to Smith. Host-controlled restriction, which Hamilton Smith described as 'an apparently insignificant bacteriological phenomenon', had yielded an enzyme that, he saw, had 'unexpectedly far-reaching implications'.[16]

Things get easier

Almost as soon as Smith had discovered the first specific restriction enzyme, his colleague Daniel Nathans was putting it to work in the service of molecular biology. Nathan's target was a little virus that infects the cells of monkeys, hence its name simian virus 40, or SV40. SV40 can, when conditions are right, transform the cells it has infected and make them grow like cancerous tumours, so it has not unnaturally been the subject of intense interest by many groups of researchers. But before examining the developments, in SV40 and elsewhere, that followed Smith's work with the *Haemophilus influenzae* enzyme, it is worth looking at the way in which interest in restriction enzymes took off.

Meselson and Yuan had an enormously hard job demonstrating that the various fractions they collected were, or were not, possessed of restricting activity. They had to use modified DNA labelled with one type of radioactive isotope and unmodified DNA with a different label. Then, after incubating a mixture of the two with the putative enzyme, they had to spin the products down a sucrose density gradient. Dividing the gradient into portions and counting the different types of radioactivity in each took yet more time, and at the end the results had to be examined carefully to see which fractions were able to destroy unmodified DNA. It worked, but it took time.

Smith and Wilcox went one better. No longer were they dependent on tedious density-gradient separations and radioactivity assays (though they still used those for confirmation); they had the viscometer, which gave a purely physical indication of whether the DNA was being broken or not. In the right hands, this was a much speedier process for testing the various fractions, and enabled Smith and his helpers to progress rather rapidly. Still, the techniques were not as fast as they were to become, and it was Nathans and his SV40 who pushed the speed up another notch.

Nathans's intention was to divide the DNA of SV40 up into manageable fragments, the better to understand how the entire virus worked. He quickly established that Smith's restriction enzyme did indeed break open SV40's circle of DNA, and that it created several fragments. The next goal was to resolve the mixture of fragments into its component parts, and for this Nathans enlisted the help of Kathleen Danna, a graduate student in his laboratory. The technique they used was electrophoresis, but rather than using cellulose as a supporting medium for the mixture of fragments they used a gel containing polyacrylamide. This is a long thread-like molecule that links to form a mesh permeated by small pores. The amount of polyacrylamide sets the average size of the pores, which in turns restrict the passage of molecules through the gel. Small molecules always travel faster, but by adjusting the amount of polyacrylamide in the gel the biochemist can fine-tune his molecular sieve to sort out a particular size most efficiently. Nathans and Danna put the sample of radioactive SV40 DNA, digested by the restriction enzyme, at one end of a 13 cm strip of polyacrylamide gel. The DNA, of course, is completely invisible, so to keep track of it they added a dye, bromophenol blue, that moved a little faster than the smallest chain of DNA. Sixty volts from one end of the gel to the other provided the motive power to separate the fragments of DNA, smaller fragments racing ahead of larger ones, and at the end of eight hours the blue band of dye had travelled 13 cm and reached the end of the gel. The problem now was to make the invisible visible, and see what had become of the DNA.

Danna froze the 13 cm strip of gel to make it easier to handle and then cut it into about a hundred bands, each just 1.2 mm wide. Each band sat for a while in solvent, and then the amount of radioactivity that had leaked out into the solvent was counted with a superior sort of geiger counter. The results showed clearly that the fragments of nucleic acid had indeed separated out. The column of numbers, counts of radioactivity from 100 or more samples, produced a clear pattern of peaks and troughs; nine peaks and ten troughs. Two of the peaks contained more than their fair share of DNA, an anomaly that autoradiographs of the gels explained by showing two bands close together at each of the two positions. The restriction enzyme from *H. influenzae* chopped the DNA from SV40 into 11 chunks, and a whole series of different measurements proved that the amount of DNA in the 11 fragments added up to the total amount of DNA in the whole virus. 'We conclude,' wrote Danna and Nathans, 'that every molecule of SV40 DNA yields one of each of these fragments.'[17] That was why each of the fragments formed a band in the polyacrylamide gel. They were always the same set of fragments, and they lined up in the gel according to size. It was just the result Nathans needed.

It was also ideal for identifying new restriction enzymes. If some portion of purified cell extract gave evidence of breaking DNA, the products of the digestion could be layered on a gel and separated by electrophoresis. If the enzyme was truly a restriction enzyme, breaking the DNA at a set number of specific sites, then it would produce the same set of fragments from every molecule of DNA, and the fragments would line up to form the tell-tale bands. One had to use radioactive DNA, it's true, and follow up the electrophoresis by slicing up the gel and counting the radioactivity, or else by allowing the fragments to photograph themselves; but Danna and Nathans had made it possible to look for restriction activity even more efficiently than had Smith and Wilcox.

Another advance came a couple of years later, in 1973, from Cold Spring Harbor Laboratory. Phillip Sharp, Bill Sugden and Joe Sambrook streamlined the search for restriction enzymes still further. Their breakthrough was in two parts. First, they changed the electrophoresis gel, from polyacrylamide to agarose. DNA fragments are large molecules, and a polyacrylamide gel with holes large enough for the DNA to get through contains so little polyacrylamide that it forms an impossibly mushy gel. Agarose, a long-chain polymer rather like starch, can provide additional support for a weak polyacrylamide gel and is better than polyacrylamide because agarose is not as sensitive to the concentration of electrically charged particles in the solution. When a protein mixture of enzymes has been separated chromatographically the different components are washed out of the column with different concentrations of solvent. Previously, each fraction had to be adjusted to the same concentration before being tested with DNA and electrophoresed. With agarose, the fractions could be taken straight from the column, incubated with DNA, and put through electrophoresis.

The second improvement was perhaps even more important, for it got rid of the lengthy procedures needed to make the DNA in the gel visible. Slicing and counting, staining with dyes (which needed to be removed again before anything else could be done with the DNA), and autoradiographs were all time-consuming and tedious. Sharp added a simple chemical, ethidium bromide, to the gel and the mixed fragments of DNA. Ethidium bromide inserts itself between the bases of the DNA and stretches the helix out slightly, but that is neither here nor there. Much more important, the DNA makes the ethidium bromide glow in ultraviolet light. No staining, no radioactivity, no lengthy wait for autoradiographs; you simply take the agarose gel into a darkroom, switch on an ultraviolet light, and there it is. Bands containing as little as 50 billionths of a gram (0.05 microgram) of DNA light up yellow-orange; to the eager researcher the glowing bands can seem as bright as neon signs and just as conspicuous. Sharp's technique made searching for restriction enzymes a dream. Or, in the dry prose of a scientific paper:

the lengthy staining and destaining or autoradiographic procedures which are an integral part of most of the techniques that are used for electrophoresis of DNA are eliminated. . . . In our hands the technique has proved to be a very useful and flexible tool for assaying restriction enzymes.[18]

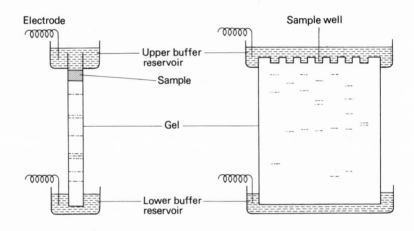

Figure 2.3
Electrophoresis apparatus. The sample mixture is carried through the gel by an electric current, which separates out the fragments according to size.

Sharp's method made everything much easier; separating and seeing DNA was now relatively simple, and the community adopted the method with alacrity. 'Agarose gel electrophoresis did not originate with our *Biochemistry* paper,' Sharp has told me, 'but was certainly popularized by it.'[19] The DNA detection was another matter. Sharp had spent a year with a postdoctoral fellowship at the California Institute of Technology, where he had seen how the dye ethidium bromide fluoresced much more brightly when bound to DNA. He remembered this at Cold Spring Harbor when he wanted to visualize DNA fragments.

I decided to try to stain gels with ethidium bromide as a means of detecting the bands formed by different length fragments. The minimum concentration of ethidium bromide necessary for saturation of DNA was calculated and within 3 hours I had successfully detected DNA bands in gels with ethidium bromide.[20]

Another conceptual leap came from Camil Fuchs, a statistician at Wisconsin university. Fuchs made it vastly easier to discover the recognition site of a new restriction enzyme. Working from the starting point that the enzymes recognize a palindromic site, Fuchs wrote a computer program to detect 4-, 5- and 6-base palindromes, and set the program to work on the complete sequences of two viruses, SV40 and ΦX174, both of which were known in their entirety. The computer told Fuchs how many fragments would be generated, what length they would be and so on for every palindrome in the two genomes. To discover the enzyme's most likely recognition sequence, the researcher had only to use the new restriction enzyme on SV40 and ΦX174, measure the fragments so easily separated and visualized, and simply read the tables that Fuchs published in *Gene*.[21] It was a simple matter then to confirm that sequence by more pedestrian methods.

The contrast between then and now, between sucrose gradient separation and fluorescent bands, is hard to imagine. Robert Yuan remembers that 'in those early days, such assays served their function well, but they were arduous, time-consuming, and extremely boring. The intellectual elegance of some of the experiments was tempered by the laboriousness of many of the methods.'[22] Now, nobody gives a second thought to the ease with which results can be obtained. There's no substitute for elegance, which still needs to be there, but the tedium is not quite so overwhelming.

The naming of parts

When Sharp and his colleagues published their paper in 1973, there were perhaps eight known restriction enzymes. They added one by showing that *Haemophilus parainfluenzae*, which had previously been thought to contain a single enzyme, actually had two which acted at different sites. Richard Roberts had already begun a concerted search for these enzymes in all sorts of bacteria. He 'felt sure they must exist. . . . This was a somewhat heretical view at the time, in that most of my colleagues told me that it was unlikely that there would be more enzymes of this sort.' Roberts's conviction proved correct; a steady stream of new restriction enzymes with new recognition sites followed, and with them a similar 'continuous stream of visitors with DNA samples who wished to see which enzymes would cut them'.[23] This led to the first, private, catalogue, in 1974, and by the published list of 1976 Roberts had documented more than 80 restriction enzymes.[24] The number now is above the 300 mark.

The plethora of enzymes could have become a source of confusion, but very early on Smith and Nathans, with remarkable prescience, saw where they were heading and polled many of their colleagues in the field to bring some order to it all. Every restriction enzyme would have a specific name which would identify it uniquely. The first three letters, in italics, indicate the biological source of the enzyme, the first letter being the initial of the genus and the second and third the first two letters of the species name. Thus, restriction enzymes from *Escherichia coli* are called *Eco; Haemophilus influenzae* becomes *Hin; Diplococcus pneumoniae Dpn;* and so on. Then comes a letter that identifies the strain of bacteria: *Eco* R for strain R (strictly for *E. coli* harbouring a plasmid called R), *Eco* B for B. Finally there is a roman numeral for the particular enzyme if there is more than one in the strain in question; *Eco* RI for the first enzyme from *Escherichia coli* R, *Eco* RII for the second.

The enzymes, having been named, can also be divided into three groups. Class I enzymes are the troublesome ones like Meselson ⏐ *Eco* K, which recognize a specific sequence but don't cleave the DNA at a specific point: they walk a random distance from the recognition site and break the DNA there. Class II enzymes are the workhorses of the genetic engineer. Like Smith's *Hin*, they recognize a specific site and break the DNA at a particular place within that site. A very few class II enzymes are a bit odd: like all restriction enzymes, they recognize a specific sequence, but they don't cleave the DNA within the recognition site; instead, they make a break a set number of nucleotides away. *Mbo* II, for example, from the bacterium *Moraxella bovis* (which causes pinkeye in cattle), recognizes

$$5'—G—A—A—G—A—3'$$
$$3'—C—T—T—C—T—5'$$

but makes its break some way down stream of this, to create a fragment with

$$5' —G—A—A—G—A—N—N—N—N—N—N—N—N— 3'$$
$$3' —C—T—T—C—T—N—N—N—N—N—N—N— \qquad 5'$$

at the end. These 'odd' class II enzymes used to be placed, by European molecular biologists in particular, into a third class, class III. But American workers, and Roberts in particular, adopted a slightly different classification. Their class III contained enzymes like *Eco* PI, which 'have characteristics intermediate between those of the Type I and Type II restriction endonucleases'.[25] 'The original classification made more sense,' says one European biologist, 'but Roberts has become pre-eminent and so . . . we have adopted the current usage.'[26] For practical purposes, the random effects of class I and class III restriction enzymes means that they don't find much use in applied genetic engineering. The real stars are the class II enzymes.

What they do

By making a wise choice from the catalogue of known enzymes, the genetic engineer can find one to perform practically any task. Almost any sequence of bases can be located and cut at will. Some enzymes recognize a long sequence, six or seven bases long: they are often useful for opening a circular strand of DNA at just one point. Others have a much smaller site, four or even three bases long: these will produce small fragments that can then be used to determine the sequence of bases along the DNA. Enzymes from different sources often recognize the same site. They are called isoschizomers, and while some cleave at the same place in the site, others cleave at different places. Nobody knows whether isoschizomers are 'the same' enzyme, in terms of their exact structure;

it seems unlikely. Enzymes such as *Hin* dII, the first to be characterized, allow some flexibility within a rigid site and are very
useful. So cuts can be made anywhere along the DNA, dividing it
into many small fragments or a few longer ones, and in an utterly
repeatable fashion. The cuts made by a type II enzyme on a given
sort of DNA will always be the same.

Strictly speaking, an enzyme qualifies as a restriction endonuclease only if the bacteria also has a specific modification
enzyme to protect its own DNA; but in many cases the restricting
activity is all that the genetic engineers are interested in. Nevertheless, some of the modification enzymes have been isolated and
characterized, and they inevitably do mirror the recognition site of
the restriction enzyme, possibly because the two sorts of enzyme
share a sub-unit that is dedicated to seeking out a particular
sequence of bases along the chain. But there are some oddities in
the restriction–modification pattern. *Diplococcus pneumoniae* has
two enzymes, *Dpn* I and *Dpn* II, that recognize the same four-base
site, GATC. *Dpn* II is completely normal, and works like any other
type II enzyme, but *Dpn* I will break the strand only if the site *is*
modified by having a methyl group attached to the adenine. This is
extremely odd. Why should the normal run of events be upset in
this way? And how does *Diplococcus pneumoniae* protect itself
from its two potentially devastating restriction enzymes? Perhaps
the bacteria don't use this enzyme as a restriction enzyme. As
Hamilton Smith says, 'it is difficult to rationalize this reversal of the
normal role of methylation'.[27]

Like the recognition site, the cut that each enzyme makes varies
from enzyme to enzyme. Some, like *Hin* dII, make a clean cut
straight across the double helix. Fragments from *Hin* dII have ends
that are flush. Others make a staggered break. *Eco* RI, for example, recognizes

$$5'\text{——}G\text{—}A\text{—}A\text{—}T\text{—}T\text{—}C\text{——}3'$$
$$3'\text{——}C\text{—}T\text{—}T\text{—}A\text{—}A\text{—}G\text{——}5'$$

but makes its cut between the G and the A in each strand. This
leaves each fragment with a protruding single strand at the 5' end.
Pst I, from the gut-living bacteria *Providencia stuartii*, does the

reverse. It recognizes the sequence

$$5'{----}C{---}T{---}G{---}C{---}A{---}G{----}3'$$
$$3'{----}G{---}A{---}C{---}G{---}T{---}C{----}5'$$

and cuts between the A and G, leaving the protruding end at the 3′ end of the double helix.

Enzymes that make a staggered cut are especially important, because the single strands that they leave protruding are complementary in base sequence. Under the right conditions, the complementary bases will pair up again, so if you cut two different sorts of DNA with one of these enzymes and mix all the fragments, the chances are that fragments from the two sorts of DNA will come together in a new hybrid molecule. You will have made a new combination of genes – recombinant DNA.

What's it all for?

There are two ways to answer this simple question. One is the answer that occupies much of the rest of this book, that restriction enzymes are 'for' genetic engineering. Certainly it would be impossible without them. But they didn't evolve to help us manipulate DNA. So what, in the evolutionary sense of 'what good', are restriction enzymes really for?

The obvious answer would seem to be that they are a defence against viral infection. This certainly seems reasonable enough. After all, that is how the phenomenon was first uncovered. Unmodified bacteriophages cannot grow very well in hosts that possess restriction enzymes, so restriction enzymes do protect cells from viruses. But is that all? Probably not, because if restriction really is a defence against viruses it is a very inefficient one. There is no defence against viruses that carry the modification, and it seems a little far-fetched to say that the whole elaborate mechanism evolved to protect bacteria of one strain from viruses that had most recently grown on a different strain. In any case, a far better evolutionary defence against viruses would be to lose, or modify, the sites on the outside of the bacteria that the virus recognizes and

Table 2.1 A sample of restriction enzymes

Source organism	Abbreviation	Recognition and cleavage site $(5' \rightarrow 3')$ $(3' \rightarrow 5')$
Bacillus amyloliquefaciens H	*Bam* HI	G|G A T C C C C T A G|G
Escherichia coli RY13	*Eco* RI	G|A A T T C C T T A A|G
Haemophilus aegyptius	*Hae* II	Pu G C G C|Py Py|C G C G Pu
Haemophilus aegyptius	*Hae* III	G G|C C C|G G
Haemophilus haemolyticus	*Hha* I	G C G|C C|G C G
Haemophilus influenzae R_d	*Hin* dII	G T Py |Pu A C C A Pu |Py T G
Haemophilus influenzae R_d	*Hin* dIII	A|A G C T T T T C G A|A
Haemophilus parainfluenzae	*Hpa* I	G T T|A A C C A A|T T G
Haemophilus parainfluenzae	*Hpa* II	C|C G G G G C|C
Providencia stuartii 164	*Pst* I	C T G C A|G G|A C G T C
Streptomyces albus G	*Sal* I	G|T C G A C C A G C T|G

attaches to before inserting its DNA into the host. And if restriction were a protection against infection, we should expect to see far more of it in higher organisms, which are just as prone to viral attack as bacteria. In fact, there is still very little evidence of any restriction activity in any eukaryote cell.

So it looks as if restriction did not evolve to protect bacteria from invading phage DNA, although it incidentally serves that purpose now. What is left in the way of invading DNA? DNA from other bacteria. When bacteria mate, they exchange DNA. If different strains were to mate, restriction enzymes in the recipient would usually ensure that the DNA from the donor was from a cell with the same restriction–modification complex. The system would act to keep strains pure, by destroying DNA from different strains. The same could be true of higher organisms. A single-celled green alga, *Chlamydomonas*, does have a restriction–modification enzyme system, but the enzymes do not seem to have anything to do with attack by viruses. Instead, they destroy *Chlamydomonas* DNA after mating. The DNA in the chloroplasts from the male partner is not methylated, and is destroyed by the female's restriction enzyme, ensuring that the offspring inherit their chloroplasts exclusively in the maternal line.[28] Salvador Luria, talking about bacteria, says:

The branding-and-rejection system facilitates the evolution of bacterial strains in diverging directions, in the same way that isolation mechanisms in cross-fertilization play a role in the evolution of plant and animal species.[29]

More important than the evolution or purity of strains and species is the restriction–modification complex itself. By destroying DNA associated with any other modification enzyme, the recognition part of the complex ensures the survival of copies of itself, regardless of what species or strain they may be in.

Restriction enzymes pose fundamental questions, not only about their evolutionary *raison d'être* but also about the mechanics of how they work. The interaction between protein, the recognition portion of the enzyme, and nucleic acid, the DNA it cleaves, is at the heart of understanding how cells regulate the expression of their genetic material. Not all the genes are being listened to at once, and proteins play a vital role in controlling and orchestrating the operation of the whole genome. Restriction enzymes, as models of more general protein–nucleic acid systems, will doubtless provide fascinating insights to those prepared to pursue them. But for the vast majority of molecular biologists, restriction enzymes are of importance not because they might provide fundamental insights or anything like that: they cut DNA, and that's what counts.

3

TOOLS

Other enzymes used in genetic engineering

The restriction enzymes have offered a glimpse at the tools that living things themselves use. That genetic engineers also find them useful is undoubted – in fact, they are more than useful, they are indispensable – but there is a host of other biochemicals that the engineers are equally dependent upon. Ordinary chemical synthesis and manipulation cannot compare with the powers of life's chemicals, a fact that has led people to treat biochemicals as mysterious. And in a sense they are mysterious, as we shall see; but they do not break any of the fundamental laws of physics or chemistry, as they were once thought to.

Historically, the vitalists believed that the chemicals made by living things were very special, imbued with a vital quality that was in some sense the essence of life. The molecules of life were themselves organic and possessed of life. This mysticism reflected, then as now, the inability of chemists to duplicate the processes of life in the laboratory. Gradually, however, understanding dawned; and the chemistry of life, while intriguing, was seen to be qualitatively the same as the chemistry of the laboratory. Individual milestones on this road are hard to discern, but one was certainly the manufacture, in the laboratory, of an organic compound – urea – from an inorganic predecessor, ammonium cyanate. Friedrich Wöhler achieved this feat in 1828, and although there were objections that urea, being a waste product, was not really an organic compound, vitalist notions began slowly to fade.

There was, however, one little problem. Wöhler, to make urea, had to put vast amounts of energy into his mixtures. High temperatures were needed to persuade the constituent elements to join up and stay joined. The energy is stored in the chemical bonds that hold the organic molecules together. But the living cell apparently achieves the same end without recourse to such violence. Urea, like all the other thousands of biochemicals, is manufactured at an extremely low temperature, one that the organic chemist would find hopelessly inefficient for synthesis. Cells achieve this superb manufacturing capacity as a result of the proteins called enzymes.

'Zyme' is from the old Greek word for leavening, or yeast; quite apart from intellectual curiosity, it was the economic importance of the wine trade, which rests solidly on the biochemical factories of yeasts, that fostered the investigations of pioneers like Louis Pasteur. Pasteur demonstrated in the 1850s that fermentation – the transformation of the sugars in fruit juice to the alcohol in wine – was brought about by micro-organisms. Semantic arguments raged to and fro over what constituted a ferment and what fermentation, and for quite some time there was a lively debate over whether it was the living organisms themselves that caused the fermentation or whether there were chemicals within the yeasts that could do it. So-called soluble or disorganized ferments, which brought about a biochemical change in the absence of the organism that produced them (like pepsin and trypsin, discovered in digestive juices), had been known for some time. Their existence served mainly to confuse the semantics and fuelled the substantive debate.

The semantic argument was solved, at least partially, by Willy Kühne in 1878. Kühne suggested that whatever it was that caused fermentation be called an 'enzyme'. In doing so, he steered well clear of the other arguments, asserting that his name

is not intended to imply any particular hypothesis, but . . . merely states that in zyme [yeast] something occurs that exerts this or that activity, which is considered to belong to the class called fermentative. The name is not, however, intended to be limited to . . . yeast, but it is intended to imply that more complex organisms, from which the enzymes pepsin, trypsin, etc., can be obtained, are not so fundamentally different from the unicellular organisms.[1]

Kühne's neologism came to be widely accepted, but didn't really help to settle the issue of whether enzyme activity was a *constituent* of living things or a *property* of living things. The soluble ferments suggested strongly that they were constituents. Pasteur was violently opposed to this notion, not least because nobody had succeeded in producing a disorganized ferment of the yeast enzyme. But despite Pasteur's opposition to the idea, and the considerable combative skills he deployed in defending his own position, it eventually became clear that he was wrong. The source of the ferment didn't have to be alive to do the trick.

In 1897, Eduard Buchner had been grinding yeast cells with fine sand and *kieselguhr*, an earth composed largely of the tiny but hard skeletons of long-dead diatoms. Biologists had been grinding cells with sand for decades, but the addition of *kieselguhr* gave the paste a strength and consistency that enabled it to be put into a powerful hydraulic press. The yeast juice that dribbled out decomposed rapidly, so Buchner, with his brother Hans and their assistant Martin Hahn (who had discovered the valuable properties of *kieselguhr*), added various substances as preservatives. One that they tried was sugar, which they knew preserved fruits. To their surprise, the yeast juice converted the sugar into alcohol and carbon dioxide. They had prepared a soluble ferment of yeast.

Having shown that a simple extract of the juices inside yeasts would convert sugar to alcohol, Buchner named the enzyme 'zymase'. (It took a great deal of subsequent work by many others to show that zymase was in fact a complex cascade of some 14 separate enzymes, each doing its own job in the conversion of sugar to alcohol.) Succeeding efforts showed that enzymes were large protein molecules. They could be extracted from living organisms, purified to the point where they would form crystals, and would still demonstrate the ability to enhance the chemical reactions that gave the organism life.

Enzymes, technically speaking, are catalysts. They enable a chemical reaction to proceed with much less energy than is required without the catalyst. The catalyst itself doesn't take part in the reaction; it merely makes the reaction go faster, so that a single molecule of enzyme can bring about the chemical transformation of many thousands of other molecules. The molecules that the enzyme works upon are called the 'substrate', and one of the great finds of the past 40 years has been that other large biochemicals, notably the nucleic acids, are the substrates for particular enzymes. That opened the possibility of using enzymes to manipulate nucleic acids, a possibility that has been amply realized.

We have already looked in some detail at one such group of enzymes, the restriction endonucleases, and in passing at some of the enzymes used in the search for restriction enzymes; these have provided a taste of the capabilities of biological systems. Incredibly specific, enzymes can catalyse a particular chemical reaction with inordinate efficiency. To recognize a set sequence of bases and then break the sugar–phosphate bond that holds the DNA backbone together at one point and no other is a feat of chemical engineering that the organic chemist is nowhere near. But in the unending struggle against entropy that is life, biochemicals perform feats like these all the time. Furthermore, as cannot be repeated too often, without enzymes none of the things in this book would be possible.

The revolution in understanding that accompanied the emergence of enzymes as a biological force was no less important than the genetic revolution that followed Crick and Watson's structure for DNA. But it was a revolution that took place long before most of the young genetic engineers learned their trade; Maxine Singer, head of the Biochemistry Laboratory at the National Cancer Institute in Bethesda and a leading light in recombinant DNA research, sensed this when asked to contribute an introduction to a volume of papers at the cutting edge of the field. She described the modern genetic engineers and their feelings for their tools as follows:

They will not usually concern themselves with the remarkable nature of the enzymes used to manipulate and construct precise DNA molecules. Most often those enzymes are perceived only as tools and are confronted in practice as a rather disorganized array of odd shaped tiny tubes inside a freezer. The sight inside the freezer carries no reminder that the fruits of a revolution are at hand. Nor will the investigator be reminded by the means he uses to acquire the enzymes. Some of them are now as easy to come by all over the world as a bottle of Coca-Cola – only more expensive. Others may be obtained by persuasive begging and borrowing, and, in a tight squeeze, even stealing. But when all else fails, and it is necessary actually to prepare one of the enzymes, the impact of the revolution may be sensed. Delight and amazement inevitably accompany the emergence of a clean, exquisitely specific reagent from the equally inevitably messy beginnings. Dismay coupled with awe of successful predecessors accompany the frequent frustrating failures.[2]

Enzyme types: an incomplete catalogue

Singer chose to remind her forgetful audience that many of the tasks they routinely performed were absolutely dependent on using the powers of enzymes. She did so by going one at a time through the enzymes that underpin genetic engineering; I can do little better than follow her and select some of the more important enzyme tools.

Alkaline phosphatase we have already encountered; Smith and Kelly used it to remove the phosphate group from the end of a restriction fragment of DNA. That, indeed, is its major task. In DNA it breaks the bond that holds the phosphate to the sugar, but it is not terribly fastidious as to what exactly the phosphate is attached to, and will break RNA with equal ease (see figure 3.1). Alkaline phosphatase is part of the cell's mechanism for recycling phosphorus. Bacteria deprived of phosphate continue to grow, making new DNA and proteins, but they do so at the expense of their RNA. When starved of phosphate the cells make alkaline phosphatase to recover the phosphorus from unwanted RNA, and this single enzyme can then account for up to 6 per cent of the cell's protein. Cells given phosphate immediately stop making the enzyme, and surplus phosphate also inhibits directly the action of the phosphatase. So this simple enzyme, so useful for removing phosphate groups and breaking up nucleic acids, is very finely controlled by its own product. In the short term, phosphate stops alkaline phosphatase working, and in the long term it stops the cell from making the enzyme.

Smith and Kelly removed the terminal phosphate from their DNA fragments because they wanted to replace it with a labelled tag, a phosphate group made with a radioactive isotope of phosphorus. To do this they used another enzyme, polynucleotide kinase. This is more or less the reverse of alkaline phosphatase. It transfers a phosphate group from the high-energy compound ATP to the unphosphorylated sugar at the end of the nucleic acid chain (see figure 3.1). If the phosphate happens to be radioactive, the strand will now carry a radioactive tag. For Smith and Kelly this tag meant that they could follow the final nucleotide in the fragment through their various procedures.

Another enzyme that acts upon the end of the DNA chain is called terminal nucleotidyl transferase, or just plain terminal transferase. This, unlike polynucleotide kinase, adds an entire nucleotide to the 3' end of the chain (see figure 3.2). It requires a source of energized nucleotides and simply adds these to the growing chain. This means that, if some DNA is mixed with terminal transferase and just one nucleotide, say the adenine nucleotide, the chain will grow a succession of adenines at the 3′ end of the strand. If another chain is incubated with terminal transferase and thymine nucleotides, it will have a protuding strand that is all thymine. Mix the two sorts of strand together and the complementary bases will attract one another, linking the different fragments. Terminal transferase, then, can be used to attach sticky ends to fragments of DNA, enabling the fragments to be joined at will – the heart of the recombinant aim. Not surprisingly, though, the technique requires yet another enzymes in order to work properly.

First, terminal transferase works best if there is a single-stranded stretch of DNA for it to add to. If the end of a fragment is flush, the engineer may prefer to digest it with lambda exonuclease: in

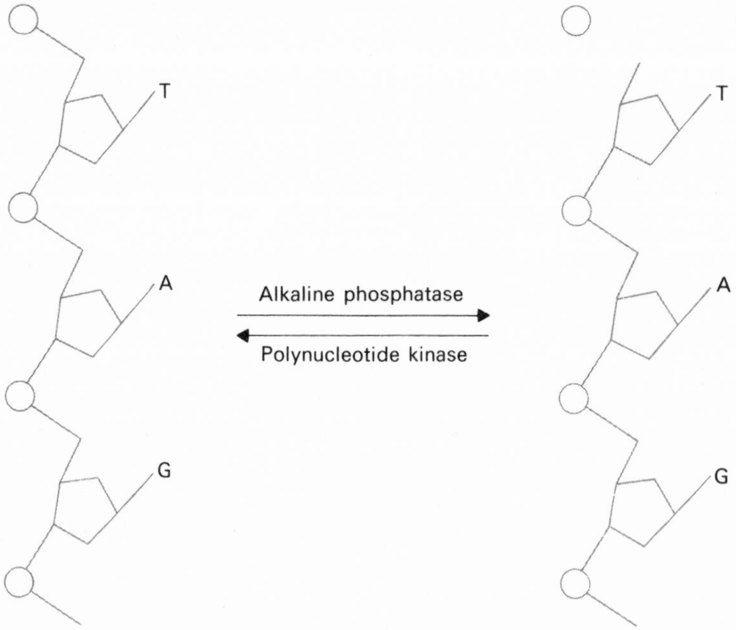

Figure 3.1
Adding and removing phosphates. Alkaline phosphatase (left to right) removes the 5′ phosphate group and so can be used to prevent DNA fragments joining up. Polynucleotide kinase (right to left) adds a phosphate group, and can be used to attach radioactive phosphorus as a label.

contrast to an endonuclease, which cuts the middle of a DNA strand, a exonuclease nibbles away at the end. Lambda exonuclease comes from phage lambda, and is one of the suite of genes that lambda employs. The exonuclease removes nucleotides from the 5' end of the strand, progressing steadily along the helix and destroying it as it goes (see figure 3.2). A brief incubation with lambda exonuclease removes just a few residues from the 5' end of the strand and leaves the single 3' end of the other strand protruding somewhat, a perfect substrate for terminal transferase to add the sticky end to.

The sticky ends may bring strands together end to end to form recombinant molecules, but the DNA will be no good unless the gaps between the fragment ends are sealed. This is the job of DNA ligase. This enzyme, now isolated from a variety of sources, repairs

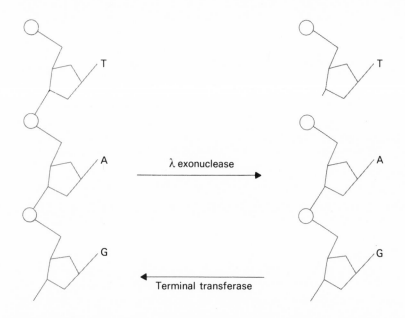

Figure 3.2
Adding and removing nucleotides. λ exonuclease (left to right) removes entire nucleotides from the 5' end and is useful for nibbling back one strand of duplex DNA. Terminal transferase (right to left) adds a nucleotide to the 3' end (there are other transferases that add to the 5' end) and is useful for attaching labelled bases.

nicks between adjacent nucleotides by building a bond between a
5' end that has a phosphate group and a 3' end that does not. It is
absolutely essential to make recombinant molecules whole. Given
this pre-eminence, Maxine Singer notes that 'it is satisfying to
realize that one of the earliest predicted results of recombinant
DNA research, the construction of bacteria that would be efficient
sources of proteins, was first realized with DNA ligase itself.'[3]

Just how we will see later.

Three-way action: the Kornberg enzyme

One of the ultimate scientific accolades is surely to have a law,
effect or some such named after you. Common enough in medicine, where the number of name-bearing diseases is legion, the
phenomenon is less prevalent in molecular biology. Watson–Crick
base-pairing is one, but there is also an eponymous enzyme. This is
the Kornberg enzyme, named for Arthur Kornberg, who did so
much of the work with it. The Kornberg enzyme is more formally
known as DNA polymerase I. He found it in cells of *E. coli* in 1956,
and subsequent studies have shown that it is a fascinating molecule.

Being a polymerase, the Kornberg enzyme might be expected to
catalyse the growth of a DNA chain, polymerizing the nucleotides
into the long sugar–phosphate chain. This indeed it does, and it
needs only magnesium ions, a supply of activated (that is, triphosphate) nucleotides, and a little DNA primer. Given these, it will
add nucleotides to the 3' end of a strand at the rate of roughly 1000
bases a minute. But it also breaks DNA down, and in either
direction. It can remove a nucleotide from the 3' end of the chain
and do exactly the same at the 5' end. The purified enzyme has a
molecular weight of about 109 000, and it can be split into two parts
by another enzyme extracted from *Bacillus subtilis*. One part,
called the Klenow fragment, has a molecular weight of about
76 000; it will polymerize DNA and break off nucleotides at the 3'
end. The smaller part will remove nucleotides only from the 5' end.
(*B. subtilis* polymerase I cannot remove nucleotides from the 5'
end.)

Those three activities, which can be visualized as being on
different heads of the enzyme, are the basis for its fascinating
action. It recognizes and binds on to a nick in one DNA strand.

(Another enzyme, horribly named DNase I, is just the job for creating a few nicks at intervals along the strand.) One head then breaks off the nucleotide at the 5' side of the nick, while the other head adds a nucleotide to the 3' side. Another nucleotide removed from the 5' side, another one added to the 3' side, and the nick moves along the chain, taking the enzyme with it until it reaches the end of the strand and falls off. All this at 1000 bases a minute. The progression of the nick along the chain has been called 'nick translation' (see figure 3.3). It is an extremely useful activity, because it means that DNA can be radioactively labelled to an extraordinarily high degree. If DNA of interest is incubated with labelled nucleotides and DNA polymerase I, then provided there

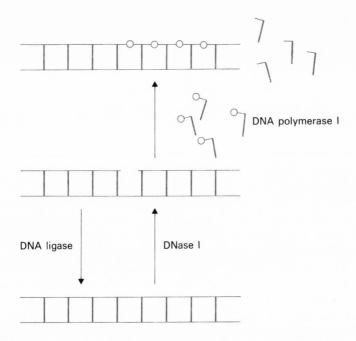

Figure 3.3
Nick translation. DNase I makes breaks (nicks) between sugar and phosphate; DNA ligase repairs them. DNA polymerase I removes nucleotides from the 5' side of a nick and adds a nucleotide to the 3' side. The nick is thus translated along the strand, so that if the DNA polymerase I is provided with radioactive nucleotides the whole strand can be labelled to a very high level, making it much easier to track small fragments.

are some nicks for the enzyme to start at the nucleotides will be incorporated into the DNA so that practically every base is label-led, and that means that minute quantities can be studied, and studied in more detail.

As with restriction enzymes, we are entitled to ask what part DNA polymerase I plays in the normal life of the cell. It is tempting to suppose, as Kornberg did when he began, that it is the enzyme responsible for DNA replication, but this is probably not so. For one thing, it won't actually reproduce double-stranded DNA semi-conservatively. For another, it is too slow. Even 1000 base-pairs a minute is much too tardy for DNA replication, which takes place at the mind-boggling rate of 100 000 bases a minute. Finally, there are mutant strains that lack the Kornberg enzyme and yet are able to grow and replicate satisfactorily, making new copies of their DNA. So it seems that the Kornberg enzyme is certainly not essential for DNA replication.

What, then, does it do? It is a repair system and proofreader all in one. Mutants that lack it are overly sensitive to mild disruptions to the DNA that normal strains cope well with. Probably DNA polymerase I removes bases that may have been mispaired. Should a mismatch occur in replication, a T might find itself opposite another T rather than an A; if DNA polymerase wanders past that stretch of the nucleic acid it will remove the offending T and replace it with an A. This corrects the mistake, provided that the enzyme is going along the newly synthesized strand, and there are suggestions that it does just that, travelling along the new strand of DNA after replication, proofreading and making corrections as it goes. But, as with the restriction enzyme, the function of DNA polymerase I is less important to the genetic engineer than is its action, which provides a very neat way of obtaining very highly labelled DNA. And, like DNA ligase, polymerase I was one of the first products of genetic engineering.

Dogma undone

The last enzyme we will look at in this chapter catalyses the formation of a DNA strand, but uses as its template not a com-plementary DNA strand but a strand of RNA. Howard Temin predicted that just such an enzyme would have to exist from his studies of RNA viruses. These viruses – the one that causes poliomyelitis is an example – store their genetic information as RNA rather than DNA, but are nevertheless able to infect cells and direct synthesis according to their own genetic message. In polio virus the RNA simply directs synthesis of more RNA and the manufacture of viral necessities. No DNA is involved in its replication. But the virus that Temin worked with, the so-called Rous sarcoma virus (which causes some bird cells to become cancerous), is a member of a different group from the polio virus; while it stores its information as RNA, it nevertheless requires DNA to be synthesized if it is to infect a cell.

Temin discovered that the Rous sarcoma story wasn't quite as simple as the other RNA viruses. He isolated from the infective virus particles an enzyme that catalysed the synthesis of short chains of double-stranded DNA. These were identical to regions of the viral RNA, and the enzyme, and synthesis, were vital if the virus was successfully to infect a cell. At first this was felt to undermine Francis Crick's Central Dogma of molecular biology: DNA makes RNA makes protein. What Crick meant was that the flow of information in living things was from nucleic acids to proteins, and not the other way round. As Crick himself put it,

Once 'information' has passed into protein *it cannot get out again*. In more detail, the transfer of information from nucleic acid to nucleic acid, or from nucleic acid to protein, may be possible, but transfer from protein to protein, or from protein to nucleic acid, is impossible. Information here means the *precise* determination of sequence, either of bases in the nucleic acid or of amino acid residues in the protein.[4]

Changes to the proteins could come about only as a result of changes to the DNA. The fact that information on RNA could be transferred on to DNA called this dogma into question, but in point of fact Crick himself never ruled out the possibility of transfer of RNA to DNA; it was just that many molecular biologists assumed that he had, and that Temin's results broke the rules. Looked at from a different point of view, they uphold the central place of DNA even more strongly; why would the virus bother to synthesize DNA from its RNA if DNA weren't supremely important? Indeed, several sorts of RNA virus can spend many generations living harmlessly within a cell as DNA, fully integrated into the host's own DNA and being reproduced along with it, which again confirms the central importance of DNA.

At first Temin called his enzyme RNA-dependent DNA polymerase. Then, as it became clear that the enzyme could also catalyse synthesis from a DNA template, he changed 'dependent' to 'directed', calling the enzyme RNA-directed DNA polymerase. The journal *Nature*, which published Temin's announcement that he had purified and characterized this odd enzyme, began referring to it as 'reverse transcriptase', 'a name,' Temin says, 'that I do not like because of its ambiguity but that has gained wide currency.'[5]

Reverse transcriptase is the name by which the enzyme goes these days, especially among people who make use of it in their work but don't work on it (see figure 3.4). They use it to make pure

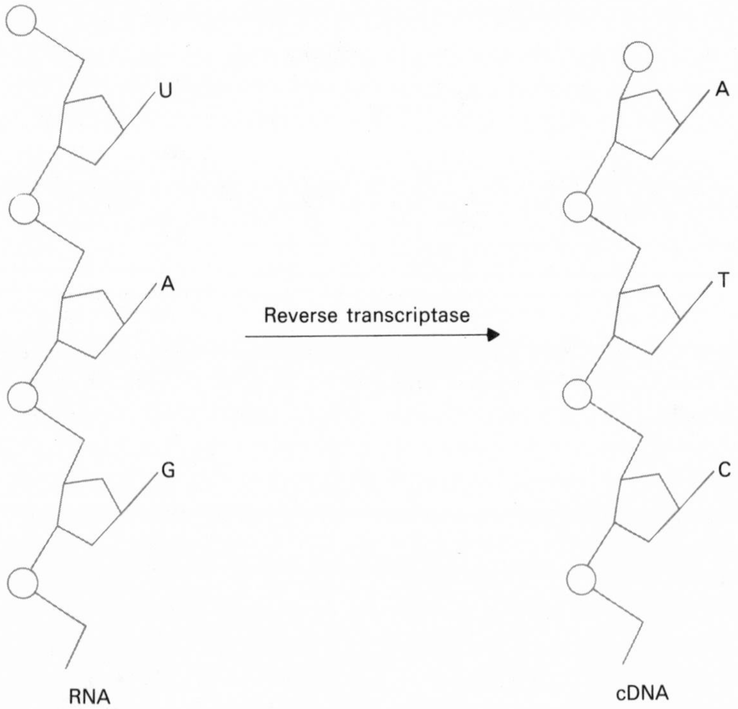

Figure 3.4
Reverse transcriptase. Normally DNA is translated into RNA; reverse transcriptase makes a single strand of DNA on an RNA template. It is very useful for making DNA copies of messenger RNA. (This figure shows the cDNA schematically; in reality it has the complementary orientation, as well as the complementary base sequence.)

DNA for a single gene. The starting point is purified mRNA from the gene in question. If this is incubated with reverse transcriptase and a supply of activated nucleotides, the complementary DNA strand will be made on the RNA template. That done, the RNA is destroyed by mixing with alkali, which attacks RNA but not DNA. Now, the single strand of DNA is offered as a template to DNA polymerase, which synthesizes the complementary strand to create duplex DNA. The result: a faithful complementary DNA (usually called cDNA) copy of the messenger RNA for a particular protein. This technique for getting the DNA that corresponds to the protein you are interested in is a very valuable one because it cuts out many of the niggling steps that living cells are good at but that the biochemist still finds incredibly difficult. The mRNA is the step just before protein; catch the message there, and it's a good bet that the cDNA will, if all the other stages succeed, be translated into that protein and no other.

The ability to interfere

These, then, are the enzyme tools of the genetic engineer. There are a few others that find specific uses from time to time, but by and large our survey of the toolbox is complete. The exciting prospect is that there may yet be undiscovered enzymes that will perform different, but equally useful, tricks. Some scientists doubt this, arguing that the search for enzyme activities has been so intense that, as far as ones that operate on nucleic acids are concerned, we have found all the enzymes that we are going to find. Perhaps there are better sources of these enzymes waiting to be discovered, but that is all. There are no stunning new powers out there.

Others are more sanguine. They feel that there could well be enzyme activities around the corner that will make even today's marvellous tools seem as clumsy as pneumatic drills. I tend to favour this view. After all, who could have foreseen that the enzymes in such general use today would ever have been isolated? And given the track record of molecular biology, it is extremely likely that, if an enzyme of unparalleled usefulness is to emerge, it will do so from a study quite unrelated to genetic engineering. The engineers will take it up and put it to work, but their toolbox is so full that they are unlikely to go looking for more.

Alone, neither the revelations of the Crick–Watson structure for DNA nor Buchner and his intellectual successors could have brought us to our present position of understanding and ability. The two had to be brought together. Maxine Singer stresses that

by itself, the DNA revolution was insufficient to permit detailed and designed manipulation of genetic systems. . . . The enzyme revolution is as central to the successful manipulation of biological systems as the DNA revolution. . . . Chemistry itself has not yet provided techniques for the precise manipulation of macromolecules.[6]

The key is the ability to go beyond simply interpreting and understanding what one sees and to interfere purposefully. Without enzymes, none of that interference would be possible.

People use the word 'biotechnology' to refer, among other things, to the application of recombinant techniques to the production of chemicals. Bacteria that produce insulin and yeasts that produce alcohol are both examples of biotechnology, although only the insulin bacteria have been engineered. But the word has, I think, been misapplied. If it means anything, it is surely the ability of life to do the things that man needs technology for. We can make alcohol without the help of enzymes, but it takes a pretty large and complicated set of equipment. That equipment is technology. The enzyme equipment that living cells use to carry out their chemical reactions is life's technology – biotechnology. What cannot even be contemplated with ordinary technology is done all the time by biotechnology in the sense that I use it, and the genetic engineers make use of those tools to perform impossible magic. But it is time to move out of the toolbox and on to the shop floor.

4

MANIPULATION

The essentials of genetic engineering, and how scientists learned to manufacture DNA

At this stage, things begin to snowball. We have the elements of a toolkit for combining the DNA from different species, and a growing group of people able, and willing, to use those techniques. Each discovery feeds off previous ones and nourishes those that follow, and the whole enterprise begins to roll with ever-increasing momentum. Stanley Cohen, the Stanford biochemist who (as we'll see) developed some of the great recombination tools, pinpointed the requirements of any attempt to create a new form of DNA:

There are four essential elements: a method of breaking and joining DNA molecules derived from different sources; a suitable gene carrier that can replicate both itself and a foreign DNA segment linked to it; a means of introducing the composite DNA molecule, or chimera, into a functional bacterial cell, and a method of selecting from a large population of cells a clone of recipient cells that has acquired the molecular chimera.[1]

Conceptually, the four are to some degree distinct, but each is also intertwined with the others. For example, new ways to cut and join enable the use of different methods of getting the chimera into the cell, and new methods of selection enable the use of different cutting and joining procedures. Still, Cohen's list provides a good guide through the tangle.

Joints

The Royal Swedish Academy of Sciences credited Paul Berg with being 'the first investigator to construct a recombinant-DNA molecule, i.e. a molecule containing parts of DNA from different species'.[2] For this, and his 'fundamental studies', Berg received a half share in the 1980 prize for chemistry. This development stemmed from Berg's interest in the way that higher, eukaryote, cells regulate and control the operation of the many genes that go to make up the hereditary message. To study the whole seemed needlessly complex, so Berg started looking for ways to isolate sets of genes in a simple environment where he could study them in detail. Berg 'began to think of using SV40 to carry genes into mammalian cells'.[3] SV40 – simian virus 40 – causes cells to become cancerous by insinuating its DNA into the DNA of a host cell. It can also exist in the cell on its own, and it was these abilities that Berg sought to take advantage of, using the virus to put the mammalian genes in which he was interested into a simple bacterial cells. The fact that very few mammalian genes had been isolated, so that there was no immediate prospect of success, didn't deter him: 'I anticipated that a variety of suitable genes would eventually be isolated. Therefore, the first task was to devise a general way to join together in vitro two different DNA molecules.'[4]

That 'general way' worked like this. There was already a class of enzymes, the DNA ligases, that would join bits of DNA together. Discovered by Khorana's group in 1970, the ligase from phage T4 would seal the flush ends of two DNA fragments together, but it was hopelessly inefficient because the enzyme couldn't work unless the fragments were aligned end to end. Concentrated solutions of DNA and low temperatures helped, but still the procedure was far too haphazard to be of much use to Berg. What he needed was a way of holding the fragments together while the enzymes went to work. Berg already knew that the DNA of phage lambda would, under the right conditions, close up into a circle of DNA. This was because there were two protruding strands at the end of the lambda genome that were complementary. The two strands attract one another and hydrogen bonds between the complementary bases held the ends together while repair enzymes closed the circle properly by sealing the nicks between adjacent nucleotides at the ends of the strands. This ability of lambda showed Berg the general way he sought. He would create cohesive complementary terminals, sticky ends, and use them to join the DNA from different species.

We have already glimpsed the basis of the method, called 'homopolymer tailing' because it involves adding a tail made of just one nucleotide to the DNA fragments. Berg, with David Jackson and Robert Symons, began by extracting and purifying the DNA from SV40. To mix with the SV40, because there were few mammalian genes around and the method was still unproven and hardly worth wasting valuable material on at this stage, they chose lambda DNA – not the ordinary lambda genome, but a smaller version in which the lambda genes had become mixed up with some *E. coli* genes (which allow the bacteria to make use of the sugar galactose) to form a small circle of DNA called a 'plasmid'. Plasmids are not uncommon (see below), and have the very special property of being able to replicate inside a cell independently of the cell's chromosome. They broke open the circles of DNA – lambda and SV40 – with a restriction enzyme, *Eco* RI, which cleaves each of them at just one place. Next came the addition of the sticky ends. This required terminal transferase, but because that enzyme works best on the 3' end of a single strand, Berg needed to strip away some of the bases at the 5' end of the fragments. Exonuclease from phage lambda did the trick. The SV40 DNA was mixed with terminal transferase and a supply of just one activated nucleotide, the one containing adenine. The enzyme added a short tail of 50 to 100 adenines to the 3' end of the DNA strands. In the same way, a thymine tail was added to the lambda DNA. Now the two species of DNA could be mixed. The adenine tails on the SV40 and the thymine tails on the lambda DNA came together and were held by hydrogen bonds. The DNA of SV40 and lambda had been combined into one chimeric molecule in the test-tube. All that remained was to repair the new molecule; a brief incubation with DNA polymerase, to fill the gaps, and DNA ligase, to seal any remaining nicks, and the first recombinant molecule was complete (see figure 4.1).

Berg and his colleagues had succeeded in their project. They now had a way to join DNA molecules to order. As they said when they announced these results, 'the methods described in this report . . . are general and offer an approach for covalently joining any two DNA molecules together'. But the experiment was intended to go beyond the general method itself: 'These molecules should be useful for testing whether those bacterial genes can be introduced into a mammalian cell genome and whether they can be expressed there.'[5]

The chimeric molecule was a monster in more ways than one. It

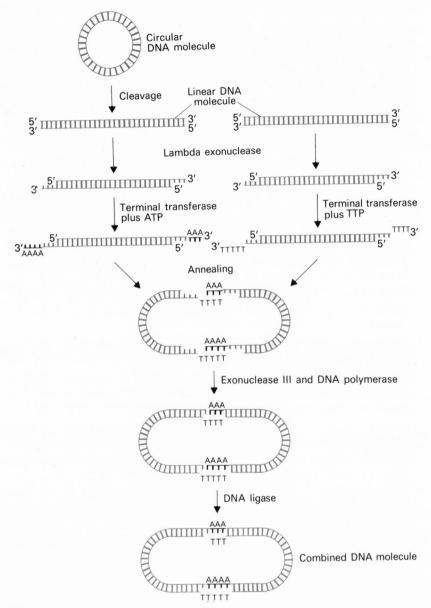

Figure 4.1
Recombination by homopolymer tailing (sticky ends). Terminal transferase is used to add complementary bases to the 3′ end of the two sorts of DNA. The bases must be in the form of activated nucleotides; these have three high-energy phosphate groups, and are called adenosine triphosphate (ATP) and thymidine triphosphate (TTP). The complementary bases attract one another and hydrogen bonds hold the molecules together while exonuclease III and DNA polymerase fill in any gaps. Finally, DNA ligase seals the joints. (*Copyright © 1975 by Scientific American, Inc.*)

was three times the size of the normal SV40 DNA, so there was no question of it becoming packaged into viral coats and then being allowed to infect cells in the normal way. Instead, Berg intended to get it into animal cells himself and see whether the *E. coli* genes would work there. And, because the lambda plasmid that they used would replicate on its own in *E. coli*, they also planned to put the recombinant DNA into *E. coli* to see whether any of the SV40 genes would operate in their new environment. Things, however, took a very different turn.

In the summer of 1971, Janet Mertz, a student of Berg's, went to a workshop course on culturing mammalian cells at Cold Spring Harbor. There, right at the end of the meeting, during a discussion of safety and ethics, she mentioned Berg's plans to infect cells with recombinant SV40. Robert Pollack, course instructor, was filled with alarm. A tumour virus inside a bacterial cell that normally lives in the human gut was an entirely unknown quantity. If SV40-containing bacteria escaped and found their way into people, the consequences could be dire. Pollack telephoned Berg and asked him to reconsider, pointing out some of the dangers. Berg accepted Pollack's arguments, and decided not to do the experiment; the 'recombinant DNA debate' had begun. Research workers, led by Berg, ended up deciding voluntarily to suspend certain types of work until the hazards had been assessed and guidelines for recombinant research drawn up.[6] Ironically, had Berg gone ahead with his experiment, it would have been a total failure, and no one would have had the slightest idea why. We shall come back to this later (see page 86).

Homopolymer tailing, as devised by Berg (and independently confirmed by Peter Lobban and Dale Kaiser)[7], provided exactly the general method Berg had sought. But while the researchers temporarily abandoned their plans to introduce the recombinant molecules into living cells, pure research work continued, and came up with different and much simpler methods for joining DNA fragments together. In Berg's biochemistry laboratory Mertz, with Ronald Davis, was examining *Eco* RI in some detail; while just across the Stanford campus in the Department of Genetics Vittorio Sgaramella was doing the same. Their targets, however, were different; Mertz set her *Eco* RI to work on SV40 DNA, while Sgaramella concentrated upon the DNA of a phage that attacked *Salmonella* bacteria: phage P22. What they both discovered was that Berg's elaborate procedure to attach sticky ends to the DNA fragments produced by *Eco* RI was, ironically, entirely unnecessary. The enzyme, on its own and unaided, produced sticky ends all the time.

You will recall that restriction enzymes frequently recognize a site that is palindromic; the two strands read the same in 'opposite' directions. (Of course, it is really the same direction, 5' to 3', on opposite strands.) If the enzyme makes a break that is not in the centre of the palindrome, then naturally it will leave complementary tags on the ends of the fragments. Mertz and Davis cut DNA with *Eco* RI and looked at the strands with an electron microscope. They saw that, having cut SV40 once with *Eco* RI, the linear DNA had a tendency to join up again into circles, which could be sealed with DNA ligase. Cut and restored, SV40 DNA was fully infectious. They also showed that all the ends of fragments produced by *Eco* RI were identical and complementary, so that any two fragments created by *Eco* RI could be joined together. Mertz and Davis said quite bluntly: 'any two DNAs with RI endonuclease cleavage sites can be "recombined" at their restriction sites by the sequential action of RI endonuclease and DNA ligase. These hybrid DNAs can be cleaved by RI endonuclease to regenerate the original DNAs.'[8] Tracing the birth of words is a frustrating business, but this seems to be the first time that molecular biologists used the word 'recombined', hesitantly and in apologetic quotation marks, to describe the chimeric molecules.

Sgaramella came up with very similar results and conclusions; he found that the DNA ligase that T4 bacteriophages produce when they infect *E. coli* cells was able to join single P22 DNA molecules into chains that were twice, or three times, or occasionally even four times, as long as the customary P22 DNA. The ordinary DNA ligase produced by uninfected *E. coli* could not do this trick. SV40 DNA, made linear by chopping it with *Eco* RI, could be rejoined by either ligase, but a mixture of P22 and SV40 never gave rise to hybrid molecules (which Sgaramella called 'molecular translocations'[9]). Sgaramella's conclusions were not as readily identifiable as Mertz and Davis's, but the promise of being able to join DNA molecules at will was there nevertheless. The two groups published in the same issue of the *Proceedings of the National Academy of Sciences* of the USA, just 15 pages apart.

The explanation for the two sets of observations was that *Eco* RI always creates sticky ends on the fragments it produces. Later, Herbert Boyer and his colleagues (who had discovered *Eco* RI in the first place) sequenced the ends of the fragments directly and confirmed that this was correct. The enzyme recognizes the six-base palindrome

$$5'\text{——}G\text{—}A\text{—}A\text{—}T\text{—}T\text{—}C\text{——}3'$$
$$3'\text{——}C\text{—}T\text{—}T\text{—}A\text{—}A\text{—}G\text{——}5'$$

and cuts between the G and the A. This leaves a four-base sticky end that will automatically hydrogen-bond with other fragments cleaved by the same enzyme. To make a recombinant molecule, all that is needed is to digest the two sorts of DNA with *Eco* RI (or one of the other type II enzymes that make a staggered break and so create sticky ends) and anneal the two sets of fragments with DNA ligase (see figure 4.2).

A third method combines some facets of homopolymer tailing with some facets of restriction enzyme-produced sticky ends. Devised by Richard Scheller at the California Institute of Technology, it requires the scientist to add small 'linker' molecules to the flush ends of fragments. The linker strands may be 10 or 12 nucleotides long and they are palindromic, so that they are self-complementary. It isn't difficult these days to synthesize short stretches of DNA to a specific sequence (indeed, there are commercial companies that offer just such a service, for a fee of course), and the linkers can be made so that they contain the recognition site for a specific enzyme, say *Eco* RI. These linkers can be joined to blunt-ended DNA fragments with T4 ligase and then digested with *Eco* RI; this gives the fragments sticky ends so that they can be recombined with other molecules that have corresponding sticky ends (see figure 4.3).[10]

The three methods for making recombinants all have their advantages and disadvantages. Homopolymer tailing is good for pairing specific fragments; because the researcher adds the sticky end he can ensure that some fragments get them and others don't. It also enables randomly broken fragments to be linked, and prevents the fragments simply recombining with themselves to form circular DNA. The two sorts of DNA, with their different tails, can only join with one another, whereas a restriction enzyme puts the same sticky end on to all the fragments, so that each fragment can swallow its tail and form a circle. These factors make homopolymer tailing an ideal way of creating a library of a species' genome, fragmented at random and inserted into a carrier DNA

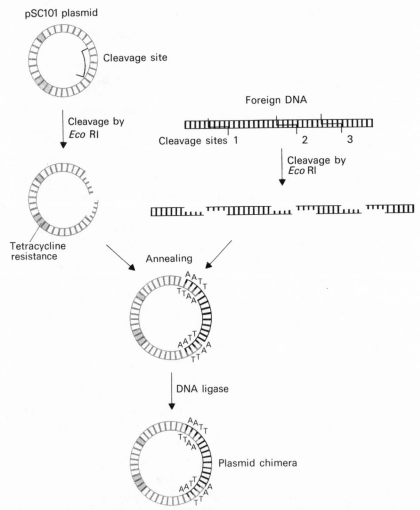

Figure 4.2
Recombination by staggered-end restriction cuts. Some restriction enzymes automatically create cohesive ends. If the vehicle and the insert are both cut by the same enzyme they will come together and join up. DNA ligase seals the joints between the two sorts of DNA. (*Copyright © 1975 by Scientific American, Inc.*)

(see chapter 5). On the other hand, homopolymer tailing creates problems when it comes to recovering the gene of interest at some later stage. There is no easy way to retrieve the gene from the carrier DNA. S1 nuclease can be used to cut DNA preferentially at regions that have an excess of AT pairs, so that if the sticky ends were made of adenine and thymine this would be one solution, but it isn't terribly efficient. A restriction enzyme, when its sticky ends

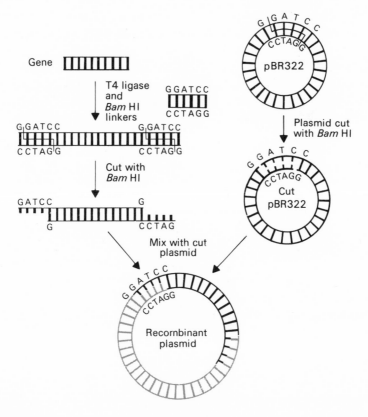

Figure 4.3
Recombination by synthetic linkers. Short strands of DNA synthesized to contain a specific restriction enzyme recognition site are attached to flush-ended DNA fragments with T4 ligase. The fragments should first have been treated with the corresponding modification enzyme, because once the linkers are attached the fragments and receiving vehicle are treated with the restriction enzyme to create sticky ends. The procedure is now as for staggered-end recombination.

have been annealed, recreates its recognition site, so the same enzyme can be used to chop the gene out of the DNA. But a restriction enzyme may not have a recognition site near the gene of interest. Homopolymer tailing, especially with the use of linkers, then becomes more appropriate.

The different methods, then, have their different uses. If the details of the genome are known, one can target the areas of interest with specific restriction enzymes. Otherwise, one can use random cleavage and add tails to get the molecules to recombine. Either way, it is no great problem to join DNA from different species. That brings us to the second and third of Cohen's necessities: a suitable carrier that can not only replicate itself and the piggyback gene but also get our gene into the new host we have chosen for it.

Search for a suitable vehicle

Paul Berg's original intention had been to introduce the recombinant molecules he had made into cells of *E. coli*. The problem was how, in reality, to do so. The search was on for a cloning vehicle. 'Cloning' because the idea was to enable the gene to reproduce freely, producing a clone of daughters that would, like all clones, be identical copies. And a 'vehicle' because the foreign genes had to be got into the host cell, and a vehicle was needed to get them there. Getting DNA into the cell turned out to be quite easy; persuading it to grow and multiply was more of a problem, and that is where the vehicle becomes important.

Bacteriophages sometimes pick up a little stretch of host DNA in their own genome and carry this with them until they infect another host. When they do so, the non-viral DNA can change the properties of the recipient host. The phage is said to have transduced the host. Bacteria can also be affected by naked DNA. This process, harking back to Avery's work with the transforming agent before he knew it to be DNA, is called transformation. But the bacteria have to be persuaded to take up the naked DNA. Morton Mandel and A. Higa, working at the School of Medicine of the University of Hawaii, discovered in about 1970 that cells would absorb, and be transformed by, viral DNA if the cells had been soaked in a solution of calcium chloride at 0 °C.[11] The solution doesn't need to be very strong, nor the soaking prolonged. Twenty minutes is enough, and for reasons that aren't entirely obvious the calcium chloride tends to make the cell walls leaky, so that smallish DNA molecules in the surrounding fluid very quickly make their way into the cell. Test-tube transformation, then, offered a way to put DNA molecules into cells. But would it work for non-viral DNA?

Stanley Cohen and Annie Chang did a very simple experiment which demonstrated that it would.[12] They knew that some *E. coli* strains were resistant to antibiotics, and that this resistance depended on genes that were not on the chromosome but on a piece of extra DNA, a plasmid. Plasmids are small circles of non-chromosomal DNA; they often carry genes for resistance to anti-biotics, though there are also plasmids that carry all sorts of other genes, and they are generally not essential to the life of the cell. Some plasmids confer on their carrier the ability to swap DNA with another organism, a form of sexual reproduction during which the plasmid may be transmitted to a different strain. On another categorization, some types – relaxed plasmids – are usually found as multiple copies within a cell, while others – stringent plasmids – are somehow constrained in number. As an autonomous self-duplicating piece of DNA, plasmids might make ideal cloning vehicles.

Extracting the DNA from an *E. coli* strain in which they knew resistance depended on a plasmid, Cohen and Chang had to separate the plasmids from the chromosomal DNA. This they did by mixing the DNA with ethidium bromide and then spinning the molecules in a caesium chloride density gradient. The ethidium bromide molecules insinuate themselves between the bases of the DNA, opening up the double helix and lowering its density. Because plasmids are closed circles they cannot unwind as much as linear pieces of DNA. That means that they take up less ethidium bromide and so stay at a higher density. In the high-speed centrifuge they end up lower in the density gradient than the linear DNA, which because it can unwind has taken up more ethidium bromide and become more buoyant.

Cohen and Chang then took a strain of *E. coli* that was sensitive to antibiotics and bathed the cells with the denser closed circles from the DNA purification, doing so in a calcium chloride medium that would certainly have enabled the bacteria to take up viral DNA. After a while they spread the cells on to an agar plate that contained antibiotics in addition to the normal nutrients that promote cell growth. Only cells that had been transformed by absorbing the 'foreign' plasmid would be able to grow, and in time each would give rise to a small colony of identical clones, all resistant. Indeed, the whole colony is a clone comprising the descendants of one resistant cell. The vast majority of cells simply died, but the ones that had been transformed selected themselves for Cohen and Chang by growing where their untransformed comrades could not. By this method, Cohen and Chang established that they could use plasmids to transform *E. coli*, and that about one bacterial cell in a million would take up the plasmid. The beauty of the method was that, by conferring antibiotic resistance on that one in a million, Cohen and Chang made it very easy to find.

As soon as Herbert Boyer had demonstrated that *Eco* RI produced sticky ends, Cohen began to search for a plasmid that *Eco* RI would cleave without destroying the plasmid's ability to replicate. This was the step that Berg had not gone through, and as a result of which his planned experiment would not have worked. He had inserted the SV40 genes into a region of the plasmid that was essential for it to be able to replicate. Later, when the methods came into use again, knowledge of plasmid functioning was sufficiently advanced to take advantage of this sort of thing. 'We hoped,' Cohen says, 'that if such a plasmid could be found, we could insert a segment of foreign DNA at the *Eco* RI cleavage site, and that it might be possible to propagate the foreign DNA in *E. coli*.'[13] They found what they were looking for in the collection at Stanford. (The collection had been gathered in earlier days, when they used mechanical force to break up the resistance plasmid into easy-to-study chunks.) A plasmid called pSC101 (p for plasmid, SC for Stanley Cohen, 101 for that one), was just one-twelfth the size of the major resistance plasmid (see plate 4.1). But it had retained the region that allowed it to replicate independently and an antibiotic-resistance gene, that for tetracycline. *Eco* RI, to Cohen's delight, broke pSC101 at just one spot, and the reconstituted plasmid was fully functional; it transformed cells and made them tetracycline-resistant.

So far, so good. But was it possible to insert foreign DNA into the plasmid without interfering either with replication or with the tetracycline resistance? Cohen and Chang (helped by Boyer and Robert Helling) went to a different *E. coli* plasmid – pSC102 – one that conferred resistance to kanamycin, another antibiotic. They created recombinant molecules of this plasmid and pSC101 and used them to transform sensitive *E. coli*.[14] The transformed cells were plated on to a medium that contained tetracycline and kanamycin. Only if both genes were working would any cells grow. It was a nail-biting time for Cohen and Chang, but when they came to examine the plates, there were the tell-tale colonies, growing happily despite the double dose of antibiotic. Not many, just one for every 40 million molecules of DNA, but that didn't matter in the least to Cohen: 'The results meant that the pSC101 could serve as a

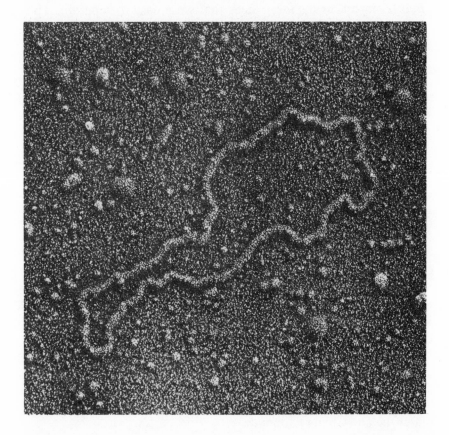

Plate 4.1
Plasmid pSC101. This little loop of DNA made genetic engineering possible. (*Courtesy Stanley N. Cohen*)

cloning vehicle for introducing at least a nonreplicating segment of a related DNA into *E. coli*. And the procedure was extraordinarily simple.'[15]

Once again, things were looking good. Cohen's plasmid would transfer *E. coli* genes into other *E. coli* cells. Would truly foreign genes be as easy? Such genes might, after all, have special signals that would prevent them working in any environment other than their own species. Cohen decided to try with a plasmid from a different host, p1258 from the bacteria *Staphylococcus aureus*. This plasmid certainly could not replicate in *E. coli* on its own, but it might work if spliced into an *E. coli* plasmid, and it was cleaved by *Eco* RI into four distinct pieces that were easy to separate. The *Staphylococcus* plasmid carried a gene that conferred resistance to yet another antibiotic: penicillin. Fortunately, *E. coli* in nature were often resistant to penicillin (as they were to tetracycline and kanamycin). In keeping with the mutually agreed guidelines, Cohen could perform this experiment and still ensure that he did not extend the resistance capabilities of *E. coli*. Cohen and Chang repeated the experiment that they had done with two *E. coli* plasmids, but this time used pSC101 and the utterly foreign p1258 from *Staphylococcus aureus*. Again, success. Colonies grew on a medium that contained tetracycline and penicillin.

The triumph is hard to imagine. It certainly doesn't come through in the scientific report, though a shadow of the future is dimly visible:

The replication and expression of genes in *E. coli* that have been derived from a totally unrelated bacterial species (i.e., *Staphylococcus aureus*) now suggest that interspecies genetic recombination may be generally attainable. Thus, it may be practical to introduce into *E. coli* genes specifying metabolic or synthetic functions (e.g., photosynthesis, antibiotic production) indigenous to other biological classes.[16]

That was in 1974. Chang and Cohen had created a stretch of DNA that was an artificial hybrid, working perfectly normally inside an otherwise unremarkable bacterium. As Cohen remarked later, he and Chang had made

a breach in the barriers that normally separate biological species. The bulk of the genetic information expressed in the transformed bacteria defined it as *E. coli*, but the transformed cells also carried replicating DNA molecules that had molecular and biological characteristics derived from a different species, *S. aureus*.[17]

The techniques were simple, they were easy, and they had practically unlimited potential – if they would work with animal genes. One difficulty would be that animal genes don't code for such easily detected things as resistance to antibiotics. Another was that there weren't, as Berg had noted, very many animal genes around on laboratory shelves. Nevertheless, Cohen had to try. He and Chang got together with Herbert Boyer and three of his colleagues to mix a eukaryote gene with their plasmid.[18] The gene they used was one that carried the code for part of the ribosomes (the protein factories) of the toad *Xenopus laevis*, better known perhaps as the African clawed toad. They sliced the toad genes with *Eco* RI, spliced the fragments into pSC101, pushed the plasmid into *E. coli* cells, and grew the cells in the presence of tetracycline. That told them which cells had taken up a plasmid and been transformed. Now they needed to examine the descendants of each transformed cell to discover which, if indeed any, contained a little bit of toad. They found them: *E. coli* cells that were busily manufacturing RNA that hitherto had been made only in toads.

Cohen's pSC101 was an ideal cloning vehicle. It had a cleavage site that didn't interfere with vital functions, and carried a tetracycline-resistance marker that was extremely handy for detecting cells that had taken up the plasmid. And cells could easily be induced to take it up. Inspired by Cohen's success, other labs quickly followed suit, and more cloning plasmids were rapidly developed.

Now there are plasmids for every purpose, each carefully tailored – by the very techniques that it allows – to permit it to perform special tasks. One of the most popular of these is pBR322, a beauty of a plasmid made by Francisco Bolivar and his colleagues (see figure 4.4).[19] pBR322, one of a whole family of vectors, is small and easy to use. It has a single cleavage site for each of five popular restriction enzymes, and offers resistance to two antibiotics. (Selection is not difficult. Inserts within the tetracycline-resistance gene can be picked up because cells fail to grow – though they are not killed – in tetracycline. To recover those cells one adds cycloserine, a drug that kills only cells that are growing fast. Those

cells will be tetracycline-resistant cells that do not harbour the
foreign gene; the ones left are the ones that have been transformed.) The combinations that the double antibiotic resistance
allows make certain types of recombinant work a great deal easier,
and yet still the work goes on to construct ever better plasmid
cloning vehicles. Many of the more common plasmids are available, like the enzymes, reagents, and bespoke DNA, off the shelf.
The choice can be bewildering. And yet plasmids are not by any
means the only cloning vehicles in use today.

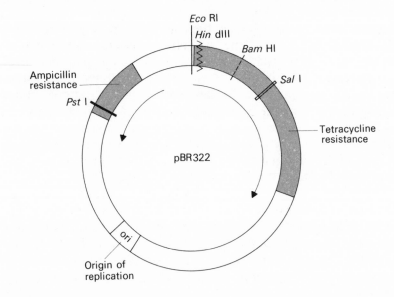

Figure 4.4
A map of plasmid pBR322. The recognition sites of the enzymes that cut the circle only
once are shown. The arrows show the directions in which the two antibiotic resistance
genes are transcribed.

Ferrymen: phage vectors

In nature, phage can pick up bits of non-viral DNA and transform
successive hosts with them. Not unnaturally, then, while Cohen
and others focused on plasmids as cloning vehicles, different workers turned to phage, and especially to lambda. It is a close-run thing

as to which of the many millions of living organisms man understands best, but lambda is certainly near the top of the list. We have a very good map of its 47 000 base-pair genome, and a broad understanding of what the various genes do. In particular, we know that there is a central region on the chromosome that isn't really needed for the infectious cycle of the phage. Even without that region, the phage can still parasitize susceptible strains of *E. coli* and multiply within them. This is important, because it means that the central portion can be replaced with recombinant genes.

Ordinary 'wild' lambda, however, is not very well suited for use as a cloning vehicle. For one thing, it has a number of restriction enzyme cleavage sites that are badly placed for the genetic engineer. That, however, has proved no hindrance. The engineers have simply gone out and manufactured two different sorts of lambda specifically for cloning purposes. Some are *insertional* vectors: they contain a single site at which DNA from a foreign gene can be spliced into the lambda chromosome and, provided that the gene does not make the chromosome too big to fit in the viral coat, these are efficient cloning vehicles. Then there are *replacement* vectors: these contain a pair of sites that allow a piece of viral DNA to be snipped out and replaced with a piece of foreign DNA. Replacement vectors allow more genes to be inserted into lambda phage.

The special genetics that allow phages to be used as vectors are, compared to plasmids, complex. Nevertheless, such vectors do find a use. As an example, we can look at two popular phage vectors. Lambda WES.B' was built by Marjorie Thomas at Stanford (and by others independently), and has a number of interesting features.[20] These include so-called amber mutants in three of the genes (see chapter 1, page 22). Amber mutants stop these genes being fully expressed; in the laboratory their effect can be overcome by growing the phage in special suppressor strains of *E. coli* that have the ability to suppress the harmful effects of the amber mutation and so permit expression. In the wild the suppressor genes are very rare, so that an escapee lambda vector, unable to make any of its components, would have a very slim chance of successfully infecting a cell. Two chunks of DNA have been removed from lambda WES.B', which leaves space for foreign DNA to be inserted, and two of the five *Eco* RI recognition sites have been altered so that the genome has both a replacement and an insertion site. The beauty of lambda WES.B′ is that, unless the foreign DNA has been spliced in, the phage DNA is too small for the viral machinery to package it properly and so no plaques are formed. Only recombinant phage can form plaques, which makes the job of selecting recombinants that much easier.

Charon, in Greek mythology, was the ferryman of the dead, who conveyed departed spirits across the river Styx. In a rather nice piece of christening, his name has been bestowed upon another group of cloning vehicles derived from lambda; these are the Charon phages made by Frederick Blattner and his colleagues.[21] Like WES.B′, Charon phages (there are 16 of them, for different purposes) have amber mutations to prevent their escape. And they have a variety of restriction sites that make it easy to insert fragments produced by any of the more popular restriction enzymes. What is more, Charon phages often have their restriction sites cunningly attached to specific genes that make picking up the recombinant clones easy (see below, page 97).

Wrapped DNA and man-made vehicles

Persuading leaky cells to take up recombinant molecules works, but it isn't terribly efficient. One-millionth of a gram of lambda DNA that has not been tampered with in any way will give about 100 000 plaques, but a bit of gene manipulation reduces that figure to something between 10 000 and 1000. If that sounds like a lot, be assured that it isn't. A million plaques from a millionth of a gram represents just one plaque for every 20 000 DNA molecules. For many genetic engineering experiments, that simply isn't good enough. Fortunately, there are ways to multiply the efficiency by more than a thousandfold.

The secret, as Sydney Brenner realized, is to package the recombinant DNA into virus particles, rather than simply bathing cells with the naked DNA. The whole particle is a much more efficient vehicle for getting DNA inside cells. Acting on Brenner's suggestion, Barbara Hohn and Kenneth Murray at Edinburgh worked out a scheme to package lambda recombinants into the customary viral coat; going through this extra stage can shoot the yield of recombinant plaques up to 100 000 000 from a millionth of a gram of DNA, an increase well worth the effort.[22]

Lambda packages its DNA into a coat made of different proteins, each coded for by a different gene on the DNA. Two proteins make up the bulk of the 20-sided head, while others form the tail and unite tail and head. The virus normally churns out its DNA in long strands, each made up of a number of copies of the single genome. Between each segment is a region called *cos*, and it is here that one of the virus enzymes produces nicks 12 bases apart on the two strands, giving rise to lambda's sticky ends. The single segments are packaged with the head proteins, and then another set of gene products welds head to tail. To package recombinant lambda DNA one needs to mix the DNA with all the proteins that the virus uses to assemble the mature particle. The best sources of these are special mutant strains of phage. One produces head proteins but lacks the enzyme to package the DNA; the other produces tails and the packaging enzyme. Between them, the two mutants take the DNA and produce from it millions of mature particles that can be used to infect cells in the normal way. The viruses seek out an attachment site on the surface of the cell, the tail sticks on, and the DNA is injected into the cell to begin the cycle of infection. And doing it this way, as I mentioned, multiplies the yield of transformed cells by more than a thousand.

The packaging system of lambda is not, actually, terribly fussy. It will snip and wrap any piece of DNA that carries two of the *cos* recognition sites roughly the right distance apart. That makes it possible to use the phage to package DNA that, apart from the *cos* sites, is not from lambda particles at all. The packaged DNA is then part of a pseudo-virus vector. These vectors are called 'cosmids', and they enable genetic engineers to combine the superior properties of phage particles as vectors with the undoubted advantages of plasmids as instruments for cloning. John Collins and Barbara Hohn made the first cosmids in 1978 by inserting the *cos* site of lambda DNA into a plasmid carrying an antibiotic resistance marker.[23] The plasmid has an *Eco* RI site, so incubating it with *Eco* RI fragments and DNA ligase produces the recombinants. The cosmid itself is about 7500 base-pairs long, and as lambda coats will hold a DNA strand of between 35 000 and 47 000 base-pairs, this leaves room for a much more sizeable gene insert than a normal lambda vector will permit (see figure 4.5). Once packaged, the recombinant DNA will be injected into a suitable host as if it were lambda DNA. In the cytoplasm, the *cos* sites attract one another

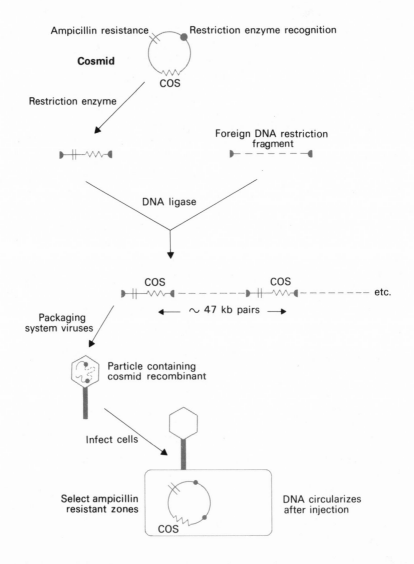

Figure 4.5
Outline scheme of cosmid vector. The phage packaging enzymes recognize the end of a stretch of viral DNA by the presence of the *cos* site. They will package any piece of DNA that carries two *cos* sites about 47 000 bases apart.

and hydrogen bond and the molecule becomes a fully functional circular plasmid, capable of replicating and coding for proteins, but not producing any viral products.

Cosmids represent in the clearest possible way the fruits of genetic engineering in the service of genetic engineering. They allow researchers to insert long stretches of DNA into host cells, particularly useful in building up a comprehensive library of the genome of an organism, and are very efficient. The background number of clones that are not recombinants is very low, without the rigmarole associated with plasmid vectors, and the efficiency of infection is high. Cosmids certainly look to be a very promising avenue to explore and they could not have been created without a backdrop of genetic engineering, not only for the techniques and expertise to make them but also for the intellectual understanding that allowed them to be made.

Needles and haystacks

Making recombinant molecules is a game with very long odds against success. Even when the bits of DNA have been joined up and inserted into cells, only a very few cells out of many tens of thousands will contain the recombinant molecule, and all the technical expertise in the world is no use whatsoever unless you can find the cells that contain the recombinant DNA. Techniques for selecting the few valuable cells from the mass of useless ones – Cohen's fourth necessity – are thus of paramount importance.

Cohen himself showed the way, with his early studies of plasmids as cloning vehicles. The plasmids brought with them resistance to antibiotics, so any cell that had received a plasmid would grow where no others could, on a medium containing antibiotic. Selection under those circumstances is simplicity itself. So, too, when the recombinant confers resistance to two different antibiotics: again, the successful cells identify themselves by being able to grow. It is no problem to screen huge numbers of cells for the few that might be valuable, and because the host cells multiply so quickly under favourable conditions a single cell, once found, will rapidly turn itself into a colony, and the colony into a massive stock, which then becomes the basis of whatever further work needs to be done. This principle, of putting a marker gene on the cloning

vehicle or ensuring in some other way that the cells will show
themselves in a special environment, is the basis of many selection
techniques.

A neat twist to the use of resistance markers can be employed to
make it easier to select genuine recombinants from a background
population of cells that have been transformed by a copy of the
plasmid that does not carry the foreign DNA. If the restriction site
for insertion of foreign DNA is in the middle of a resistance gene,
then cells that have taken up the recombinant will be sensitive to
that particular antibiotic. Those that have absorbed a non-
recombinant plasmid will not be sensitive. All transformants select
themselves on a medium containing one antibiotic. A sample from
each colony that grows is then plated on to a medium that contains
the other antibiotic. The colonies that do not grow are recombinants in which the foreign DNA has inactivated the second
resistance gene; they can be picked off the original plate.

Bolivar's pBR325 plasmid is just such a useful vector. It confers
resistance to three antibiotics – ampicillin, tetracycline and chloramphenicol – and the chloramphenicol gene contains the plasmid's
single recognition site for *Eco* RI. If an *Eco* RI fragment is inserted
into pBR325, the chloramphenicol gene no longer works. Transformed cells will grow on ampicillin or tetracycline, but cells that
contain truly recombinant plasmids cannot grow on chloramphenicol.

A slightly different approach to selection uses a technique called
'complementation'. Host strains that lack a specific gene will not be
able to grow if they need the enzyme coded for by that gene. If the
cloning vector contains the missing gene, it will supply the missing
enzyme and the cell will be able to grow.

Phage vectors have the very desirable quality of producing new
phages in the cells they have infected. The presence of a plaque on a
lawn of cells indicates that here was a successful transformation,
with hundreds of daughter phages going out and continuing the
infective process. In the first phage vectors, this was all that was
needed to select successful recombinants; if the DNAs had not
recombined properly, the hybrid would not be able to produce new
phages. Of course there were slight problems, and phage vectors
were soon modified to take care of these. For a start, there was the
difficulty that might be caused by fragments of phage coming
together without the inserted foreign DNA. This hurdle was

jumped by deleting inessential regions of the phage so that the resulting recombined DNA, if it did not contain the inserted foreign sequence, would be too small to be packaged into the phage's protein coat. No packaging means no further infection once the host cell has burst, and so no plaque.

Phage vectors, like plasmids, can be fitted with special regions that allow genuine recombinants to be picked up quite easily. Many of the Charon phages, for example, are themselves recombinants. They contain a gene called *lac* Z, derived from *E. coli*, which produces an enzyme called β galactosidase. This enzyme breaks down the sugar lactose, but in Charon phages it provides a neat tag that distinguishes recombinants. The makers of one of the Charon vectors – number 16a – put the phage's two special restriction enzyme sites, one for *Eco* RI, the other for *Sst* I, in the middle of the *lac* Z gene. Successful insertion of a fragment thus destroys the lac gene, which means that the cell cannot use lactose. In itself, this does not matter because the phage does not need to use lactose to multiply. But there is a chemical, called 5-bromo-4-chloro-3-indolyl-β-D-galactoside (or Xgal for short) that resembles lactose to the extent that galactosidase will act upon it. One product of the reaction is a blue-coloured derivative that shows up nicely in plaques that contain a working copy of the *lac* Z gene. Plaques that don't contain this gene, in other words those made by the progeny of a successful recombinant, are colourless, and can be picked out with hardly any effort at all. (The Xgal system can also be used to detect plasmid vectors that contain the *lac* genes.)

Selection methods that exploit the genetics of the host cell are particularly useful when the recombinants have been made with foreign DNA that is already fairly pure. The recombinants will contain the inserted sequence and it is no great hardship to select a few transformed cells and establish that they contain the engineered stretch of DNA. This was exactly the approach that John Morrow used to find the first ever recombinants of prokaryote and eukaryote genomes. Morrow and his colleagues knew that the toad ribosomal sequence they had inserted into the plasmid had certain physical characteristics. On the basis of antibiotic resistance, they selected 55 clones that had apparently received the cloning vector. Those 55 cell lines were grown up and the DNA in them extracted, purified and digested again with *Eco* RI. This reconstituted the fragments that had gone into the recombinant molecule. An agarose gel served to separate the fragments, which could be measured by the speed at which they travelled through the gel. Every one of the 55 clones provided a fragment the same size as the original pSC101 plasmid, which was just as well, for every one of them had been selected on the basis of antibiotic resistance carried on that plasmid. Thirteen of the 55 also produced fragments equal to the four fragments that *Eco* RI produces from the *Xenopus* ribosomal gene. Those 13 formed the basis for a whole series of further experiments investigating the way toad genes worked inside a bacterium. The point is that, because he knew what DNA fragments they had put into the recombinants, Morrow could discover which of the transformed cells contained those particular DNA fragments. (It is worth remembering that most of the other methods, discussed below, had not yet been developed as there was not yet any call for them; I doubt if Morrow would use the same technique today.)

Physical characterization was a good method to use under the circumstances, but it is slow and can be tedious. And when the recombinants might contain any one of a whole series of inserted sequences, or when you are looking not just for recombinants but for recombinants in which the inserted sequence is being decoded and turned into protein, this can be a little more difficult. It isn't enough simply to detect recombinants: you also have to select those recombinants that are working in the way you want. One method for doing this relies upon the immune system, the natural defence mechanism of the body.

Just as enzymes are able to perform reactions that are beyond the capabilities of even the best organic chemists, the immune system is an identification system better than any physical system available. When the cells of the immune system contact a foreign protein (which might be the coat protein of a bacterium, the toxin of a bee, or any other protein that finds its way into an animal's blood-stream) they manufacture special proteins of their own. These are called antibodies, and they contain specific sites that recognize, and bind tightly to, sites on the foreign protein. The antibody acts as a label, identifying the foreign protein (or antigen) so that scavenger cells can come along and destroy the antigen. A single protein may have many different sites capable of acting as antigens, so that many different antibodies will be produced, each corres-ponding to one of the antigenic sites.

The beauty of antibodies is their specificity – proteins that differ by just one amino acid in hundreds can be separated by appropriate antibodies – and their sensitivity – antibodies will react reliably to very few molecules of the antigen. And the antibody molecules are easily labelled with radioactive iodine, which makes them easy to trace. Together, these properties make immunochemical methods the most exquisitely sensitive techniques for detecting proteins.

In the service of genetic engineering, immunochemical methods enable researchers to find those clones that are producing particular proteins, even if the proteins are present in minute amounts and are only fragments of the original protein. Many procedures have been developed, but the one devised by Stephanie Broome while working at Walter Gilbert's laboratory at Harvard is perhaps the most popular.[24] The starting point is so-called immune serum, a mixture of antibodies in blood plasma. If you are looking for human haemoglobin genes, for example, you need to make antibodies to the various components of human haemoglobin. This you do by injecting rabbits with the purified haemoglobin. The rabbits make antibodies to the foreign protein, and these are present in the blood serum. A small amount of purified serum contains enough antibodies for many screening tests.

Broome and Gilbert's method requires two lots of serum antibodies, one plain and the other labelled with radioactive iodine. The cold antiserum is washed over a small disc of plastic. The antibodies stick tenaciously to the plastic, which is then laid on top of colonies of cloned recombinant DNA recipients. The bacteria have been broken open, by infecting them with phage or spraying with chloroform, so that the cell contents of the colonies are in contact with the antibodies on the plastic disc. Any antigens, even fragments of the protein provided that they contain one of the antigenic sites, bind tightly to the antibodies. The plastic disc can be washed now, and the antibodies, perhaps with a precious burden of antigen, remain stuck to the plastic. Now the hot, labelled, antiserum is swilled over the disc. Those protein molecules that are bound to an antibody will almost certainly attract another antibody, this time one labelled with radioactive iodine. Again the disk is washed, and now it is laid on top of an X-ray film for a couple of days. The radiation from the iodine exposes the film, creating a round patch wherever there was a colony producing the protein target. With the autoradiograph developed, it's back to the copy

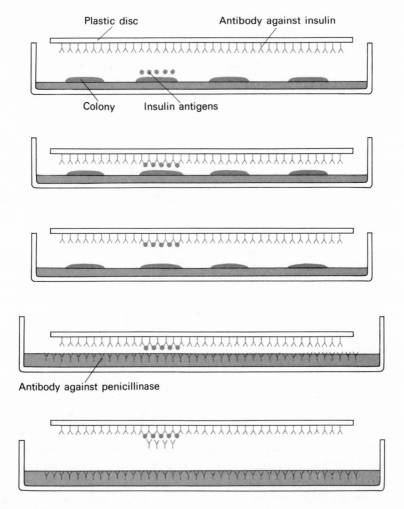

Plastic disc   Antibody against insulin

Colony   Insulin antigens

Antibody against penicillinase

Figure 4.6
Clone detection by radioactive antibody. Cells are broken open (after making a replica of the plate) and a plastic disc coated with antibody placed over the colonies. Antigens bind to the antibody on the disc, which is now washed to remove debris. Radioactive antibody is then added, and binds to the antigen captured by the disc, revealing the location of positive colonies in an autoradiograph. If the antigen is a composite protein (insulin fused to penicillinase, for example), two different antibodies can be used to detect only the hybrid protein. (*Copyright© 1980 by Scientific American, Inc.*)

plate of the colonies (you have to make a copy, because lysis destroys the cells) to pick the ones that showed up (see figure 4.6). The method is sensitive – each cell need produce only a few molecules of protein – and simple. With suitable modifications it can be used to detect hybrid proteins, engineered or accidental, that would be invisible to most other methods. For Gilbert, who was looking for a stretch of insulin attached to the penicillin-resistance enzyme, this was a particularly important property.

As an alternative to using immune methods to detect specific proteins, one could attempt to detect specific DNA sequences within the transformed colonies. This might be an especially good idea when there are reasons to suppose that the DNA is not being translated into protein or when, regardless of whether it is or is not being translated, the RNA that it would produce is available. These methods depend on using a 'probe' of RNA to find the relevant stretch of DNA, and, as with immune methods, a number of different techniques have coalesced into one that seems to be preferred over all the others. This is the method devised by Michael Grunstein and David Hogness while they were both at the Biochemistry Department of Stanford University Medical School.[25] Their method makes use of the great affinity that single-stranded DNA has for nitrocellulose. Having selected transformed colonies by some other method, the colonies are transferred to a nitrocellulose filter on top of a plate of nutrient agar. Colonies grow up on the filter, which is then removed for further treatment. The filter is soaked from below with sodium hydroxide (caustic soda), which breaks open the cells and separates the double strands of the DNA from one another. A gentle and brief incubation with proteinase gets rid of contaminants, and a wash with chloroform and saline solution removes other debris and leaves a little patch of denatured DNA for each colony. The whole filter is now slipped into an oven at 80 °C for two hours to bake the DNA strands on to the nitrocellulose. Once that has been done, the probe can be flooded on to the filter to find the DNA. The probe, in these cases, is generally a purified sequence of messenger RNA from the gene in question, labelled with a radioactive isotope. After allowing enough time – 16 hours or so – for the RNA to find complementary stretches of DNA and bind to them, the whole filter is placed on top of X-ray film. The radioactive hybrids take a picture of themselves, and the researcher once again can go back to the reference plate of colonies and pick the ones that showed up in the autoradiograph (see figure 4.7).

The method is not as sensitive as immune detection, but it is more general. It does not need the DNA to be translated into protein, and although it originally required the use of RNA probes, it works just as well with DNA fragments, which are so easy to label by nick translation. But it does require a copy of the gene, or mRNA, in question. Even so, the ability to use a small amount of DNA or RNA as a probe to locate clones that can provide far greater amounts of the same sequence means that researchers are willing to go through the various steps necessary. They can find one clone, grow it up to provide themselves with unlimited quantities of probe, and use the probe to find other clones that contain the desired sequence.

Put the sensitivity of immune methods together with the recognition capabilities of one nucleic acid strand for its complementary

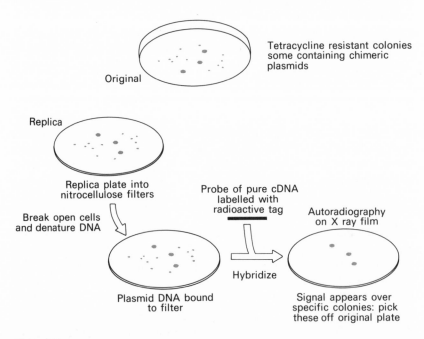

Figure 4.7
Clone detection by colony hybridization. A labelled DNA or RNA probe is used to bind to the DNA of interest. Only colonies that contain the complementary stretch of DNA will show up on the autoradiograph.

partner, and you have the basis of one of the most powerful methods for finding that clone in a million, It is called 'hybrid arrested translation' (or HART), and it is the brainchild of Bryan Roberts at Harvard Medical School.[26] HART can identify a given DNA in a clone even if neither DNA nor RNA probes are available, so long as you know what protein you are looking for. Each clone's DNA is extracted and purified, and the two strands are separated from one another. The strands are mixed with the raw RNA from the donor cells whose DNA was recombined with the vector. Each bit of donor mRNA binds to its complementary DNA if that DNA is present. The whole lot is then put into a cell-free synthesis system, like the ones pioneered by Marshall Nirenberg to crack the genetic code, in which everything needed to synthesize proteins from mRNA is present. All the mRNAs in the mixture begin busily directing protein synthesis, except for any that are bound to DNA. So if the protein you are looking for *is* present in the mixture, the gene you want *is not* present in the clone.

To find the protein, use a radio-labelled antibody. If the protein is being made by the cell-free system, then it will bind to the antibody and the radioactivity will reveal it. But if the purified recombinant DNA from the clone contains the gene you are interested in, the mRNA will have bound to the gene and none of that protein will have been synthesized. As a check, if you separate the mRNA and DNA, by gentle heating, synthesis of the protein *will* now take place (see figure 4.8). Again, having used hybrid arrested translation to find one clone with the desired bit of DNA, that clone can be grown up to provide probes for use with the other, simpler, methods.

Strategy

Genetic methods, immune methods, hybridization methods all have one goal: to detect a particular cell from among many millions. When that cell has been found, we have accomplished the last of Cohen's four steps. We can break and join DNAs from different sources, with homopolymer tailing, straightforward restriction enzyme ligation or linkers. We can insert fragments into cloning vectors, which might be bacterial plasmids, bacteriophages or chimeric combinations of the two, and these can be inserted into

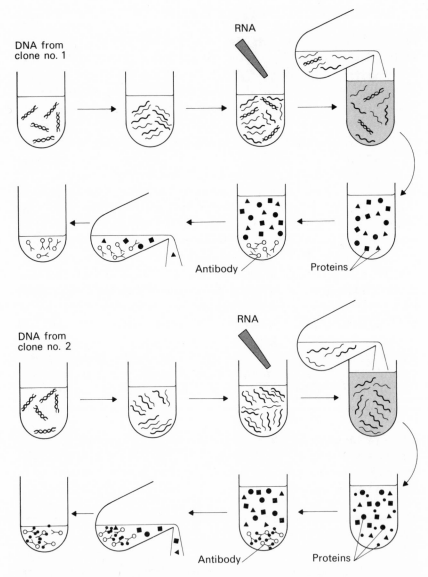

DNA from
clone no. 1

RNA

Antibody

Proteins

DNA from
clone no. 2

RNA

Antibody

Proteins

Figure 4.8
Clone detection by hybrid arrested translation (HART). DNA from the clones being tested is denatured and mixed with the unpurified RNA used to make the inserted DNA. The RNA and complementary DNA form duplex strands. In a cell-free translation system with labelled amino acids, unhybridized RNA can direct the synthesis of radioactive proteins. RNA bound to DNA cannot. The specific protein coded by the DNA sought *will not* be made in the clone that contains the sought DNA. Antibodies to that protein will be radioactively labelled in all clones except the one that contains the sought DNA (top). For further confirmation, the RNA/DNA duplex can be separated by warming; the protein will now be synthesized. (*Copyright © 1980 by Scientific American, Inc.*)

host cells. There, the cloning vehicles will multiply and thus amplify the amount of DNA at our disposal. When, finally, we select the particular clones that contain the recombinants we seek, the next phase begins. This might be to read the sequence of bases along a gene, or to manufacture the protein product of that gene in bulk, or to refine genetic engineering methods yet further. Every experiment is carried out with some purpose in mind, some question that needs an answer, and the particular question will dictate which method we employ at each stage and the overall strategy that we pursue.

If we already have a pure, or relatively pure, version of either the DNA or RNA, then the strategy is quite simple. The RNA can be turned into DNA by reverse transcriptase and the DNA purified by density-gradient centrifugation, electrophoresis or even chromatography. The vector we choose, and the method used to insert the fragment into the vector, will depend on many things. Do we want to recover the gene intact? If so, the insertion method had better create specific sites for a restriction enzyme. Do we want the recombinant molecule to synthesize some protein in bulk? If we do, we must ensure that the vehicle will enable the gene to be transcribed, and that means ensuring that the inserted fragments' codons are read from the correct reference point and that the gene is preceded by the requisite control segments that will turn translation on.

By and large, these sorts of difficulties can be overcome, as we will see when we consider specific examples of genetic engineering in progress. And if they can not, then we can manufacture new tools to solve particular problems. That is why I think of genetic engineering as a snowball, rolling unswervingly down a slope, getting bigger and going faster. And every new development steepens the slope and hastens the drop. Just when phage vectors were proving too small for certain uses, threatening to slow the ball down, along came cosmids with their vastly increased capacity, and it picked up speed. New developments come all the time, and it is fair to say that at present the genetic engineers are still novices. Going solely on the past 10 or 15 years, who knows what they will come up with next?

5

UNRAVELLING

Techniques for deciphering the message of the genetic code

When you want printed information, you go to a library. When you want genetic information, you go to a chromosome. But there the comparison ends; for, unlike a library, the chromosomes contains no reassuring cabinet of index cards, telling you where the gene you seek is to be found or, indeed, whether it is present on the shelves at all. The information is not even likely to be shelved according to subject. Genes often do occur in clusters – all the genes needed to make use of lactose, for example, are right next to one another – but they are not in a section labelled 'Sugars, how to use'. It is as if, faced with mile upon mile of shelves, you had to check every single title to find the volume you're looking for. Genetic engineers are now able to use selection and screening methods that make the checking of every item feasible, but only if the library offers ready access. One weapon, the shotgun, has made gene libraries – with index cards – possible.

The shotgun is a paradox. It offers enormous power, but little finesse. That is why it is the weapon of choice when power, rather than finesse, is at a premium. It must also be why the genetic engineers called their most powerful weapon a 'shotgun'. Quite simply, the entire genome of an organism is chopped at random into little bits. Every one of the bits is inserted into a cloning vehicle and used to transform a host cell. The multitude of hosts, each carrying some random fragment of the genome, represent that genome carved up into manageable chunks. Between them the recombinant vectors, whether inside a host (if plasmids) or outside (if phage), form a library that can be consulted for any genetic information thought to be in the genome (see figure 5.1).

The shotgun finds itself much used because it offers the only practical way to hit a small target. In the early experiments on recombinant DNA, John Morrow and his colleagues could isolate relatively pure DNA that coded for the toad ribosomal components alone and use that DNA to make their chimeras. Any cells that were transformed stood a good chance of containing the toad genes, and that was indeed the case. About one in four transformants carried the information for toad ribosomal proteins. But this was a special case, because multiple copies of the ribosomal genes are present inside the toad egg, which makes them quite easy to separate from the rest of the DNA. Many genes do exist in multiple copies, we now know, but a good many others do not. Isolating and purifying them before making recombinants would be an extremely difficult job. Of course, one can use other approaches, synthesizing the complementary copy of the purified messenger RNA, or indeed synthesizing the entire gene, though the knowledge required to do that often depends on shotgun experiments in the first place. Besides, these techniques might not be available in any specific instance. That is when the shotgun becomes invaluable.

You can blast your way into the genome by mechanical force, shoving the DNA around and breaking it into pieces. Or you can go in with restriction enzymes, preferably those that recognize a short four-base sequence which again give small pieces. One of those bits contains the real target; all that remains is to find it. If that one target is all you are interested in, then the other transformed clones, the ones that do not contain anything of interest to you now, can be destroyed. The alternative is to save those clones and keep them as a living library of the genome. Next time you want a gene from that species, you will not have to use the shotgun but can simply go to the library.

The first libraries

The very first libraries were quite small affairs. The fruitfly, *Drosophila melanogaster*, beloved of geneticists everywhere, was one of the first species to be so enshrined. Pieter C. Wensink and his colleagues at Stanford University School of Medicine did so in 1974. They chopped the *Drosophila* chromosomes up mechanically, by squirting them through a small needle, added sticky ends of adenines and thymines, spliced them into pSC101 vectors, and transformed *E. coli* cells with the recombinant plasmids.[1] Next to get this treatment was *E. coli* itself. Louise Clark and John Carbon at the University of California at Santa Barbara used first mechanical shearing and then *Eco* RI to break up *E. coli* and insert it into plasmid vectors.[2] More importantly, Clark and Carbon carefully worked out how large a library would need to be if it were to be considered complete. ('Complete', somewhat quaintly, was not 100 per cent complete: 99 per cent was all that was required of a complete library.) Naturally, it depended on the size of each volume, the average length of the fragment in each clone, and the size of the genome; for *E. coli*, with its 3.4 million base-pair genome divided into pieces each about 10 000 bases long, the entire library could be contained in 1440 clones. Clarke and Carbon's library actually comprised 2100 clones.[3]

For a while, though not for long, that was where things stayed. Progress was halted by three main obstacles. More complex genomes were larger and so required special techniques. The size of the genome meant that the cloned library would be contained in a very large number of volumes, so that the screening procedures to find information would have to be very efficient. Second, the scientific community had, itself, decided to forbid certain types of shotgun experiment until safety conditions could be met (see chapter 6). One of the requirements was for vectors and hosts that had been biochemically crippled to make them unable to live outside the laboratory, and these had not yet been constructed. (Indeed, the guidelines made it necessary for Carbon to destroy two libraries of yeast and *Drosophila* DNA because he had put the gene fragments into a strain of *E. coli* that had not been approved for this type of experiment.) Third, there was the problem of inefficiency. Almost a million clones would be needed to contain the entire genome of an average mammal. Transforming cells with naked DNA produced about 1000 clones for every millionth of a gram of DNA. So a complete library would need about a thousandth of a gram of DNA. That doesn't sound like much, but it would take the DNA from billions of cells. Laid end to end, one-thousandth of a gram of DNA would stretch nearly 300 000 kilometres. No wonder, then, that the people who finally solved the problem laconically described this as 'an amount difficult to obtain'.[4]

That was how things stood in 1976. By 1977, all three problems had been overcome. Indeed, two of the three solutions were published in one special issue of *Science*. The issue was devoted almost entirely to genetic engineering, and it included two of the three much needed items. There was a rapid screening procedure, based on hybridization, which enabled workers to look at thousands of recombinant plaques a day, and there were the lambda vectors that Philip Leder and Frederick Blattner had developed, which satisfied the need for crippled cloning vehicles that would fail to thrive outside the laboratory. Finally, and this did not appear in *Science*, there was the packaging system that Barbara

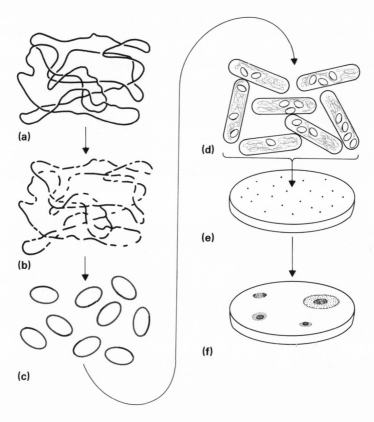

Figure 5.1
Shotgun experiment. The total DNA (a) is broken into random fragments (b) mechanically or by a restriction enzyme. The fragments are recombined with a vector (c) and inserted into host cells (d). The hosts are allowed to grow (e) and the collection of transformed colonies represents a library of the original total DNA, which can be screened (f) for DNA segments of particular interest. (*Copyright © 1977 by Scientific American, Inc.*)

Hohn and Ken Murray had developed, which dramatically increased the efficiency of transformation, giving more clones for the same amount of DNA. Together, these three facilities made a reference library of a mammalian genome a distinct possibility.

Tom Maniatis, then at the California Institute of Technology in Pasadena, was one of the first people to apply the rapid screening techniques and improved cloning vehicles to the need for genome libraries. Maniatis led a large team, which had created three separate libraries by June 1978. Two months later, in August, another Cal Tech group, which also included Maniatis, announced that it had created a human gene library.[5] The steps that Maniatis took to build his libraries are worth going through in some detail, not only because they provide a glimpse of the genetic engineer at work but also because they show how far the science had come in just three years.

Maniatis set his sights on three species: *Drosophila* (which Wensink had used earlier), the silkworm and the rabbit. He also, at the same time, intended to create the human library. In each case the approach was more or less the same, but because it is closer to home, we will follow his steps for the human genes. The primary requirement was a source of human DNA. The liver of an unborn foetus provided the DNA, which was purified according to more or less standard techniques. After the usual cleaning stages the mixture of nucleic acids was spun for 2½ days at 45 000 r.p.m. to separate the longer, heavier DNA molecules from everything else. This DNA formed the basis of the library.

Next, the DNA had to be broken into manageable chunks. There were two possibilities, mechanical breakage or restriction enzymes. Shearing the DNA mechanically – by squirting it rapidly through a small hypodermic needle – is a very inefficient process. The large size of the genome makes efficiency important if the library is to be complete, which leaves restriction enzymes to break up the DNA. As the fragments were eventually to be inserted into the *Eco* RI site of a phage vector, the obvious solution might have been to break up the DNA with *Eco* RI, but this obvious approach has many hidden difficulties. The sticky cohesive ends that *Eco* RI produces would again be a threat to efficiency, for they would allow the fragments to join to one another rather than to the vector. A blunt-ended restriction enzyme provided a better alternative, but it had to be one with a short recognition site because a six-base sequence, like the one that *Eco* RI recognizes, poses a different sort of problem. Maniatis wanted an essentially random collection of fragments. There was every possibility that the sites recognized by restriction enzymes were not randomly placed along the DNA. There might be too many in some places and not enough elsewhere, and the longer a recognition site was, the more likely that it was non-randomly distributed. The solution was to use the enzymes *Hae* III and *Alu* I, both of which recognize four-base sequences and produce blunt-ended fragments. (*Hae* III recognizes GGCC and *Alu* I, AGCT.)

Four-base restriction enzymes, however, create yet more problems. Any four-base sequence is liable to arise roughly every 256 bases. With two enzymes, the average DNA fragment would be just 128 bases long. The human genome is 5000 million bases long. Forty million fragments is just too many to cope with, and in any case would waste the carrying potential of the vectors, which Maniatis knew could cope with an insert 20 000 bases long. To get longer fragments, he needed to ensure that he used far too little restriction enzyme. This technique, of using too little enzyme for the reaction to be completed, is called a 'partial' or 'nonlimit digestion'. Trial and error tests with the rabbit DNA had revealed the best concentration of enzymes to give the highest proportion of fragments in the desired size range, and it was with this amount of enzyme that they broke up the human DNA.

The partial digest does indeed produce a collection of fragments drawn at random from the entire genome. To make most efficient use of the vector they needed to select fragments between 18 and 25 kb (kilobases; 1 kb is 1000 bases) long; this was done by centrifuging the fragments on a sucrose gradient with markers of known length. The DNA fragments between the two markers were collected and went forward to the next stage.

Maniatis and his team now had a few hundred millionths of a gram of DNA. The fragments were the right size, but they had blunt ends. They could be joined to other blunt-ended fragments with T4 ligase, but then the researchers would not be able to recover the fragments easily. In any case, the chosen vector, one of Blattner's Charon phages (Charon 4A, to be precise), was specifically designed to accept *Eco* RI fragments. So now synthetic linkers had to be added to the fragments. Richard Scheller at Cal Tech provided some of the 12-base synthetic DNA linkers that he had

constructed to contain the recognition site for *Eco* RI; but before
these could be attached to the fragments there was more work to be
done. To make sticky ends, the fragments, with attached linkers,
would be digested with *Eco* RI. But the fragments themselves had
been made with other restriction enzymes. There was a very good
chance that each fragment contained recognition sites for *Eco* RI,
so the fragments had to be protected from the enzyme. Fortunately, *Eco* RI was a very well studied restriction system. The
modification enzyme, which protects the host's own DNA from the
restriction enzyme by adding a methyl group to some of the bases,
had been isolated, and it was a relatively easy matter to incubate
the fragments with this enzyme.

Once the fragments had been protected against the restriction
enzyme the linkers could be added and digested with *Eco* RI to
create the sticky ends. That done, the fragments were mixed with
the vector, Charon 4A. Twelve hours at 12 °C was needed to
ensure that almost all of the library DNA was taken up into the
vector DNA. Then the recombinant molecules, some made up of
as many as 14 complete phage–gene recombinants chained
together, were ready to be packaged into particles.

For the first three libraries, stringent safety checks now had to be
carried out. The possibility of dangerous recombinants was being
taken very seriously – although still an unknown quantity – and the
National Institutes of Health, in the guidelines that allowed scientists to resume shotgun experiments, had laid down tests that had to
be carried out. The cells that had been used to grow the mutant
phages for the test-tube packaging system had to be blasted with
high-energy ultraviolet light to destroy any whole phages that
might have arisen through a fluke reverse mutation, and before the
packaging viruses could be used they had to be tested to check that
the precautions had worked and that there were no living viruses
capable of producing a plaque. There never were, and so the
packaging reaction, in which the two mutant viruses make up each
other's deficiencies to package the recombinant DNA, could go
ahead. Indeed, so safe and effective were the vector and packaging
virus strains that by the time Maniatis was packaging human gene
recombinants the guidelines had been changed to remove these
safety checks.

The packaged recombinants, having passed all the safety tests,
meant that Maniatis and his team had achieved their goal. There, in

the phage vectors, was a complete library of the human genome, neatly divided into the manageable chunks they wanted. But there was not a great deal of finished material. To make the library useful it would have to be amplified so that there would be enough of it to allow people to do whatever screening and testing they needed to. The packaged recombinants – roughly a million of them – were allowed to grow for 14 hours on a lawn of fresh *E. coli* cells. Nutrient agar plates 15 cm across received roughly 10 000 Charon phages each. A hundred 15 cm plates, little more than an oven full, was enough for the complete human DNA library. Once the phage had grown and amplified their precious cargo several hundred times, the agar was scraped off the plates and mixed with a little chloroform to ensure that cells that had not yet burst to release their phage would do so. The whole lot, about one-third of a litre, was spun in a centrifuge to remove bits of agar and cell debris, and popped into the freezer for storage: a small jar, holding the entire human genome as a collection of handy ready-to-use pieces.

What you do with the contents of that jar is bounded only by your imagination. What Maniatis and his colleagues did was to screen hundreds of thousands of recombinant lambda phages that make up the libraries, searching for various genes that they were particularly interested in. The silkworm uses something like a hundred different proteins in building the shell of its egg, each switched on and taking its place in an orderly sequence of development. How is the sequence controlled? Maniatis isolated clones holding these genes by looking for ones that would hybridize with cDNA made from the mRNA of the developing egg: 350 000 plaques yielded 350 interesting clones, which are being studied intensively to unravel the control mechanisms. The rabbit, and human, libraries offered information about another puzzle. Haemoglobin contains four protein chains of two different sorts. The globins, as they are called, determine the properties of the haemoglobin, and they change as the organism develops. Foetal globins are different from adult globins and the difference is very important, because it enables the growing foetus to remove oxygen from its mother's haemoglobin. People have long suspected that the various globin genes form a kind of family, related to one another by evolutionary descent, but to tackle the problem properly they needed to get at the various globin genes, see how their sequences differ, how they are positioned on the chromosomes, how they are controlled. The rabbit library – 750 000 clones in all – yielded four different globin sequences. The human library – a million clones – has provided a similar number of globin genes. Shotguns and libraries have now offered up many globin genes from many species for further studies, and our picture of the globin gene family is much more complete as a result.[6] But there is a great deal more that one can do with library clones.

Reading the genes

The new-found ability to read genes with astounding ease is a marvellous story, one worth telling. And there is a temptation when retelling a story, especially one that describes some scientific technique or other, to follow a strictly chronological historical line, dragging you, poor reader, down all the blind alleys and back routes before finally emerging into the clear light of modern under-standing. Sometimes this can be a good method, for it points up the evolution of ideas and the ways in which developments are bound by their context. But most of the time the straightforward history works against the storyteller; no sooner have listeners absorbed an idea than they are told to abandon it and take in the next, improved, idea. At the end there may be a problem in sorting what was once useful but is now discarded from the way things are at the moment. So it is with DNA sequencing. There were many false starts, and many very laborious techniques that did, admittedly, get the job done but at a cost, in labour and tedium, that is hard to imagine. Now, however, there are two methods for reading the sequence of bases along a DNA strand, which, while they may yet be further refined, are so good, and so widely accepted, that it would be foolish to force you to follow along the paths of their discovery. That is not to denigrate earlier efforts; it is just a recognition that, while they may have shown the way, those methods have been superseded and it would serve no great purpose to go into them now.

The two current techniques are the chemical method, devised by Walter Gilbert and Allan Maxam at Harvard, and the chain termi-nator method, from Fred Sanger at Cambridge. So important are they to the growth of modern molecular biology that the Royal Swedish Academy of Sciences honoured Sanger and Gilbert with a quarter-share each in the 1980 Nobel Prize in Chemistry (Paul Berg got the other half). It was, as already mentioned, Sanger's second Nobel Prize in the same field, which put him into an elite club that contains only two members, himself and physicist John Bardeen. More interesting still, it broke with an unwritten rule of Nobel Prize aspirants – live long. The Academy often waits decades before conferring the prize on a researcher, the twin tests of time and peer acceptance counting for a great deal in its deliberations. Sanger and Gilbert published their methods in 1977, and they were almost literally an overnight success, the final seal on that success being a Nobel Prize just three years later.

The impact of the new methods was enormous. In the early 1960s Walter Fiers in Belgium began a project, as ambitious in its way as Sanger's assault on insulin, to determine the complete RNA sequence of a very small virus, the phage MS2. Fragments had to be eight nucleotides long, or less, to be successfully analysed, and the complete sequence of 3569 bases was eventually published some 15 years later in 1976. Thanks to Gilbert and Sanger, as the anonymous editorialist of the journal *Nature* put it, 'the sequencing of MS2 would now be no more than a single PhD project'.[7] Laboratories like Fiers's, which had been struggling hard to sequence short bits of nucleic acid, welcomed the new methods with open arms, and within a very short time DNA sequences sprouted in the literature like weeds on a naked patch of earth. *Nature* quickly raised 'the problem, faced by journals, of printing screeds of ATCG permutations, less appetising to those who have not acquired the taste, than even the stock exchange page of a newspaper'. (One scientist's rejoinder being that 'there are now a number in the scientific community for whom the financial advantages of scrutiny of either may be of the same order'.[8]) International repositories of sequence information have been set up, in the USA and in Europe, and the amount of startling new information to come out of these endeavours is astonishing. The Nobel committee mentioned one, that the genetic code is not as universal as it was once thought to be; and that was certainly a shock. Another was the discovery, almost as soon as the sequencing searchlights were trained on eukaryote genes, that those genes were not the simple linear stretches of DNA that had been imagined. The average gene, it seemed, consisted of a series of DNA sequences that coded for protein but were buried within long stretches of DNA that did not get expressed and appeared to be nonsense. An extreme example, revealed in November 1981, is that of the gene for collagen (one of the major components of ligaments and tendons) of the chicken. The 'gene' is 38 000 bases long. But the coding regions comprise just 5000 bases spread out over the 38 000 base stretch and interrupted by more than 50 nonsense sequences.[9] A great deal of research effort is today being devoted to understanding how this bizarre system works and, perhaps more important, why it is so.

Coding complications and intervening sequences, while undoubtedly important for molecular biology, are not central to the pragmatics of genetic engineering (though, of course, widely dispersed genes are very difficult to engineer). They simply emerged from the ability to determine sequences rapidly and accurately, and it is to sequencing that we must return. (The changed picture of molecular biology, largely the result of advances in genetic engineering, is discussed in chapter 10.)

Frederick's ladder

The concept behind gene-reading is not hard to grasp. Imagine a supply of purified DNA of the gene you are interested in. You break the DNA at a specific point with the help of a restriction enzyme. That gives you a start mark that is identical for all the strands. Then you break every strand of DNA again at a random distance from the start mark. You will now have a collection of fragments, each starting at the same position but ending different distances away. Ideally, there will be strands one base longer than the start, two, three, four and so on up to strands hundreds of bases long. If you can now separate the strands, and discover the identity of the end base, you can put the fragments into size order and work out the entire sequence. That much is common to the chemical method and the chain terminator method; but, whereas Gilbert relies on simple organic chemistry to create the fragment collection, Sanger uses enzymes. Because the technique used to separate the fragments is Sanger's, I will deal with chain termination first.[10]

The starting point, of course, is a supply of purified DNA of the gene of interest. This will usually be obtained from a library by screening the clones and selecting the ones of interest to grow up and amplify. If the clone was made with a restriction enzyme site at either end of the insert, it is a simple matter to snip the insert out and purify it by running the DNA on an electrophoresis gel. You know the rough size of the insert and can retrieve fragments of that size directly from the gel, visualizing the bands of DNA with ethidium bromide and ultraviolet light.

At this point you have double-stranded DNA of the gene you are interested in. To apply Sanger's method you need to denature the double helix into two single strands and separate the strands. That done, you anneal a small primer of DNA to the single template strand. The primer might be synthesized directly, or it might be another restriction fragment that contains a complementary sequence. The purpose of the primer is to provide a starting point for DNA synthesis. DNA polymerase I, provided it has a supply of activated nucleosides, will add those nucleosides to the primer in the correct order, as specified by the single strand of DNA. By making the nucleosides radioactive, you can ensure that the resulting synthesized fragment will carry a label enabling you to detect even tiny quantities of it later.

The polymerase will keep adding to the chain as long as there are nucleosides available to add; the trick is to stop the growth of the chain. This Sanger does by adding a little of one nucleoside in the so-called dideoxy form. Dideoxynucleosides are missing a linking group at the 3' end. As a result, they can join on to a growing chain but cannot support further growth of the chain; there is nowhere for the next nucleoside to attach to. If the incubation mixture contains a mixture of mostly normal deoxynucleoside and a little dideoxynucleoside, then most of the time a normal nucleoside will get attached to the chain, which will be able to continue growing; but occasionally, and essentially at random, a dideoxynucleoside will get attached instead, and the growth of the chain will be terminated.

Sanger divides his purified DNA, with attached primer, into four lots. Each lot is incubated with DNA polymerase I and a mixture of the four activated nucleosides, but each lot also has added a small amount of one of the nucleosides in the dideoxy form. This means that each portion will eventually contain a mixture of fragments that all end with the same nucleoside. Focus for a moment on the portion that contains dideoxyguanine triphosphate, or ddGTP. The polymerase keeps building the chain. Each time there is a C on

the template strand of DNA, the polymerase inserts a G; sometimes that G is in the form of ddGTP and the chain stops growing.
So, when the incubation is finished, the test-tube contains a collection of fragments that end with G. The other three test-tubes
contain fragments that end with A, T and C. If you have got the
amounts of dideoxy to normal nucleoside correct (and with the
detailed instructions Sanger has published there is no reason why

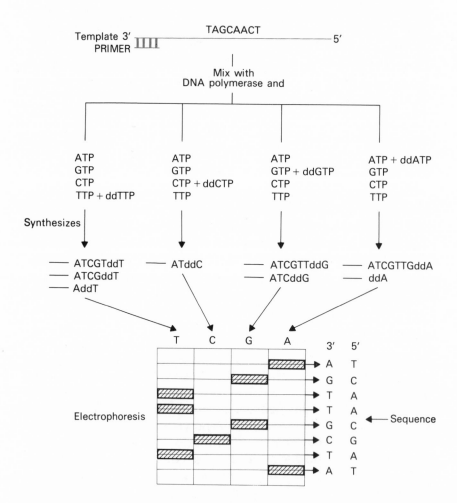

Figure 5.2
DNA sequencing by Sanger's chain termination method.

you should not), there will be at least one thoroughly labelled chain for every nucleotide position.

Now you separate the synthesized fragments from their templates and place each of the four portions into one of the wells in a polyacrylamide electrophoresis gel. Turn on the voltage, and the fragments march down the gel, smaller ones moving faster. The gel will easily separate fragments that differ by just one added base. When the smallest fragments have reached the end of the gel, you turn off the current and load the gel on to a piece of X-ray film to take its own picture. The developed autoradiograph shows a series of four ladders, each with unevenly spaced rungs. Each ladder corresponds to one nucleotide, and each rung to a chain that has ended with that nucleotide. To read the sequence you begin at the bottom and note which ladder contains the lowest rung. That is the first nucleotide. Then you move across the ladders looking for the next highest rung. That is the second nucleotide. The next rung is the third base, and so you go, climbing the ladders and shifting from side to side as you reconstruct the base sequence of the gene (see figure 5.2 and plate 5.1).

The method is sensitive, because the DNA fragments are labelled throughout and so will show up on the radiograph even if there are only a few of them. It is fast, because there is only one incubation step. And it is accurate, enabling sequences 200 bases from the primer site to be read with ease. As the sequence unfolds you can read it to decide on new primer sites further along that will enable you simply to walk along the DNA, reading it as you go.

Walter's cookbook

Gilbert's method is conceptually similar, in that it separates a collection of fragments using Sanger's electrophoretic ladder, but the creation of the fragments is very different.[11] Gilbert identifies four stages in the method, once you have the full-sized fragments produced by a restriction enzyme. First, you label one end of the DNA with radioactive phosphorus. Then you randomly break the DNA at each of the four bases separately. Then you electrophoretically order the products by size on a slab gel and make an autoradiograph of the slab. Finally, you read the base sequence off the autoradiograph (see plate 5.2 and figure 5.3). The last two are, of course, the same as Sanger's.

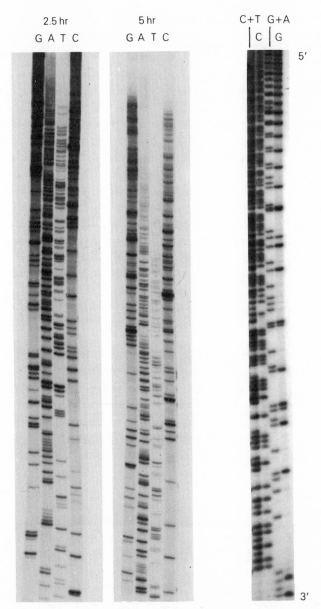

Plate 5.1 (left and centre)
DNA sequencing ladder made by Fred Sanger. *(Courtesy Fred Sanger)*

Plate 5.2 (right)
Sequencing ladder made by the Maxam and Gilbert Method. The sequence is of the boundary between the first coding sequence and the first intervening sequence of a human embryo globin gene. In the intervening sequence is a repeat pattern that may be important in shuffling bits of genes. (*Courtesy Nick Proudfoot*)

Labelling the end is a simple matter, either T4 polynucleotide kinase to attach a radioactive phosphate to the 5' end, or calf thymus terminal transferase (or T4 DNA polymerase) to attach the label to the 3' end. Now the strands have to be separated. This can be conveniently done by putting the DNA on to a so-called denaturing gel and electrophoresing it. The gel is formulated to break the bonds that hold the two strands together, and the single strands then migrate at different speeds through the gel. Nobody really knows why the strands travel at different speeds; it isn't simply a question of molecular weight, though it may be something to do with the way that single strands sometimes fold up. In any case, why the strands separate is less important than the fact that they do, and that they can be cut from the gel and entered into the next phase, the chemical reactions that break the strands.

The logic here is to attack one base selectively and then cut the chain at that base. Again, by getting the quantities right you can ensure that the bases are chemically modified (though not in the same way as modification enzymes) essentially at random to create a complete collection of fragments, each a single base longer than the next. The DNA is divided into four portions, one for each base, and put through stage one, base modification. One lot is incubated with dimethyl sulphate. This attacks purines, especially guanine, and adds a methyl group to the guanine ring. A second lot is incubated with acid. This also attacks purines, but non-selectively. It removes guanines and adenines from the strand but leaves the sugar-phosphate backbone intact. The remaining two portions are incubated with hydrazine, which opens the ring of pyrimidines; on its own it attacks both cytosine and thymine, but with salt it attacks cytosine preferentially. These chemicals – dimethyl sulphate and hydrazine – are useful, but dangerous. Both are poisonous and volatile, and hydrazine has the extra property of being rather flammable, so the reactions are carried out with care and inside a protective chamber; but the end result is four tubes, each of which contains DNA with certain bases selectively modified.

Stage two is to recognize the modified bases and break the DNA there. One reagent, piperidine, suffices. Piperidine removes methylated guanine and also attacks and removes the pyrimidines opened by hydrazine. That done, it goes on to break the sugar-phosphate chain at any point where there is no base present. The end result is four collections of DNA fragments, all of which start at the same known point. One sets invariably ends with a G. Another set ends with G or A. The third set ends with C or T, and the fourth set with C alone.

The four mixtures are loaded on to a polyacrylamide gel just 0.3 mm thick. This special thin gel was Sanger's idea, and offers three advantages. It allows you to use much greater voltages, which means faster separation; it produces sharper bands on the radiographs, because there is less scattering of the radioactive particles; and, not unimportant, it reduces consumption of acrylamide. A

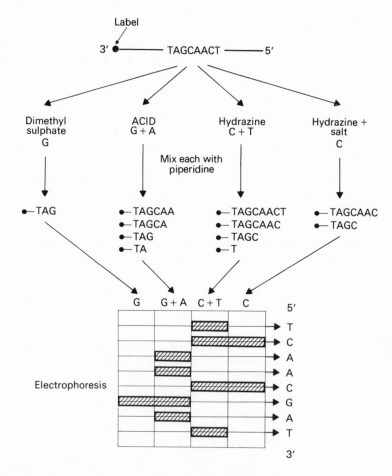

Figure 5.3
DNA sequencing by Maxam and Gilbert's chemical method.

marker of xylene cyanol, which shows up as a green band, travels as fast as fragments about 70 nucleotides long, and tells you where the fragments are; all that remains is to separate the fragments. The problem here is that the gel acts like the element on an electric radiator; as current flows through it, it heats up. Thin gels lose heat more quickly, so they can be used with higher voltages – up to 2000 volts – but still Gilbert advises keeping an eye on the voltage so that the temperature of the glass plates containing the gel stays between 45 and 55 °C. Once the run is over, you mark the gel with nifty radioactive ink and expose X-ray film as usual. The autoradiograph shows four ladders corresponding to fragments ending in G, G or A, T or C, and C alone. If there is a rung in both of the purine ladders, that base is a G, if only in the G or A ladder, then obviously it is an A. Likewise, with the two pyrimidine ladders, a rung in both indicates C, a rung in only one indicates T. As with the chain terminator method, you run up the ladder, reading the sequence as you go.

Skeleton keys

The two methods each have their advantages and disadvantages. Sanger's method is more sensitive and, because the chains are labelled throughout, requires less DNA to leave a discernable mark on the X-ray film. It is also quicker, but it needs single-stranded DNA (although exonuclease III can be used to nibble bases away from the 3′ end of a duplex strand and prepare the template, and there are now special virus cloning vehicles developed expressly for sequencing because they store the gene as single-stranded DNA[12]). Maxam and Gilbert's method requires no enzymatic copying and will work with single or double strands. Moreover, it will read up to 250 bases in either direction from a single restriction enzyme site and can provide an automatic check on results by sequencing both strands. But it needs more DNA and is not as fast. Maxam and Gilbert's method, despite the greater technical demands that it imposes on researchers, had been the more popular. Indeed, it is possible to buy, off the shelf, everything you need to sequence DNA by the Maxam and Gilbert method. The kit includes all the chemicals you need and a copy of the detailed 'cookbook' that Maxam and Gilbert published in *Methods in Enzymology.* Once you have your DNA, you need only follow instructions to read the base sequence on it. Popular though it is, the chemical method relies on Fred Sanger's electrophoretic ladders, and is perhaps not as powerful a general technique as Sanger's. In any case, there is no real rivalry between the two, and Sanger himself stresses the importance of checking sequences in several ways.

The ability to read genes is the key to many locks. Opening them has, as we've seen, exposed an enormous upset – the revelation that vast stretches of DNA are never expressed as proteins and seem to serve no obvious purpose. As an end in itself, gene sequencing has achieved great things, not least the entire genome of a number of organisms, so far mostly viruses but also the complete genomes of the mitochondria (the 'powerhouses' that supply cells with energy) of people and yeast. In about five years we have progressed from the 3569 bases of MS2 to the 50 000 or more bases of the yeast mitochondria. Wally Gilbert, in his Nobel Prize acceptance lecture, gave a lovely example of the efficiency of his method. 'To find out how easy and how accurate DNA sequencing was,' he said,

I asked a student, Gregor Sutcliffe, to sequence the ampicillin resistance gene . . . of *Escherichia coli.* . . . All he knew about the protein was an approximate molecular weight, and that a certain restriction cut on the [pBR322] plasmid inactivated that gene. He had no previous experience with DNA sequencing when he set out to work out the structure of DNA for this gene. After 7 months he had worked out about 1000 bases of double-stranded DNA, sequencing one strand and then sequencing the other for confirmation. . . . The DNA sequencing was correct. Sutcliffe then became very enthusiastic and sequenced the rest of plasmid pBR322 during the next 6 months, to finish his thesis.[13]

Thirteen months, for the entire sequence of 4362 bases on both strands, by a student with no previous experience of the method.

Rapid sequencing has done more, though, than merely unlock endless lines of bases. It has offered great insight into the way DNA controls the cell's chemical factories, with special sequences that adjust the translation of RNA into protein and others that guide newly formed proteins out through the cell membrane. Knowing the exact sequence of a gene has enabled engineers to create, from scratch, an improved version of the gene that will still code for the required protein but will be much easier to handle. There are other examples, too, of sequencing in the service of molecular biology, some of which will appear in later chapters. Disparate though they may be, they share one common feature; they all depend on the ready availability of purified DNA of the desired sequence. And that, in turn, often depends on shotgun experiments and the resultant genome libraries.

A cupboard unlocked may contain treasure such as insulin or interferon. It may equally well contain a skeleton, and in shotguns, libraries and rapid sequencing the potential for evil is always present. A gene library of the botulism bacteria (*Clostridium botulinum*) would provide a ready source of one of the world's deadliest poisons. Toxins of all descriptions could be isolated and manufactured with the help of shotgun and library and could even, in the most macabre sense, be improved by sequencing and directed mutation. The antibiotic resistance that is so useful in selecting clones could be perversely employed for malevolent purposes, intentionally to create super-resistant disease organisms that could do untold damage. It was the realization that genetic engineering offered the two faces of good and evil that led to the astounding spectacle of scientists voluntarily curbing the inquiries that are the lifeblood of research.

6

REGULATION

Scientists perceive the hazards and call a halt, but regulations and greater knowledge clear the way

Shotguns are powerful weapons, open to misuse. They are also extremely valuable in the right hands. The balance of risk and power is a fine one; it exercised the scientific community for many months, and continues to be of the utmost importance. The chronicle of concern over the safety of recombinant DNA is long and convoluted, amply documented elsewhere,[1] but a short summary of some of the concerns and some of the solutions is essential here.

In the early days of the science, heady claims rang out about the benefits of being able to engineer DNA to suit. At the same time there loomed the indistinct, but nevertheless frightening, hazards. That the dangers seemed somehow vague did nothing to ease fears. Indeed, ignorance magnified fear, so that the risks apparently were magnified. Paul Berg's intention to put SV40 into *E. coli* let the cat out of the bag at almost the last hour. *E. coli* is a natural inhabitant of man's gut. What if some bacteria had escaped from Berg's lab? What if they had infected one of the workers? What if they had passed the SV40 DNA on to some of that worker's cells? SV40 occasionally causes cancer in cells; could the escape of *E. coli* containing SV40 cause cancer in a human being? It seemed unlikely, but nobody knew. Could it, even worse, spread like an infectious disease, causing cancer in all who came into contact with the engineered escapee? Not only did people not know, they didn't even have the slightest idea.

Viral tumour DNA poses an obvious threat, but even benign experiments could go awry. What would happen if an *E. coli* able to manufacture insulin escaped and took up residence in the human gut? The victim's control over glucose metabolism might vanish completely, with dire effects. And those are accidents. What if some thoroughly misguided researcher decided to insert the gene for a toxin, botulinus for example, into *E. coli*? Could it escape and wipe out the human race?

Shotguns offered much greater danger with even less effort. The genome of an organism is not just a collection of inherited messages. It is an integrated set of genes that work well together. There are clutches of genes that do similar things, under delicate and finely-tuned feedback control, to ensure that the processes are carried out efficiently. What if, in a shotgun experiment, some genes were separated from the DNA regions that keep them under control? Might they be an entirely unknown source of danger? SV40 can insinuate itself into its host's DNA and lie there dormant, perhaps being kept down by some host-DNA suppressor. What if other genomes also contain tumour-causing viruses? Might a shotgun experiment release these from their confinement to plague the world? Shotguns are weapons of maximum uncertainty; you know you will hit something, but there is absolutely no way of knowing how exactly you will hit it.

Suppose we decide to clone the genome of a rabbit, and that by great good fortune we end up with each gene separately in a bacterial clone that starts manufacturing the gene's product. There are, perhaps, 100 000 genes. Suppose one in 1000 of those could have a harmful effect if it got out and infected a person. If we pull the genome apart one gene at a time, the risk of producing a dangerous recombinant in our first ten tries is 1 per cent; that might be deemed acceptable. But if we clone the genome in a shotgun experiment, we produce 100 harmful strains at once, and we won't know which clones contain the harmful genes. The risk of producing a harmful clone is still one in 1000, but we've done them all in one bang, and we have no way of controlling the experiment or ensuring that nothing can escape. Worse, the figures I've given are simply guesses, ones that happen to be enshrined in some of the writings on DNA safety. The number of potentially harmful genes might be much higher. Or there might be only one in 100 000. Does that make it any safer? What if that one in 100 000 were to escape and wreak devastation?

As knowledge of recombinant technology grew, worries about the risks of escape and spread of entirely new sorts of pathogen occupied many people's thought. But some worried also about the more fundamental issues. There are two major themes to life today: the prokaryotes, exemplified by *E. coli*, and the eukaryotes, exemplified by ourselves. The prokaryotes evolved first, but the two lines have been separate for the best part of a billion years. In that time, barriers to the free flow of genetic information between the two lines have sprung up, notwithstanding the viruses – neither pro- nor eukaryotes, but often go-betweens – that plague our lives. Genetic engineering purposely and wilfully penetrates those barriers and mixes DNA from the two realms. Is this a dangerous practice? And if it is, would it rob scientists of their liberty if they were totally forbidden to explore recombination? Some critics, notably Dr Robert Sinsheimer, professor of biology at California Institute of Technology, believed firmly that, intellectual freedom or no, these barriers should not be knowingly breached. 'Would we,' Sinsheimer asked, 'wish to claim the right of individual scientists to be free to create novel self-perpetuating organisms likely to spread about the planet in an uncontrollable manner for better or worse?' He answered his own question: 'I think not. . . . Science has become too potent. It is no longer enough to wave the flag of Galileo.'[2] Sinsheimer spoke for a small, but very concerned, group of scientists when he said:

People seriously wonder if through our cleverness we may not blunder into worse dilemmas than we seek to solve. They are concerned not only for the vagrant lethal virus or the escaped mutant deadly microbe, but also for the awful potential that we might inadvertently so arm the anarchic in our society as to shatter its bonds or conversely so arm the tyrannical in our society as to forever imprison liberty.[3]

Sinsheimer's solution was to imprison science, for its own good and for a short time only; but in the end other counsel prevailed.

Prisoner and gaoler at once

Arguments about probabilities and odds, worst-case scenarios and maximal disruption effects hide the fact that our ignorance of the realities was, at the time, staggering. It was, quite simply, impossible to agree to any assessment of risk, other than that there certainly was some risk. To their credit, the scientific community did not let this prevent them tackling the problem head on. Cynics may say that the threat of externally imposed legislation was the stick that drove the molecular biologists forward, but there was also a definite realization that they themselves were the people best placed to assess the risks. And while the risks were still so completely unknown, they had better slow down and consider.

New Hampton, New Hampshire, is one of the locations that annually hosts the Gordon Conferences. These renowned gatherings bring scientists together to discuss progress right at the edge between known and unknown. In June 1973 the participants in the Gordon Conference on Nucleic Acids had perhaps the first formal opportunity to discuss the potential, good and bad, of the emerging technology. They had heard from Stanley Cohen about his early work with plasmids, and in a specially convened discussion meeting they aired their concerns. The result was a spread, through that marvellous network that has been called the 'invisible college', of some of the doubts about recombinant DNA. Scientists, one hopes, left New Hampton with a slightly deeper understanding of their responsibilities. More tangibly, Maxine Singer and Dieter Soll, who jointly chaired the conference, drafted a letter that was sent to the American National Academy of Sciences and the Institute of Medicine. The letter was also published in *Science*, the journal of the American Association for the Advancement of Science, where the entire community could learn that the genetic engineers were asking for a study committee to be set up to investigate the potential risks. 'Although no hazard has yet been established, prudence suggests that the potential hazard be seriously considered.' It was, as the letter said, 'a matter of deep concern'.[4]

The National Academy of Sciences announced, in February the next year, that Paul Berg would chair the study committee. Eleven people, all in on recombinant DNA from the start, began their deliberations. They knew – Stanley Cohen and Herb Boyer were on the committee – that toad genes had been successfully engineered into *E. coli*. They could see for themselves that the pace was quickening even as they deliberated. As yet, so far as anyone knew, there had been no disasters, not even minor ones; but with each new experiment the risks apparently grew. An accident seemed imminent, even overdue. The committee wrote to *Science* – the so-called 'Berg letter' – asking colleagues to pause for a while and defer certain types of experiment, notably those that would create novel combinations of antibiotic resistance and those that involved animal viruses, whether tumour-causing or not.

'Although such experiments are likely to facilitate the solution of important theoretical and practical biological problems, they would also result in the creation of novel types of infectious DNA whose biological properties cannot be completely predicted in advance.'[5] Other experiments were to be 'carefully weighed' and were 'not to be undertaken lightly'.

The Berg Committee also called on the Director of the National Institutes of Health to set up an advisory committee that would oversee experimental plans and would assess danger, develop procedures to minimize risks, and draw up a set of guidelines to govern recombinant DNA work. Finally, they recommended that 'an international meeting of involved scientists from all over the world be convened . . . to review scientific progress in this area and to further discuss appropriate ways to deal with the potential biohazards of recombinant DNA molecules'. The Berg letter was published on 26 July 1974. In February 1975, 150 involved scientists from all over the world did indeed convene at the beautiful Pacific coast resort of Asilomar for a meeting that can honestly be described as historic.

Asilomar was an experiment. Never before had scientists gathered to discuss regulating their own activities. Naturally, all points of view were represented, from Galileo's flag-wavers, who wanted no restrictions whatsoever, to the super-cautious, who felt that there were certain areas – no-man's lands – that ought to be forbidden. Out of a great deal of debate, some consensus did emerge. Asilomar sorted the types of experiment that might be done into four categories (there were six originally, but this was felt to draw too fine a set of distinctions), which could be ordered in terms of riskiness. Then it agreed on two different sorts of protection for those four categories. The front line was to be physical; special facilities and handling procedures that would minimize the risks of escape. The lowest-risk experiments, those involving DNA from organisms that normally swap genes with *E. coli*, could be done using straightforward approved microbiological practices as carried out in good laboratories everywhere. These alone would suffice to contain the risks. The highest risk, where DNA from adult primates or animal viruses known to contain harmful genes was involved, would have to be done in a special facility of the highest security, not unlike the laboratories in which nerve gases and biological weapons are developed. This consensus represented a serious attempt to match the restrictions to the risks, and as such was welcomed by most of the participants. But the possibility remained that, however good the security, some recombinant DNA might escape to the outside world.

Here the special nature of the material they were dealing with caused particular alarm. A single molecule of even the deadliest toxin poses no great threat if it should be spilled, because once cleaned up the danger has been removed. That is not to underestimate the power for harm that toxic chemicals have – Seveso stands as testimony to that – but chemicals can be degraded and the spill can be cleaned up. Life is different. A single bacterium, given the right conditions, can double every 20 minutes. A single day, 24 hours, of unrestrained growth is enough to produce nearly 5000 million million million bacteria from a single escapee. There is no question of mopping that kind of mess up, so Asilomar decided on a second line of defence.

Sydney Brenner, as so often before in the growth of molecular biology, played a vital role in this. He managed to focus the conference's attention on a problem it could cope with, at a time when the participants were growing restless at the endless problems of putative disaster scenarios, and were beginning seriously to question the need for restraint. In addition to mere physical containment, recombinant DNA would be isolated by biological containment. The hosts and vectors would be strains selected to be cripples outside the laboratory. They might require special nutrients not found outside the test-tube, or they might grow only at temperatures considerably higher than wild *E. coli*. This notion – that researchers could exploit the conditions they provided in the laboratory to enable chosen strains to grow – was a considerable comfort to the assembled biologists. It was something they all understood, that natural selection would act with them to wipe out any undesirables that had somehow made it past the physical barriers. And the search for crippled cloning vehicles was something that the genetic engineers could undertake with alacrity and a fine sense of purpose, something that would not only help them all in the long run but would be elegant science in its own right. Brenner's suggestion (Waclaw Szybalski had earlier suggested biocontainment in a letter to Paul Berg, but it was Brenner who focused Asilomar's attention on this possibility) saved the day, and enabled the conference finally to complete its debate.

Under the guidelines envisaged by the Asilomar conference certain experiments would indeed not be permitted, but only because the biological containment systems had not yet been developed. These very dangerous experiments were not forbidden outright, but they would have to wait until the science of biological containment caught up with the researchers' aspirations.

The participants at Asilomar had been faced with a very real dilemma. No hazard of recombinant DNA technology had been unequivocally demonstrated. One might have thought, then, that no restrictions were necessary. And yet the scientists were willing to accept restrictions. Not one, apparently, argued against all restriction. If the research workers were willing to accept these checks on their academic freedom, clearly there must be some hazard. And yet, no hazard had been demonstrated . . . How could they match earlier statements about the safety of genetic engineering with their willingness to embrace restraints? The answer, it seems, is at least partly that they feared the consequences of not accepting restraint even more than the restraint itself. Had they not agreed a fairly stringent set of rules, legislators less informed about microbiology might have imposed restrictions that were far less tolerable. It was the lesser of the two evils, and it would have been very difficult for the scientists to protect themselves against draconian legislation had they not shown some willingness earlier on. As one professor of international law told the conferees, in the final legal session that related their academic concerns to the real world outside, 'it is the right of the public to act through the legislature to make erroneous decisions'.[6]

Marie Jahoda, professor of social psychology and for two years a member of the UK's advisory body the Genetic Manipulation Advisory Group (GMAG), offered a different reason in her review of James Watson's 'documentary history' of gene cloning. Asking why the scientists stopped themselves short, Jahoda answers:

At the risk of being laughed out of court by these superior minds, I suggest that they were overcome by a metaphysical awe at their own power to fiddle with the very building blocks of life. Watson's self-derogatory explanation that he acted originally in a fit of liberal conscience is a bit superficial – conscience in scientists and others had better come not just in occasional fits. That metaphysical awe was akin to Oppenheimer's experience in witnessing the first atomic bomb explosion, and when it communicated itself to the public all hell broke loose.[7]

Eventually the consensus of Asilomar was translated into acceptable legislation. In the USA, National Institutes of Health (NIH) director Donald Frederickson set up a Recombinant Advisory Committee which eventually hammered out a set of draft guidelines that was at least as stringent, and perhaps more so, than the Asilomar consensus. These set out in detail what was and was not permitted, the standards that the various levels of physical and biological containment had to reach, and a lot more besides. They made it clear that responsibility for safety devolves ultimately on to the individual investigator, though the institution and the NIH also play their part in keeping an eye on day-to-day research. Sanctions, however, were not provided. These depended on other federal agencies and legislation, for example health and safety at work legislation. The scientists' target, to regulate themselves with the minimum of external interference, had been achieved, and they had been seen to act responsibly throughout. (Not responsibly enough for some; at many debates around the country accusations of elitism were made against the genetic engineers. Often this was simply a reflection of the social concerns of the young radicals making the accusations, but some engineers undoubtedly were insensitive to public concern; by and large, though, in my opinion, they behaved well at all times.)

Events in the UK followed a very similar course. The Berg letter was published in *Nature*, the London-based journal, at the same time as it was released in *Science*, but created much more of an uproar in Europe. Scientists here saw the recommendations and responded in a tone of wounded pride. Who were these Americans to tell them what research to do and what not to do? Were they trying to prevent the free flow of scientific knowledge? The reason became apparent only after Berg came to England in September to defend the letter. *Nature* had removed the final paragraph, with its cautionary explanation of the motivation behind the letter. Those who took *Nature*, rather than *Science*, read a letter that seemed arrogant in its presumption, but this little misunderstanding was soon sorted out, and in 1974, after the Berg letter had been published, the Research Councils enforced the moratorium with a letter to all employees instructing them to obey the call for a halt. As Sydney Brenner noted, 'of course it was quite easy to obey because we weren't doing experiments'.[8] The councils also established a working party under the chairmanship of Lord Ashby. The

Ashby report urged that an advisory panel be established and that it consider drawing up a code of practice. This led to the Williams working party, whose report in turn led to the creation of GMAG, the Genetic Manipulation Advisory Group. GMAG, which was perhaps unique in that scientists were joined by trade unionists in their deliberations, issued guidelines similar to those of the NIH but relying more on physical and less on biological containment.

A change of heart

By the end of 1976 genetic engineers in the United States and Britain were working quite freely within the confines of a set of guidelines that they had imposed upon themselves. With the turmoil dying down, it became appropriate to look a little more calmly and a little more thoroughly at some of the assumptions that had been made. The guidelines allowed for experiments specifically directed at the infectivity, survival and so on of recombinant DNA molecules provided that these experiments were carried out within suitably secure physical containment systems. Such experiments would assess safety directly, and the results were very reassuring. Workers handling, without special precautions, ordinary K12 *E. coli*, which possessed a resistant plasmid, were examined every day for two years. Neither K12 nor the resistance plasmid appeared in their faeces at any time. The risk of transmission and contamination was apparently very low, perhaps because the K12 strain, by virtue of its half-century history of cushy life in laboratories, cannot compete with wild *E. coli* even if it does escape to a worker's gut. The resistance plasmid never showed up either, perhaps because no *E. coli* carrying it ever infected the workers, but perhaps also because the DNA was destroyed by nucleases among the digestive enzymes.

As they examined the risks, molecular biologists became more knowledgeable and more sanguine. Roy Curtiss III, professor of microbiology at the University of Alabama, exemplifies the process. In 1973, Curtiss was more cautious than Berg; he wanted all recombinant DNA work to stop until the risks had been satisfactorily assessed. As a member of the NIH advisory committee he was a tireless advocate of maximal caution. By 1977, when he wrote a letter on the subject to NIH Director Frederickson, Curtiss believed that 'the introduction of foreign DNA sequences into EK1 and EK2 host-vectors offers no danger whatsoever to any human being', apart from misguided souls who deliberately choose to infect themselves.[9] Between his earlier position and his revised view, Curtiss had not simply allowed others to assess the safety of the systems. He had been instrumental in developing the first safe crippled strain of *E. coli*, a fragile beast that he christened χ1776 in celebration of the American bicentennial. Curtiss had also turned himself into an expert on biohazards, and his change of heart was not lightly reached. 'The arrival at this conclusion has been some-what painful and with reluctance since it is contrary to my past "feelings" about the biohazards of recombinant DNA research.'[10] Nevertheless, reach it he did, by soberly assessing the evidence and overcoming his earlier 'feelings'; nor was Curtiss alone in his change of heart, for many scientists examined the evidence and changed their views.

While the molecular biologists were assessing the risks of working with particular bacteria in particular ways, epidemiologists and microbiologists pored over the safety record of other workers exposed to similar hazards. Pathogens are dangerous, of that there is no doubt, and even with precautions there are cases of workers catching diseases in the laboratory. Indeed, because microbiology laboratories are often working expressly with dangerous pathogens, the risks of disease and death are not inconsiderable. But, and this is important, the incidence of laboratory-related infections has been declining steadily over the past few decades as techniques improve and security becomes tighter. More important still, very rarely do diseases spread from one laboratory worker to an outside person, and never has a laboratory been the centre of an epidemic. There is, the scientists argued, little reason to fear that laboratories as such are dangerous places. Their record is not perfect, admittedly, but it is good and getting better.

The American apparatus of control has been exercised in only two infractions. In the spring of 1980 graduate students in the laboratory of San Diego researcher Samuel Ian Kennedy discovered what they thought was a violation of the NIH guidelines. Kennedy had permission to work with Sindbis virus but had, it seems, cloned Semliki Forest virus, which was not permitted. The students' charge brought in Kennedy's department, the University of California at San Diego's Biosafety Committee, and eventually the NIH. Kennedy resigned his post while the NIH deliberated on his transgressions. They discovered that he had indeed cloned Semliki Forest virus, but they did not try to find out whether this had been done intentionally in defiance of the guidelines or whether Kennedy's Sindbis virus was contaminated. The NIH says it was Kennedy's responsibility to ensure the identity of his stocks and that he did not discharge this responsibility. While investigating this charge, the committee came across another transgression that was potentially more harmful. In applying to the NIH for funds, Kennedy mentioned recombinant experiments on mouse cells that had not been cleared by his institutional Biosafety Committee. Because Kennedy resigned his position, there was little that the NIH could do. If he applies for NIH funds in the next two years a copy of the transgressions report will be forwarded to the appropriate grant review board, and if he succeeds in getting funds he will be subject to extra impositions on his recombinant DNA work. In all, Kennedy seems to have been let off rather lightly, though what would have happened had he not resigned is anybody's guess.

Marty Cline was equally fortunate. He broke the guidelines by performing experiments with recombinant vectors on human patients. Cline, who resigned as head of UCLA's Haematology and Oncology Division in the Center for Health Sciences, though he remains a full professor, planned an attack on two genetic diseases, sickle cell anaemia and beta thalassaemia. Both diseases are painful, incurable and lethal, and are caused by defective haemoglobin genes. Cline planned to insert engineered haemoglobin genes into patients but came up against red tape in the form of recombinant DNA committees and human experimentation committees. Neither would give permission for the experiment until the other had considered it. Cline eventually got permission to do the experiments in Israel and in Italy, but at the last minute changed the protocol slightly. Instead of inserting the naked human globin genes, as he said he would, he used the genes in their pBR322 vector. UCLA assumed jurisdiction over his work abroad and brought the NIH in on the case. After seven months' deliberation, the NIH gave Cline much the same treatment as Kennedy. He too has to submit a copy of the NIH report with any new application for funds, and has to obtain special permission for future research that involves government money and genetic engineering of any kind.

In December 1981 the NIH's National Heart, Lung and Blood Institute stripped Cline of his funding, worth \$244 000, but two other agencies that support Cline decided to do nothing.

These two examples are the only ones that have come to light so far. They are hardly the horror scenarios that were once imagined. Kennedy's case is hard to assess, but Cline certainly appears to have acted thoughtfully throughout and with his patients' best interests at heart. The punishments, I think, reflect this. The guidelines served their purpose well, and there will always be some need for control. Nevertheless, as researchers learn more about the risks and dangers the controls will need to be adjusted to keep up with the state of knowledge. Probably this will mean a progressive relaxation, but there is every possibility that certain well-defined areas may come under even stricter control, should the need arise.

The new consensus emerging from the molecular biology community is that recombinant DNA experiments are no more hazardous than non-recombinant experiments on the same microorganisms. If you're working with *E. coli*, for example, inserting foreign DNA does not of itself create any substantial increase in the likelihood of a dangerous outcome. Simply inserting new DNA into a bacterium does not turn it into a dangerous pathogen. Indeed, with eyes open to the possibility of genetic transfer between strains and even between species of bacteria, researchers have discovered that it goes on all the time. There is nothing about recombination *per se* that poses a threat. It happens all the time in sexual reproduction. Indeed, shortly after Asilomar, at a meeting to begin the business of turning the conferences will into guidelines, Jane Setlow, now at Brookhaven National Laboratory in New York, had a sudden flash of insight. 'Do you realize,' she asked her colleagues, 'what this means? It means we've just made human sex a moderate-risk experiment.' 'But only in the laboratory,' someone else pointed out, after a brief silence and some hesitant laughter. Nor is there anything special about recombination in a test-tube compared to recombination out in the world. Brenner pointed the paradox out quite forcefully:

What a genetic manipulator does is to do things *in vitro*. In theory, if you could do genetic manipulation by avoiding the use of test-tubes, then in fact you would be doing something that was a natural mechanism and so in theory you might argue that you could escape from the GMAG regulations. . . . Work on recombinant influenza viruses, work on recombinant

bacteria . . . goes on, but doing the same work – indeed, the identical
experiment could be formulated – with a restriction enzyme would put
you under the GMAG regulations.[11]

Brenner said this in October 1978, and although he didn't men-
tion it, England had recently seen a horrifying example of exactly
the sort of thing he was talking about. A little more than a month
before, on 11 September 1978, Janet Parker, a photographic tech-
nician, died of smallpox. Parker worked in the Anatomy Department above Birmingham University's smallpox laboratory. Her
disease was traced to that lab, and accusations were made that the
smallpox laboratory had been genetically engineering more virulent strains. The lab had, it is true, created more virulent strains,
but it had done so by the time-honoured method of selection, not
by the new-fangled recombinant techniques. It was an old-
fashioned smallpox virus that was responsible for the death of Janet
Parker, one that was immune to genetic engineering regulations.
Had the smallpox laboratory been using recombinant techniques,
the accident might not have happened. Microbiological smallpox,
not genetic engineering, killed Janet Parker.

Of course, some recombinants are going to be dangerous, just as
some pathogens are dangerous and others are not. With knowledge
has come greater understanding. What were once unimaginable
horrors are now seen to be acceptable risks, and not very dangerous
risks at that. The benefits of creating recombinant molecules of
DNA shine even more clearly now that the risks have been illumin-
ated and shown to be smaller than imagined. The result has been a
clamour from scientists for a loosening of the reins.

Comforting truths

Even as the guidelines were being drawn up, there was a feeling
among some scientists that they might have exaggerated the danger, and that the alarm they sounded was all the more worrying
because it came from a group not traditionally associated with
enormous public altruism. If scientists had blown the whistle
because they perceived a danger, the disaster must be imminent
indeed. People said that, having drawn the picture they did, the
researchers would find it hard to persuade the regulatory bodies to

relax their grip on the work. In the event this has proved partially true, but the regulations have been revised and generally in the direction of less, not more, control. In September 1981 the Recombinant DNA Advisory Committee recommended to the NIH that the guidelines be changed from a compulsory set of rules that federally funded laboratories *had* to comply with (industry was exempt) to a voluntary code of practice that laboratories *ought* to comply with. Allan Campbell of Stanford and David Baltimore of the Massachusetts Institute of Technology told the director of the NIH that there was every reason to ease the restrictions and no case for increasing the levels of containment required in any experiment. 'The benefit,' they said, 'is likely to be zero.'[12] Recognizing that there was a 'good scientific case' for relaxation, the committee suggested that containment for recombinant DNA experiments be at least as high as containment for non-recombinant experiments with the same organisms, but not necessarily higher. The committee also suggested that large cultures, 10 litres or more, be permitted without special clearance, and that experiments in which recombinant molecules are deliberately released into the environment be permitted. Along with the slackened guidelines, some members of the advisory committee also felt that the committee had played its part and ought to phase itself out of existence.

The Recombinant DNA Advisory Committee informally endorsed the proposal from Baltimore and Campbell, and judging by the response from scientists it seemed that the guidelines would indeed be not only relaxed but also made voluntary. The edifice of control would have been constructed and razed in less than a decade. *Nature*'s editorialist was led to ask: 'Has the whole exercise been a waste of busy people's time?'[13] But then state legislatures, notably in California, threatened to introduce tougher local measures of their own if the guidelines were dismantled, and in the end this threat, essentially the same one that permitted the guidelines to arise in the first place, swayed the committee. In February 1982 it adopted, by 17 votes to 3, an alternative proposal from Susan Gottesman of the National Cancer Institute. The containment categories will be revised, and some will surely be relaxed, but researchers will still be required to comply with the guidelines.

In the UK too there have been attempts to relax the guidelines. Sydney Brenner, instrumental in setting up Asilomar and provocative at all times, pointed out long ago that GMAG's categories, like the NIH's, were not based on biological knowledge; that a classification according to the known threat posed by well understood pathogens provided a far better model for containment. Categorization is now based on risk assessment procedures, but opinions vary on the validity of some of the calculations involved. Local safety committees have some influence over low-risk experiments, and contain representatives of all groups in the laboratory. They should be ideal watchdogs, but may be open to manipulation and abuse. And the Confederation of British Industry, which bridles at most forms of regulations, delivered a strongly worded proposal recommending broadly based relaxation of the guidelines. The Confederation would make no distinction between laboratory manipulation and large-scale industrial applications, but GMAG does not see eye to eye with industry. Indeed, GMAG and the CBI have agreed on very little, and the CBI's proposals would have wrested control over industrial genetic engineering from GMAG, giving it instead to other regulatory bodies that might be more malleable. The revised UK guidelines have yet to appear, but they too will echo the feeling of safety and, perhaps, sheepishness at having made such a fuss over a threat that turns out, so the scientists say, to be more illusory than real.

Dangerous lies

This is a far cry indeed from the suasive arguments voiced at Asilomar and elsewhere in favour of a scientific watchdog, but the mood has changed. The genetic engineers seem to be saying that, because they have demonstrated their responsibility, by opening their own cupboard and examining the skeletons while desisting from further work voluntarily, they should now, having shown that the skeletons were largely imaginary, be permitted to get on with their work without restriction. As an example, James Watson wrote in an article in 1978: 'I'm drawing up the Whole Risk Catalog. Under D I have dogs, doctors, dioxin. Where do I put DNA? Very low.'[14] Should we believe Watson? Can we trust the scientists?

Jonathan King, professor of biology at MIT, thinks not. He has been an implacable foe of unrestrained genetic engineering since the inception of the debate, and declares that he is not really heartened by the recent experiments that apparently demonstrate how safe recombinant DNA is. King points out that industry is getting involved in a big way, and that industry just cannot be trusted in the same way that scientists at the research bench can.

The risk-assessment research hasn't been done – in the United States it has been blocked, and in my estimation it's been blocked because some risk is going to emerge. . . . A fortune is going to be made from the cloning of insulin in bacteria. Four million doses are sold three times a week in the United States. They are not going to sell that insulin cheap; they are going to sell it expensive because it's human insulin. They are going to *produce* it cheap. That is a very very powerful force behind the scenes, but it penetrates the scientific deliberations. . . . [The companies'] front men may be research scientists who say 'we are only interested in the expansion of human knowledge', but the background there is very different.[15]

King's warnings are ominous. They fall, by and large, on deaf ears. Genetic engineers have shown themselves concerned, and have demonstrated the safety of what they do. But King reminds us that it is not the engineers themselves who pose the dangers but the application of their discoveries. There is an uncomfortable parallel to be drawn between genetic engineering on the one hand and nuclear power on the other. Both of the technologies can indeed be shown to be safe, on paper and in small-scale tests of specific links in the chain of disaster. And both technologies harness knowledge and are operated for profit. That imposes constraints upon the operation that jeopardize its safety.

After the disaster on Three Mile Island, one critic of the nuclear power lobby reminded people that there are only two kinds of nuclear power stations: those on paper – safe as houses – and those finally built – risky, to put it mildly. The catalogue of error, oversight and plain bad practice that has been uncovered at nuclear power stations is long. Some items, like the basketball used to plug a waste-water outlet, would be funny if they weren't so frightening. Others have no redeeming qualities. The promise of nuclear power – endless clean and cheap electricity – has been partially met, but the dangers have not been completely contained, not so far. Genetic engineering also holds out great promise. So far there has been no biotechnological Harrisburg. So far.

7

APPLICATIONS

How bacterial factories that make human hormones fulfil the early promise of recombinant DNA

Forty million people around the world suffer diabetes. The pancreas – more specifically, the beta cells of the islets of Langerhans – cannot make enough of the hormone insulin, and as a result cannot accurately control the amount of sugar in their blood. Many diabetics can achieve a modicum of control by taking tablets and watching what they eat, but for the rest, an outside source of insulin is essential. That insulin, which must be injected once or twice a day, comes from pigs and cows, which in itself creates problems. For one thing, insulins from different animals are not quite identical, and those subtle differences can cause a reaction in the patient. Then there is the question of purity; getting the insulin out of the pancreatic cells is a complicated business, and it is all too easy for minor impurities to find their way into the injection along with the insulin. These impurities also cause adverse reactions. The ideal replacement for missing human insulin is, of course, human insulin. Beef and pig insulins are, fortunately, close enough to control human blood sugar – if they weren't, diabetes would still be a fatal incurable disease – but it has always been a dream to develop an inexhaustible supply of completely pure human insulin. Genetic engineering is well on the way to making that dream reality.

Insulin is just one of the biochemicals with real practical benefits. Other hormones, like growth hormone and the reproductive hormones, interferon (a defence against viruses and possible cancer cure), arcane and exotic proteins responsible for such things as blood clotting – all are relatively simple proteins made by the body's cells. With care and attention, and a ready supply of suitable cells from fresh corpses or cultures, the important proteins can be, and have been, extracted to treat those who lack them. But all these vital chemicals could be made even more readily by new cells created by genetic engineering, and all have been made by genetic engineering.

The diseases that could be treated if an inexpensive and obtainable source of specific proteins were available are legion; and in the early days of genetic engineering, when it became clear that bacteria could be instructed to make specific proteins to order, the carrot of medically valuable substances lured people on. The stories told in those early days, of endless supplies of therapeutic proteins, are coming true; and they are provoking interest not just among those who would benefit medically, but among investors who see in genetic engineering a market crying out for products. When Biogen, the Harvard and Swiss bioengineering company, announced that it had cloned human interferon, the value of one of the investors in the company rose by $425 million. Other companies have similar tales to tell, but the real star of these glamorous gene-splicing businesses was Genentech.

In May 1980 Genentech had permission from the National Institutes of Health to proceed to large-scale culture with three major products; human growth hormone, human anti-growth hormone, and human insulin. On 14 October of that year, Genentech offered its shares to the buying public. They opened at $35 dollars each, and minutes later were trading at $89. Lab technicians – and indeed researchers – who had accepted shares in lieu of payment found themselves unimaginably wealthy. Wall Street valued the company as a whole at $530 million, and Herb Boyer's original $500 investment had become $82 million. The promise of genetic engineering, at least in one area, had been made good. Ironically, by early 1982 not one single genetically engineered therapeutic compound has arrived at the market place, and there is evidence of some disillusion. Genentech shares hover around the $35 mark again, and there is difficulty raising fresh capital. The abandoned optimism has given way to caution, but the work goes on, and the much-vaunted benefits of genetic engineering are beginning to appear.

Engineered help for the engineers

The glamour of being able to engineer products that many people depend on tempted a lot of scientists into recombinant DNA technology. But one of the first successful applications of that technology was to manufacture a product that the genetic engineers themselves depended on: DNA ligase. The ligase from *E. coli* is useful because it will seal the nicks between strands of DNA, but extracting it from a mass of *E. coli* cells is tedious, complex and inefficient. The ligase is an enzyme, a protein, so all the steps of separation and purification must be travelled, and in the end the amount of enzyme obtained is quite pitiful. So it was very good news when, early in 1977, Sharon Panasenko announced that she had engineered a strain of *E. coli* that would produce 500 times more ligase than the ordinary bug.[1] Panasenko and her colleagues at Stanford had already inserted the ligase gene into a lambda vector, cutting the gene out with *Eco* RI and inserting it into the gap in the lambda vector. The gene came from a mutant that was already overproducing ligase by about five times, and when they infected ordinary *E. coli* with the recombinant lambda the cells overproduced by about ten times. It was a doubling, and a good start, but it wasn't enough.

Panasenko set about improving the engineered virus. The first thing she did was to remove one of the lambda's *Eco* RI restriction sites by mutation. This meant that the lambda would, after treatment with *Eco* RI, retain a gene that, while not essential, enabled it to grow more efficiently. Without that gene, which it lost during the *Eco* RI digestion, the phage was not able to grow terribly well. Panasenko then swapped one fragment of the lambda she was using with the corresponding fragment from a mutant lambda. The mutant section would allow the new vector to insert itself into the host's chromosome and remain there as a dormant prophage until the experimenters decided to induce the virus to begin multiplying. The replacement also enabled Panasenko to insert a larger *E. coli* fragment into the lambda DNA. The new vector was chopped up with *Eco* RI, as was the old vector with its cargo of ligase genes. After mixing and joining, the recombinants were selected and tested to see how much ligase each was making.

The result, when all was done, was a new recombinant lambda that carried the gene for *E. coli's* DNA ligase and that would be able to grow efficiently in *E. coli*. Under normal circumstances it would infect *E. coli* and become incorporated into the DNA, replicating along with that DNA, so a large vat of the cells could be grown from a few starters. To get the DNA ligase, the bulk of the cell soup would be removed and subjected to heat shock – a short period at 43 °C instead of the usual 37 °C. (A few cells would be left behind to start the next batch, rather like a home-made yoghurt operation.) The heat shock induces the viral prophage to dissociate itself from the host chromosome and begin replicating, eventually breaking open the host and releasing hundreds of new infective particles. While the rest of the virus is replicating, the ligase gene on the viral DNA directs the synthesis of DNA ligase, and the engineered cells, after induction, produce a hundred times more ligase than ordinary *E. coli*. With that increase in concentration, the tedium of protein purification became much more worthwhile, but there was yet another piece of engineering to increase the yield even further.

Manufacture of ligase stopped because the cells broke open to release the newly synthesized lambda phages. Panasenko delayed the cell lysis by putting an amber mutation into the lambda S gene, which controls lysis. Viruses with the mutation were unable to break out of the host; they kept replicating – and making DNA ligase – much longer. With this final modification the engineered lambda would produce about 500 times more ligase than untouched *E. coli*. In fact, DNA ligase made up about 5 per cent of the protein in the engineered cell, an amount that made it very easy to extract and purify quite large amounts of the enzyme. And of course, readily available large amounts of DNA ligase made it easier to do more elaborate genetic engineering, so the fruits of the pioneering efforts to harness the manufacturing capabilities of microbes began a sort of cascade system. Genetic engineering for certain products made the whole of genetic engineering easier, which made it easier to create yet other products.

A giant step: anti-growth hormone

Of course the genetic engineers are pleased that they can obtain purer, and cheaper, DNA ligase for their work; engineering makes for easier engineering. But what about those high hopes for health products? They too have been successfully engineered.

The first human gene product to be grown in a bacterium was the hormone somatostatin. Normally produced by the gut and pancreas, but mostly by the hypothalamus, somatostatin acts as a brake on the growth of the body. It counteracts the effects of growth hormone (and, incidentally, insulin), and can be thought of as anti-growth hormone. People who have a somatostatin deficiency often turn out to be giants called acromegalics. (The ends of their bones are abnormally large.) Unfortunately, it is all but impossible to purify somatostatin from normal biological sources. It can be manufactured chemically by tediously stringing the 14 amino acids together in the correct order; a single gram made this way costs about $50 000. A more plentiful, and cheaper, supply would be very useful to treat certain types of gigantism.

Somatostatin, then, offers a number of advantages to the genetic engineer. It is small, just 14 amino acids long, and the sequence of those amino acids is known. Assays of exquisite sensitivity exist, so that the presence of even minuscule quantities of the hormone can be readily detected. Finally, it is a hormone of some biological importance, and therefore of theoretical and practical interest. It seems ages now since 1977, when Keiichi Itakura and his colleagues – who included Francisco Bolivar and Herb Boyer – announced that they had successfully cloned somatostatin. (Actually, they weren't in all that much of a hurry to announce; the news leaked out when Paul Berg told the US Senate's Subcommittee on Science, Technology and Space about it as an example of the potential benefits of genetic engineering.) But those efforts are important because they illustrate not only the tricks of the trade but also the fantastic advances that had been made even in the two years after Asilomar.[2]

The first point is that Itakura did not get his somatostatin gene from a living cell. He made it. As he knew the 14 amino acids it was a conceptually simple, but chemically sophisticated, exercise to manufacture a string of nucleic acids that would direct the synthesis of the hormone. Itakura had been instrumental in developing a new way for biochemists to join bases together into longer sequences. Previously, they had joined pairs of bases into so-called dimers, and then linked the dimers. Itakura devised a way to make threesomes – trimers – and join these. Each of the 64 possible trimers, representing the 64 codons, could be made in bulk and strung together to order. To make somatostatin, Itakura and his colleagues looked at the amino acid sequence for the protein and devised a sequence of coded nucleotides that would produce that sequence of amino acids. They divided the two strands of the artificial gene into 16 segments, between 11 and 16 bases long, and then linked the segments together. The design had been carefully contrived, not only to have an *Eco* RI recognition site at one end and a *Bam* HI site at the other (to ease later handling of the gene), but also to ensure that the smaller subunits would link together. So clever was the design that, in their own words, 'the somatostatin gene self-assembles'.[3] (It isn't clear how long all the preliminary assembly work on the artificial gene took, and I have been unable to find out, but this technology too has leaped ahead. Companies now advertise gene manufacturing machines that will string 16 bases together in predetermined order overnight.)

The somatostatin gene that Itakura made may, or may not, have had the same sequence as the genuine article on a human chromosome, but that matters not a bit so long as the end product – the protein – is the same. And, given that he had used the universal genetic code and the known sequence for somatostatin to construct the gene, there was every expectation that the bacterial and natural products would be identical. Apart from the two restriction enzyme recognition sites that he put at either end of the gene, which would enable him to play about with it subsequently, Itakura also put an additional amino acid, methionine, at the start of the protein; this would prove to be very important later in the game.

With the gene made, the next step was to construct a vector to get it into the *E. coli* cells, and that was where Bolivar came in. The basis for the vector was his plasmid pBR322, which he engineered to insert part of the *lac* operon from *E. coli*. The point of this was to provide a start mark – the region switching the genes on and part of the first gene – that the bacterium would recognize. One of the problems with bacteria is that they don't recognize the same control codes that higher animals use, so to get the bacterium to obey the synthetic foreign somatostatin gene Itakura had to provide the bug with a start signal that it could recognize. The *lac* operon was that signal, and whenever the bacteria made the enzymes in the *lac* operon, which it would do when using lactose sugar, it would also make the somatostatin. The new plasmid, with the *Eco* RI insertion sites, would respond to the presence of lactose by switching on the *lac* operon, and in so doing would make somatostatin. To find the ideal plasmids, they infected *E. coli* with the modified pBR322 vector and grew the infected cells on agar that contained tetracycline, ampicillin, and the lactose analogue X-gal (see page

97 above). pBR322 is resistant to ampicillin and tetracycline, but only those colonies that had taken up the *lac* genes would show up as blue on the X-gal medium. Forty-five blue colonies were picked and screened to find those with the correct orientation of the *lac* fragment; three of the 45 had the goods, and the best of these was grown up and christened pBH10.

The trouble with pBH10 was that the very act of inserting the *lac* fragment had created a second *Eco* RI site, and to make sure that recombination would be efficient the cloning team wanted only one. In the absence of ribonucleotide bases, RNA polymerase will bind to the start of the *lac* operon and stay there. One *Eco* RI site is nearby, and is protected from the restriction enzyme because it is covered by the polymerase molecule. The other is further away, and can be broken by *Eco* RI. That done, the single-stranded sticky ends can be nibbled away with S1 exonuclease and the molecule then joined head to tail with T4 DNA ligase. The resultant plasmid, with just one *Eco* RI site near the start of the *lac* operon, and resistance to ampicillin and tetracycline, was dubbed pBH20. They were now ready to insert Itakura's synthetic somatostatin gene (see figure 7.1a).

The pBH20 plasmid was digested first with *Eco* RI and then with *Bam* HI, yielding a small fragment, which could be thrown away, and a large fragment, which would be used to receive the somatostatin gene. Only proper recombinants had a working ampicillin resistance gene, so it was a simple matter to select the colonies that would grow on ampicillin. The plasmid pSom I has everything needed (see figure 7.1b). DNA sequencing showed the presence of the artificial gene exactly where it was supposed to be, but alas, the cells containing pSom I did not seem to be making any somatostatin. Radioimmunoassay, sensitive enough to detect a few molecules of the stuff, found nothing.

The engineers had noticed that, when they added somatostatin to extracts of *E. coli*, the hormone was rapidly broken down. So could it be that the plasmid was making the hormone, but that the cell's degenerative enzymes were breaking it down as fast as it was made? To find out, they inserted almost all of the gene for the enzyme β-galactosidase in front of the somatostatin gene. Fortunately, β-galactosidase has an *Eco* RI site near its far end, and even more fortunately, the site is placed so that it would not affect the reading frame of the triplets that coded for the somatostatin. They

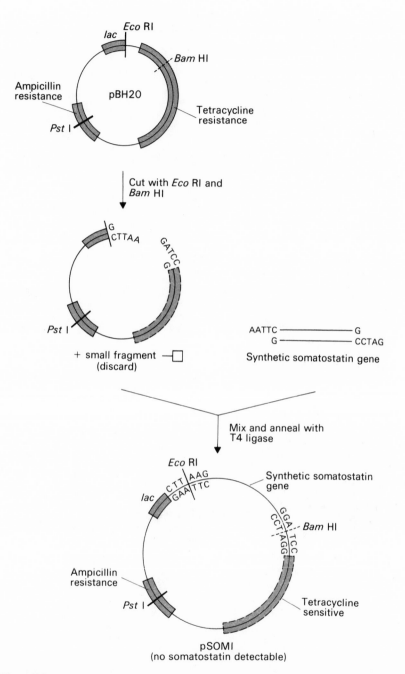

Figure 7.1
Construction of somatostatin plasmid. (a) The synthetic gene is inserted into pBH20.

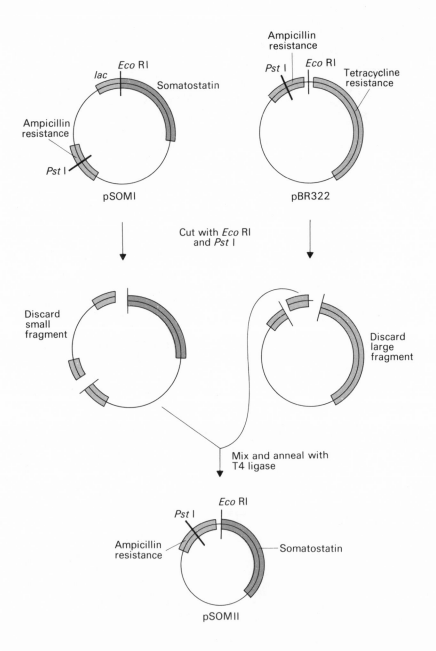

(b) The ampicillin resistance gene from pBR322 is added to pSom I to make pSOM II.

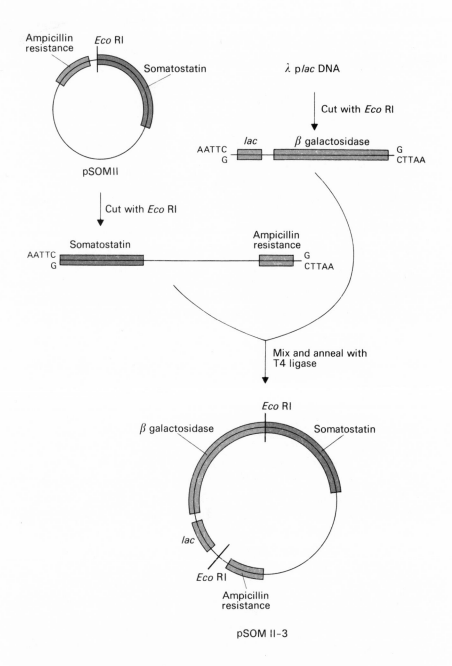

(c) Part of the *lac* operon is inserted in front of the somatostatin gene. pSom II-3 secretes somatostatin fused to β-galactosidase.

would still produce the somatostatin, but it would be tagged on near the end of the much larger β-galactosidase molecule. The result was a few clones that had all the desirable properties; they were resistant to ampicillin, turned X-gal blue, and manufactured something very like β-galactosidase. When that something was mixed with a compound called cyanogen bromide, which breaks proteins specifically after methionine residues – remember the methionine at the front of the synthesized somatostatin gene? – all the tests confirmed the presence of somatostatin. pSom I probably had been making somatostatin, but had also been destroying it. In pSom II-3 the large fragment of β-galactosidase wrapped around the somatostatin and protected it from enzyme breakdown (see figure 7.1c). The combined molecule could be removed and purified, and then split with cyanogen bromide to release the hormone.

Itakura, and Boyer's company Genentech (which had supported the research), had obtained a human protein from a genetically engineered colon bacillus, a hormone that would prevent genetic giants from becoming too outsized. When endocrinologists were working on the structure of somatostatin, they had to use nearly half a million sheep brains to get five thousandths of a gram of the hormone: 2 gallons of culture of the early Genentech somatostatin bacteria produced the same amount.

A little more help: growth hormone

The other side of the growth coin is the hormone that promotes bodily growth, called somatotropin, or human growth hormone (HGH). This peptide, 191 amino acids long, encourages bones to grow and bodies to put on weight. In medicine, it is used mainly to treat children with a growth hormone deficiency, who without it would end up dwarfs, but also to help broken bones to join, to mend burned skin, and to heal bleeding ulcers. Before genetic engineering, the only source was human cadavers, and ironically, it was the early promise of genetic engineering that led, in Britain, to a severe shortage of the natural product.

About 800 children in Britain need regular doses of growth hormone to ensure that they will reach a normal stature. That growth hormone was extracted from the pituitaries of corpses collected by mortuary workers, who received a small additional payment for each pituitary. This system worked well, and in 1978 the mortuary workers gathered some 70 000 pituitaries. These were more than enough for hormone needs, and the excess pituitaries were stockpiled. Alas, the Department of Health and Social Security decided to incorporate the small pituitary bonus into the mortuary workers' wages. As might have been predicted, the number of pituitaries that the workers collected fell drastically. The stockpile waned as the pituitaries were used up, and the DHSS found itself faced with a shortfall of growth hormone. This would not have mattered too much if the early claims of Genentech for bacterial production of human growth hormone had been met, but there have been delays that, coupled with the shortage, produced a large rise in the price of HGH: in 1978 the price was £1.25 for a 5 unit ampoule, while in November 1981 the same ampoule cost something like £15.00. The delays arose partly in production and partly with the quality of the bacterial compound. Early doses had pronounced side-effects, notably fevers and destruction of the body's protective white blood cells, which were almost certainly the results of contamination by bacterial toxins. In any event, the DHSS's response to the gap was to reduce the therapeutic dose offered to children with growth hormone deficiency. The net effect of that reduction should not be too drastic – one expert thinks that children given the lower doses will end up at worst about 3 cm short of their potential maximum height – and future generations of pituitary dwarfs should be much better off.[4]

The cloned gene for growth hormone was one of the reasons that Genentech's stock changed hands at $89 – after opening at $35 earlier that day. So what had the company's scientists done? The principle, again, was simple; to engineer a growth hormone gene into *E. coli* cells and persuade the cells to make the hormone. But the techniques were more complex than had been needed to get bacteria to manufacture somatostatin.

When the body manufactures growth hormone, it does so in stages. The messenger RNA made from the gene contains a extra region called a signal that seems to tell the cell that the protein behind the signal is destined to be exported outside the cell. Complementary DNA, made from purified messenger RNA, told the Genentech team all they needed to know about the structure of the gene. There was a recognition site for *Hae* III in the region that specifies amino acids 23 and 24 of the hormone, so the engineers

planned to clone the natural gene below that site but to manufacture an artificial gene for the first part of the molecule and attach
it to the cloned natural DNA. The plan was to ensure that the
manufactured leader section contained the right signals to start
synthesis, while the rest specified the bulk of the hormone. The
hybrid growth hormone gene simplified the amount of sheer chemistry needed while still offering control over the contents of the
vital first section of the gene.

Having gone through the steps leading to the somatostatin plasmid, the details of the somatotropin scheme would be superfluous.
In essence, David Goeddel succeeded beyond the expectations of
almost everybody, and the announcement of Genentech's success
(a detailed paper appeared in *Nature* in October 1979[5]) took people
rather by surprise. But the recombined plasmid, pHGH107, was
real enough and produced something remarkably like human
growth hormone. The Genentech scientists tested it exhaustively,
comparing it to human growth hormone from humans in all sorts of
ways. The two proteins migrated step for step in an electric field.
They reacted against the same antibodies in the same way. The
sequence of the inserted gene would, by all that's known in molecular biology, have produced a protein identical to human growth
hormone. As far as everyone was concerned the stuff that Goeddel
and his colleagues had persuaded *E. coli* to make *was* human
growth hormone. It was, they announced, 'the first time that a
human polypeptide has been directly expressed in *E. coli*', and the
engineered strain with its specially created plasmid 'produce[d]
HGH in large amounts'.[6] But before the product would be
accepted by the medical fraternity it would have to be *proved* to be
human growth hormone, identical or superior to the stuff from
cadavers.

That took another two years, till October 1981, when a ten-man
team announced that 'purified human growth hormone from *E.
coli* is biologically active'.[7] (That team, incidentally, included only
one person who was also on the team, also ten-strong, that had
engineered the growth hormone bacteria.) Again, they tested it
against genuine human HGH, and again it was indistinguishable.
Given to rats, the human and bacterial hormones produced identical patterns of growth, and 'no adverse effects were observed in
the rats . . . , even in those given the highest HGH dose'.[8] Indeed,
on several of the physical and chemical tests it was clear that the

HGH purified from human pituitaries contained contaminants that the bacterial HGH did not. These contaminants are believed to be the source of insulin-related problems that can turn a dwarf child into a diabetic – of normal stature. The bacterial HGH looks like a better bet in the long run.

At one point it looked as if human growth hormone would be the first product to come on to the market and justify the wild welcome offered to recombinant research, but still there are problems. The first clinical trials were cut short because of the side-effects, the result of bacterial toxins; the manufacturers say that the purification process is now much improved and have restarted trials. Even this, however, does not persuade some sceptics. They point out that the bacterial protein is not quite identical to the genuine article 'Clever though Genentech's genetic engineers are, they have not been able to devise a way for their bacteria to produce growth hormone without an extra methionine at one end of the molecule.'[9] Methionine, it seems, is very powerful when it comes to stimulating antibodies, which causes some experts to predict that over the long term patients will become allergic to the bacterial hormone and unable to use it. By then, mortuary supplies may have dried up altogether.

Of course the scientists with a stake in bacterial growth hormone are working hard to eliminate the problem of this additional methionine. It may not even turn out to be a problem. The irony of it is that, in the original plan to synthesize the gene, when the methionine was inserted as part of the start-up signal, Goeddel and his colleagues were confident that it would pose no problem. 'The fact,' they wrote, 'that most bacterial proteins do not contain N-terminal methionine residues suggests that the fMet [methionine] should be efficiently removed.'[10] Alas, it isn't so, and that little amino acid is causing troubles that far outweigh its size.

A sweet victory: insulin

Growth hormones are important; nobody would deny that. But commercially speaking they are very small potatoes indeed compared with the market for insulin. The precise value of that market is hard to gauge, but Eli Lilly, which has already cornered 90 per cent of the American insulin market, invested $40 million in 1980 to set up two plants, one in Indianapolis and one in Liverpool, specifically to make insulin. And the insulin they are going to make there will be genetically engineered insulin.

From the very dawning of recombinant DNA research, insulin has been held out as one of the inestimable boons it will provide. Why? Diabetics – not all, but many – require daily shots of insulin to regulate the way their bodies use sugar. There are something like 2 million people in the US and UK who need insulin regularly, and at the moment their supply comes from slaughtered cows and pigs. There are very slight differences between pig insulin and human insulin, and some diabetics, perhaps one in twenty, develop an allergic reaction to the pig insulin. That reaction has been blamed on the subtle differences between porcine and human insulin, so, together with the shrinking availability of pig pancreas from which to isolate the insulin, the search for a source of human insulin has been a major component of genetic engineering. The human insulin gene, plugged into a bacterium and working properly, would indeed be a boon; but there are problems.

Perhaps the greatest problem is the structure of insulin; it is vastly more complicated than either somatostatin or somatotropin. The finished hormone itself isn't too bad, consisting of two separate peptide chains joined together by special sulphur bridges. One, the A chain, contains 20 amino acids, while the other, the B chain, is 30 amino acids long. But that isn't how the cell constructs insulin. The gene for insulin produces a protein 109 amino acids long, called preproinsulin. This molecule is secreted out of the cell, and as this happens the preproinsulin is stripped of the first 23 amino acids, the 'pre' tag, to make proinsulin, 86 amino acids long. The first 30 amino acids of proinsulin will later form the B chain, and the last 20 the A chain. Between them is a stretch of amino acids called the C chain. The whole proinsulin molecule folds up, and the structure of the C chain is important in bringing the A and B chains together in correct alignment so that the sulphur bridges form. Then an enzyme comes along and snips away the C chain, leaving the A and B chains properly joined as a mature insulin molecule, ready to go out and regulate cellular metabolism. The problem for the genetic engineers is to mimic the almost byzantine complexity of this action; and, in an atmosphere resembling a race rather than research, different teams approached it in different ways.

The winner's laurel, in a sense, belongs to Bill Rutter's team at the University of California in San Francisco. In May 1977 they announced that they had inserted insulin genes from the rat into *Escherichia coli* cells. They weren't human genes, because the NIH guidelines still forbade that, and they weren't working in their new home yet, but Paul Berg commented that the experiment 'has fulfilled a prediction that many people have been confident about for two years'.[11] Rutter got his insulin gene by making a copy of the messenger RNA in rat pancreas cells. He handed it over to Howard Goodman, and his group inserted it into a plasmid called pMB9. In achieving this, Goodman broke the NIH guidelines. The plasmid used in the early stages of the experiment – pBR322 – was 'illegal', because the NIH had not yet certified it as being safe for this type of work. Once he realized this, Goodman switched to a plasmid that had been approved, but the cloning wouldn't work. Finally, pMB9 was approved and, given their experience with the illicit pBR322, the team was able to clone the insulin gene successfully just three weeks after certification (see figure 7.2). The pBR322 plasmid was eventually approved, and no harm came as a result of the error, though there were those who said that the San Franciscans had gained an unfair advantage over their competitors. Certainly, the speed with which they reached their goal surprised many. The incident also revealed the complexity of the regulations, the minutiae of which even the most sophisticated genetic engineers were unaware of.

Rutter's engineered rat insulin was a considerable achievement, especially as it allowed him to sequence the gene and discover the exact code of the DNA. But it didn't produce any insulin, and the real action in the DNA story switches to two other laboratories, Wally Gilbert's at Harvard and Herb Boyer's Genentech in San Francisco. (Rutter and Goodman were associated with Boyer, but apparently did not participate in the second prong of the Californian attack on insulin.) Gilbert took a similar tack to Rutter, seeking out the natural gene and inserting it into *E. coli*. Boyer, with the services of the wizard synthesizer Keiichi Itakura, manufactured artificial insulin genes.

Close second

Gilbert's team, led largely by his postdoctoral assistant Lydia Villa-Komaroff, started with a culture of cancerous rat cells grow-

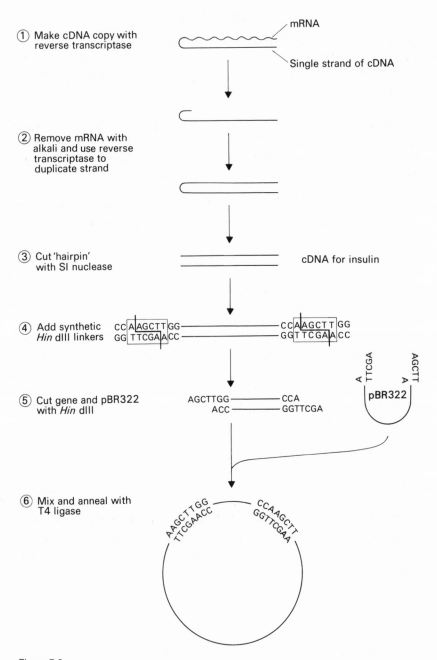

① Make cDNA copy with reverse transcriptase

mRNA

Single strand of cDNA

② Remove mRNA with alkali and use reverse transcriptase to duplicate strand

③ Cut 'hairpin' with SI nuclease

cDNA for insulin

④ Add synthetic *Hin* dIII linkers

CC A AGCTT GG———————CC A AGCTT GG
GG TTCGA A CC———————GG TTCGA A CC

⑤ Cut gene and pBR322 with *Hin* dIII

AGCTTGG————CCA
ACC————GGTTCGA

A TTCGA
AGCTT A

pBR322

⑥ Mix and anneal with T4 ligase

AAGCTTGG
TTCGAACC
CCAAGCTT
GGTTCGAA

Figure 7.2
The first insulin clone, as made by Bill Rutter and Howard Goodman. It did not secrete any insulin.

ing in the laboratory and ended with *E. coli* secreting insulin. The cells were from a tumour of the beta cells, the particular cells responsible for manufacturing insulin. The approach was to make DNA copies of the messenger RNA in those cells, insert the DNA into a plasmid, and clone it in bacteria. To make sure that they would be able to retrieve the insulin – recall the problems that Genentech had experienced in obtaining Itakura's anti-growth hormone – Gilbert decided to insert the insulin gene into the bacterial gene for penicillinase. This is the enzyme that protects *E. coli* from penicillin, and the bacteria secrete it so that the enzyme can get at any penicillin in the environment. If the insulin molecule could be attached to the penicillinase molecule, it would be secreted out of the cell, and there would be no need to kill the cells to harvest the insulin.

That was the plan, and it worked. By August 1978 they were able to announce 'a bacterial clone synthesizing proinsulin'.[12] The plasmid vehicle was Francisco Bolivar's pBR322, long since certified for safety, which has a handy single *Pst* I site. *Pst* I is a very useful restriction enzyme because it cuts a single guanine from the 3' end of the DNA. That means that the recognition site can be reconstructed by adding Gs to the cut piece and Cs to the insert. Even better, the *Pst* I site in pBR322 is close to the start of the penicillinase gene. They obtained the gene to insert by making a reverse transcriptase copy of the RNA in the tumour cells. Those cells produce a great deal more than insulin alone, so Villa-Komaroff had to employ a number of tricks to improve her chances of getting the messenger for insulin. First, she used the sequence that Rutter had published to select a primer for the reverse transcription that would favour the insulin message. The primer is a short stretch of DNA that attaches to the mRNA and provides a platform for the reverse transcription to work from. By making the primer complementary to a known portion at the beginning of the insulin message, the chances of getting a cDNA copy of that message were vastly increased. That done, cytosines were added to the mixture of cDNAs to reconstruct the *Pst* I site, and then the mixture was sorted for size electrophoretically. There was no point in inserting genes much longer or much shorter than the insulin gene, so only those fragments between 300 and 600 base-pairs long were used. The desired bits were removed from the gel and cleaned up, and then mixed with the cut pBR322. Guanine attracted cytosine, as it must, and the inserts fell into place. With no further treatment, the recombinant plasmids were used to transform *E. coli* cells in culture. The cells themselves could be relied upon to fill in the gaps between insert and plasmid, seal the breaks, and generally see to it that the plasmids were in pretty good repair.

A culture of transformed cells is the haystack, the insulin gene the needle. To find it, the cells were plated out on to agar containing tetracycline. Only cells that had taken up pBR322 would be resistant. Two days later, the surviving colonies were screened for their ability to hybridize with a fragment of DNA thought to be specific to the insulin gene. The idea here was not to find a plasmid containing a complete working copy of the entire insulin gene, but to find one that could in turn be used to locate the 'golden' goose. Nine colonies hybrized well; these were given the opportunity to block insulin synthesis in a hybrid-arrested translation system (see p. 103 above). One – plasmid pI19 – came up trumps.

A quick bit of sequencing on the *Pst* I fragment from the plasmid in pI19 confirmed that it did indeed contain the complete insulin sequence, in the right orientation. Gilbert didn't know at this stage whether the gene was in the correct reading frame to code for insulin, but that didn't matter. The importance of pI19 was that it provided a supply of insulin-sequence DNA that could be used as a sensitive probe to screen the other colonies. When they exposed those 1745 other colonies to nick-translated hot DNA from pI19, 48 showed up positive on the X-ray films: 48 out of 1745 is about $2\frac{3}{4}$ per cent. With a confirmed sequence, Villa-Komaroff could go back and look at the mRNA from the pancreas tumour in detail: less than one-third of 1 per cent coded for insulin. The enrichment procedures had worked well. But were any of the 48 colonies producing insulin?

The needle-finder here was the double antibody technique that Gilbert had developed with Stephanie Broome (see p. 99 above). Using it, they were confident that they could detect as little as 10 picograms – that's ten millionths of a millionth of a gram – of insulin. They screened the 48 colonies with antibodies to penicillinase and antibodies to insulin. Only one clone – pI47 – gave a positive response to both. It was, beyond a shadow of a doubt, manufacturing the hybrid penicillinase–insulin molecule, and secreting it to the outside of the cell. Using his rapid chemical sequencing technique, Gilbert quickly confirmed that the plasmid in pI47 contained the entire insulin gene, in the correct orientation and in the correct reading frame (see figure 7.3). The probe, pI19, also harboured the whole gene, but the reading frame was wrong so it did not produce insulin.

What Gilbert had with pI47 was a little better than Rutter's version back in San Francisco. For one thing, Gilbert's plasmid was actually producing something sufficiently like insulin to react with antibodies to real insulin. There was still the question whether the hybrid molecule would behave, biologically, like insulin, but Gilbert was confident: 'We expect soon to be able to demonstrate biological function for this, or for a similar, fused protein.'[13]

While one group pursued the biological activity of the engineered insulin, another tinkered with the plasmid to make it more efficient. Karen Talmadge attacked the problems posed by the fusion of the insulin gene to the penicillinase gene. The main thrust was to move the insulin insert closer to the 'pre' sequence of the penicillinase and so get rid of some of the bacterial protein from the hybrid molecule; but there was also a general curiosity about the signal sequences that guide proteins out through the cell membranes. Talmadge put the gene for proinsulin into the penicillinase gene and discovered that, if there was no signal sequence, the protein would not be secreted. But it didn't matter whether the signal sequence was the bacteria's prepenicillinase or the rat's preproinsulin. Either, on its own, would ferry the molecule attached behind through the cell wall. If bacteria, which have been evolving separately from rats for more than 3 billion years, can recognize the rat's signal sequence, the implication is clear; signal sequences must be, as Talmadge put it, a 'very general (and very ancient) aspect of [protein] structure'.[14] Furthermore, this similarity of behaviour towards the two types of signal raised a further question. Would the bacteria process, that is chop off, the rat's signal sequence? They would: 'Bacteria mature preproinsulin to proinsulin,' Talmadge announced a month later.[15]

Make the A chain

While Gilbert was going hard at his rat genes on the East Coast, the West Coast genetic engineers were by no means idle. Over at Genentech they took the same streamlined approach they had

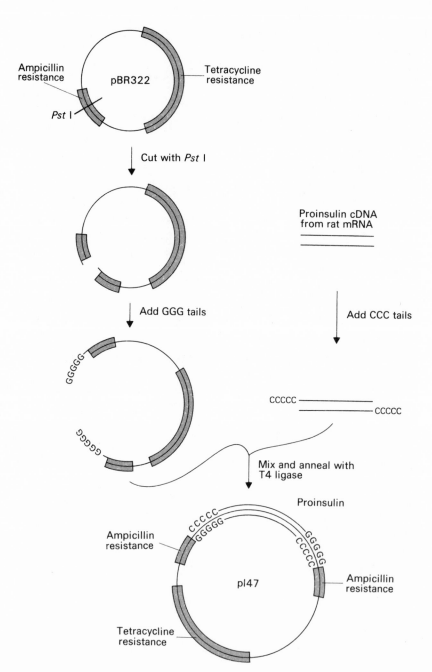

Figure 7.3
Lydia Villa-Komaroff and Walter Gilbert's cloning of insulin.

taken with somatostatin. Forget the complications of *isolating* a human insulin gene: *make* one. The 14 amino acid somatostatin had been done, so why not the 50 amino acids needed for the two insulin chains? Itakura and his colleague Arthur Riggs set to work, joining the codons together. In a corner of Itakura's City of Hope Laboratory is a refrigerator containing about 40 bottles. Each bottle contains a specific codon. To make the gene, you take out the bottles and join the codons in the correct order, using a few chemical tricks to ensure that all works as it should do. Two months for the A chain, three for the B chain, and they were ready to hand on to David Goeddel at Genentech. He then attached the synthetic genes to the *lac* operon in pBR322, just as with somatostatin. The A chain went into one clone and the B chain into another. The two clones manufacture β-galactosidase linked to an insulin chain, and it is a simple matter to split the insulin chains off with cyanogen bromide. So far so good; the tricky bit is to join the two chains together so that they form mature insulin, rather than some other strange protein. The sulphur bridges that unite the chains form between the amino acids called cysteine, but the amino acids are not very fussy. Any two cysteines will join, and the beauty of the C chain in nature is that it ensures that the A and B chains will be folded so that the correct sulphur bridges form. The Genentech scientists devised a way to get a yield of about 80 per cent, by using something like 50 times more A chain than B. They did this, they said, 'to drive the reaction', but nobody was quite sure how it worked.[16] It did work though, and Genentech succeeded, on 21 August 1978, in making the first genetically engineered human insulin (see figure 7.4).

The process was inefficient, and it didn't provide them with very much insulin, but it was enough to attract Eli Lilly into an agreement with Genentech to undertake a programme 'aimed at the commercial production of human insulin'.[17] The triumph didn't satisfy Itakura. Even as Genentech made its announcement, he was planning future steps. He intended synthesizing the C chain as well and then joining his three synthetic chains end to end and plugging them into a single bacterium. That way the C chain would do the hard work, and all the Genentech scientists would need to do would be to find a way to snip out the C chain, not too difficult a prospect.

David Goeddel, too, was not content to rest on his laurels. He

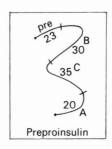

Preproinsulin

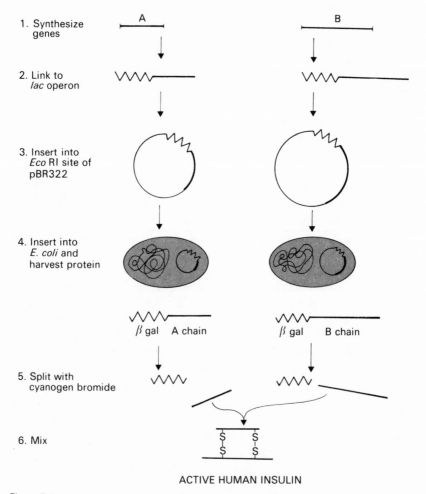

1. Synthesize genes

2. Link to *lac* operon

3. Insert into *Eco* RI site of pBR322

4. Insert into *E. coli* and harvest protein

β gal   A chain

β gal   B chain

5. Split with cyanogen bromide

6. Mix

ACTIVE HUMAN INSULIN

Figure 7.4
Insulin as originally cloned by Genentech. Small quantities of active human insulin were produced.

was after the same thing – the entire human insulin gene in a single bacterial clone – but with all the additional knowledge that had been flowing in about insulin genes he was ready to tackle it the way he knew best, by searching for the gene from a mixture of clones. The mRNA came from a human pancreas tumour, and they prepared the DNA and inserted it into pBR322 just as Rutter and Goodman had. The transformed clones selected themselves on agar containing tetracycline, and the ones with insulin genes showed up by hybridizing with rat insulin DNA, of which Goeddel now had a ready supply. Twelve clones gave good results, but Goeddel concentrated on the one with the largest insert. This clone, pHI3, Genentech sequenced both with Gilbert's chemical method and, to confirm, with Sanger's enzymatic method. (It's worth reflecting on how much a part of the scene these two methods had become in such a short time; they enabled researchers to sequence a gene almost as easily as they could go to the library to look up an obscure reference.) The gene they had was indeed the whole preproinsulin gene, and from it the Genentech team predicted the amino acid sequence of the signal region of human DNA. Once again, though, the real point of the exercise was to obtain a better tool for ultimately making bacterial human insulin, and Goeddel was quite clear about that: 'This cloned human preproinsulin cDNA will facilitate the isolation of the human insulin gene.'[18]

Bacterial insulin factories have been just around the corner since Rutter's first ground-breaking discovery. In July 1980, when the first experiments with the synthetic insulin were announced, it was forecast that the drug might be on the market a year later, by mid-1981. Later that year, in December, the date had moved forward to '1982 or 1983'.[19] Now, at the start of 1982, there's still no sign of commercially available bacterially produced human insulin, but every expectation that it will arrive before the year is out. The first trials are over. Healthy human volunteers responded to Eli Lilly's bacterial insulin almost exactly as they responded to porcine insulin. Long-term tests and clinical trials with diabetics have since been started, but even in those early days Professor Harry Keen, head of the Unit for Metabolic Medicine at Guy's Hospital and responsible for the trials, commented that 'genetically synthesised human insulin seems to be safe and effective in man'.[20] In the meantime, diabetics everywhere eagerly await the trial results and

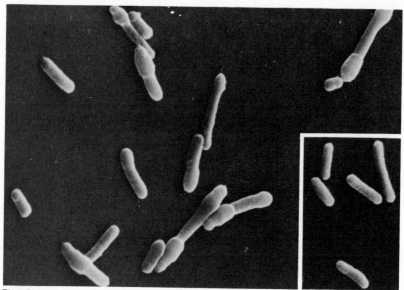

Plate 7.1
Bacteria engineered to produce insulin. The bulges are large amounts of insulin. The inset shows the same strain without the insulin plasmid. (*From Williams, Daniel C., Van Frank, Richard M., Muth, William L. and Barnett, J. Paul, Cytoplasmic inclusion bodies in* Escherichia coli *producing biosynthetic human insulin proteins, Science, 215: 687–8, 1982. Copyright 1982 by the American Association for the Advancement of Science.*)

Plate 7.2
Crystals of bio-engineered insulin. (*From Chance, Ronald E., Kroeff, Eugene P., Hoffman, James A. and Frank, Bruce H., Chemical, physical and biologic properties of biosynthetic human insulin, Diabetes Care, 4(2): 1981. Copyright 1981 by the American Diabetes Association, Inc.*)

attempts to scale up from the laboratory bench to the drug factory.

The efforts that have been invested in getting *E. coli* to synthesize human insulin have been truly prodigious. Ironically, it might all have been a waste of time; using methods devised in recombinant DNA research, it has been discovered that *E. coli* has been making something very like insulin all along.[21] Not just *E. coli* either, but also a couple of moulds and a small single-celled organism produce a protein that is exceedingly similar to insulin, both in its ability to react with insulin antibodies and in the way it alters cell metabolism. What those insulin-like compounds are doing there is anybody's guess. They may have some use as a signal between cells, or perhaps the cell uses them to regulate its metabolism. Maybe they are a primitive weapon, secreted to depress the activity of neighbouring cells. Nobody quite knows what these primitive insulins are for, though their very presence argues for an ancient origin of the hormones that we think of as typical of more organized animals. The compound has not yet been isolated, nor the gene for it pinpointed, but it is surely only a matter of time. Then, it may turn out that a far simpler route to human insulin had existed all along: to direct specific mutations to the gene for this insulin, which would transmute it into the gene for human insulin, and then engineer the bacteria to overproduce. It remains to be seen whether anyone, at this advanced stage in the cloning of human insulin, will bother.

Replacement for real

Insulin for diabetics, growth hormone for dwarfs – both are examples of the kind of medical treatment called 'replacement therapy'. The patient lacks some vital biochemical and so the doctor replaces that chemical. Many treatments, apart from the hormones mentioned, are really a form of replacement therapy, from the vitamins that prevent scurvy and beri-beri to the artificial pacemakers that keep damaged hearts ticking nicely. The trouble is, the replacement has to be kept up. A conscientious diabetic can lead a practically normal life, provided that he acts as his own pancreas, assessing his blood sugar levels and administering insulin as and when needed. But without insulin things are very different, and usually fatal. Not surprisingly, then, much effort has been invested in developing a real replacement pancreas, one that will measure sugar and infuse insulin on a continuous basis, just like the genuine article. This research is beginning to pay off, too, with small pumps and such like being tested in hospitals. But the best possible replacement would be not an artificial pancreas but the real thing: a transplant of beta cells that would work as normal. This is probably quite a way away at the moment, although it is being taken seriously. But what about replacing the defective genes that cause some diseases?

Diabetes seems to have some genetic component – identical twins share it more often than not, and it can run in families – but it isn't a question of a simple genetic distinction between those with the disease and those without. That means that genetic therapy is probably not on. But consider the genetic diseases that are the result of simple, confined mutations. Sickle cell anaemia, with its single amino acid substitution, for example, is open to the ultimate replacement therapy. Replace the defective gene.

The idea, like so much in genetic engineering, is simplicity itself. Go into the cells, and give them working copies of the gene that is damaged. That is all there is to it. If the cells accept the new genes, and if the new genes work properly, the disease is cured. Not treated, but cured. And if you go in early enough, while the organism is still just a single fertilized cell, the wonderful process of development will do all the donkey work for you, spreading copies of the new working gene to every cell of the emerging body. Even the sex cells would get their copies of the working gene, so that future generations would not have the threat of the genetic defect hanging over them. If that sounds like science fiction, be assured that it isn't. There are mice running around in several laboratories that are carrying, along their chromosomes, the genes for human interferon. Those genes were put into their parents, or in some cases their grandparents, by an experimenter. Other mice carry the human insulin gene. They are the preliminary steps of the road to the ultimate replacement therapy. And it hasn't stopped at mice; gene replacement has already been attempted – unsuccessfully, admittedly – on two humans.

Martin Cline of the University of California at Los Angeles was the author of this bold experiment – one that eventually cost him grant support worth almost $200 000, because he didn't have quite the go-ahead he needed to perform these experiments. He had the experience and the know-how, but not the permission, to transfer genes into the cells of living human animals. Putting genes into cells in culture was already routine when Cline announced, in April 1980, that he had done the same in whole mice. The idea had been to insert the genes into cells in a test-tube, and then put those cells back into the animal. To ensure that they grew and eventually dominated the other cells, you needed to give them some sort of advantage in the struggle to survive. Cline's approach was to mimic the gene cloners; he would give his transformed cells, as their extra gene, resistance to a drug that prevents normal cells growing. That way, transformed cells would select themselves. He enumerated his requirements as follows. First, the drug used to select transformed cells must not be too toxic to the whole animal. Second, it must affect the growth of the particular organ selected for therapy. Finally, that organ must be one that shows continual cell growth in the adult animal; otherwise there would be no opportunity for the transformed cells to take over. Some of the agents used in therapy to stop cancerous cells growing seemed to be ideal selective agents, and the bone marrow, which manufactures blood, was a perfect target. Or, as Cline put it in his scientific paper, 'anti-metabolite drugs used in cancer chemotherapy and blood-forming tissues . . . seem to be ideally suited for such genetic manipulations'.[22] The beauty of attacking the blood system was that there were genetic diseases, not just sickle cell but various others, collectively known as the thalassaemias, crying out for this sort of replacement therapy: simple mutations that, once reversed, would enable the patients to be well.

Cline took bone marrow from mice, mixed it with purified DNA from cells resistant to the drug methotrexate, and put somewhere between 5 and 50 million treated cells back into the mice, having first knocked out their own bone marrow with X-rays. Methotrexate is an anti-cancer drug that stops cells, especially rapidly dividing cells, growing. As cancers consist of cells that are dividing rapidly, it destroys them, but it can also kill bone marrow cells, which are dividing rapidly. Normal mice, given methotrexate, do not produce new red blood cells. While the experimental mice were recovering, Cline gave them doses of methotrexate. Ordinary cells were unable to divide and reproduce, but those that had taken up the resistance gene could. The mice thrived. The amount of red cells in their blood went up, a sure sign that the marrow cells were growing as they should, and Cline could see no abnormalities. Of course, the mice were killed to complete the investigations, but at the time of their death, Cline stated, they were 'clinically well'.[23]

Emboldened by his success, Cline outlined the two major clinical uses he saw for the technique. One was in the treatment of cancer. Genes for drug resistance would be inserted into non-cancerous organs, enabling the doctors to use higher doses of drugs targetted against the cancer itself. The other was to treat genetic defects in haemoglobin. On the cancer front, Cline told *Science* that this might be tested in human patients within '3 to 5 years'.[24] But the attack on haemoglobin defects, which Cline described as 'natural targets for treatment by gene transfer techniques', began immediately.[25]

The difficulties of gene replacement therapy are two-fold. First you have to get the desired gene into the cells; then you have to ensure that it works, that the gene is expressed. At first it seemed that delivery, rather than expression, would be the harder nut to crack, but Cline had demonstrated that the techniques for shooting new genes into cells were effective and could reasonably be expected to succeed. Expression was another matter. At the time, early in 1980, control of expression of human globin genes in the test-tube had not been achieved. This deficiency attracted criticism to Cline and his colleague Winston Salser, but their justification was straightforward. During the time it would take to modify the mouse system for use in people, someone – perhaps themselves, perhaps another group – would devise a method to bring the globin genes under control. And when that happened, they would be ready with a safe and effective treatment for a group of diseases that are painful and invariably fatal.

The design of the experiment was similar to the ones on mice. They would remove marrow cells from a human patient, mix the cells with DNA for the correct globin structure and a little gene to give transformed cells an advantage, and insert the cells back into the patients. The major differences were that in the mouse the inserted gene itself provided the edge over other cells. In human patients, the globin gene alone would be no great advantage, so Cline added another gene to give the transformed cells the boost they would need. This was the gene for an enzyme called thymidine kinase. All cells have this enzyme, which they use to activate thymidine prior to using it in nucleic acid synthesis, but Cline got his thymidine kinase from the virus that causes herpes. Herpes enzyme is more efficient than the mammalian thymidine kinase, and so would give transformed cells an advantage over those that had not taken up the new genes. At least, that is how it was in mice.[26] He chose his patients with great care. They had to be in the final phase of the illness, and sufficiently intelligent to give a genuinely informed consent for the operation. In particular, Cline stressed that the experiment itself was unlikely to benefit these very first patients, and was satisfied that they understood this but still wanted it to go ahead. In July 1980, Cline did the experiment, on a 21-year-old woman at the Hadassah Hospital in Jerusalem and a 16-year-old at the Poly Clinic in Naples. Both patients had β-thalassaemia: neither of them made any β-globin chains, with disastrous results for their ability to transport oxygen around the body. They were given the genes for a correct β-globin and herpes thymidine kinase. The patients did not improve, though it is hard to judge the success of a genuinely ground-breaking procedure. Nor is it easy to judge the furore that subsequently broke around Cline.

He had, it seems, transgressed mightily against the ethical committees that decide on the propriety of experiments on humans. It is a little hard to sort out exactly what happened, but it appears that the first attempt at gene transfer therapy was also the first use of recombinant DNA in man.[27] Cline had permission to insert the globin gene and the kinase gene separately, disengaged from the plasmid on which he had cloned them. At the last minute, and without telling the authorities, he inserted the two joined together, as they had been cut from the entire pBR322 plasmid. He did this, he says, because further work with animals made him believe that the genes would be more effective linked to the plasmid. That was the magnitude of his crime; that he used a recombinant molecule without permission. The irony of it is that the two genes he inserted were, of course, made with recombinant techniques. Separated from one another and the vector, however, they were not themselves recombinant: spliced into pBR322, they were.

Cline later admitted that he 'exercised poor judgement in failing to halt the studies and seek appropriate approval'.[28] But it is hard to believe that he had anything other than his patients' welfare in mind at all times. Asked by a reporter if he had not simply been after personal glory, Cline was emphatic. 'I say the answer is no,' he replied.

I realize that I was taking the risk of drawing criticism for such experiments. But I don't know of anyone in the country who has precisely the same type of skills that I have, with knowledge both in the animal systems and in clinical investigations in man. I think in that sense I must be unique. In the last analysis one must ask how responsible an investigator has been up to that point in time.[29]

The reporter, experienced *Science* writer Nicholas Wade (now with the *New York Times*), agreed. 'Cline and Salser took something of a gamble, skating close to the edge of what was scientifically reasonable and publicly acceptable. But there is no evidence as yet that they transgressed either boundary, although they may have given spectators something of a fright.'[30] In any event, when the evidence of Cline's transgression surfaced, he was punished severely. In December 1981 the National Institutes of Health stripped him of his research grants, having earlier marked him for careful scrutiny in the future. Cline became a whipping boy for the whole community, and the NIH's moves were seen as 'a clear signal to other researchers that violations of rules governing recombinant DNA research and human experimentation will not be condoned'.[31]

Gene replacement therapy, in the meantime, will not be held up. When it succeeds, it will almost certainly be with one of the globin disorders, but the way will be opened to treat other simple genetic diseases. Engineered growth hormone itself may not be needed then, for a very recent study had demonstrated that some dwarves lack the growth hormone gene. With gene replacement therapy, they will be given the gene they lack rather than just the hormone. Perhaps, eventually, despite the overwhelming difficulties, it will even be possible to treat the more complicated multi-gene problems, such as stroke and heart disease. Genetic engineering will, sooner or later, provide the ultimate replacement therapy.

8
VACCINES

Helping the body to fight disease and defend itself

Cleanliness is in the eye of the belolder. If you could look at yourself with the eyes of a bacteriologist you would find yourself anything but clean. Every inch of your skin teems with bacteria of different sorts, and inside is no better. Viruses too are everywhere. Many of those pathogens are the same ones that cause severe illnesses, but they seem for the most part to be impotent. For that, you have your bodily defences to thank. Day in, day out, the defence system operates to keep pathogens at bay, and most of the time it is remarkably successful. Considering the hundreds of thousands of bacteria that share our lives, it is a wonder that we survive at all. And even when the immune system does lose the battle, and we go down to an attack of mumps or measles, it is usually over quite quickly and often never happens again. The immune system is our saving.

The immune system is a complex set of interdependent sub-systems, all of which work together in an attempt to ensure that no foreign invaders get a grip on the body. The complexities merit a book of their own, and I can hardly do them justice here. Essentially, there are two components to the immune system: antibodies and killer cells. Antibodies are proteins that recognize, and latch on to, substances called antigens. The relationship between antigen and antibody has been likened to that between lock and key, but it is more than that. Not only does an antibody fit only one antigen, but the antigen in a sense creates the antibody, and no lock really creates its key. Almost any foreign substance can act as an antigen – indeed, one of the mysteries of immunology is how the body distinguishes between 'self' and 'not self' – but not all do. A foreign substance – and there may be many different antigens on the surface of a cell or bacterium – will cause special cells to make and secrete antibodies to that substance. The antibodies, once bound to the antigen, can directly neutralize its effects if, say, it is a toxin of some sort; but if the antigen is on the surface of, say, a bacterium, the antibody will bring about the destruction of the bacterium directly, assisted by various components of the blood collectively called 'complement'. Guided by the antibody, the complement breaks down the cell walls of the bacterium. The antibody can also act as a signal to the wandering killer cells, mostly white blood corpuscles, to engulf the offending antigen and destroy it. A bacterium covered in antibody will stick to the surface of a killer cell, and this makes it much easier for the killer cell to engulf the bacterium.

When we are invaded by some pathogen – chicken pox, for example – three things happen. The pox viruses have a protein coat protecting their nucleic acid, and while the immune system may recognize the protein as foreign, there is little it can do about it. First it must tool up to manufacture the antibody to those coat proteins, which will then guide the killer cells to their targets. During this stage the disease gets a grip, and we fall ill. But as the antibody production grows, the body begins to fight back. Provided we are reasonably healthy over all, the disease will be conquered. That is the second phase. Now, the third phase. As a result of the previous attack, our immune system has been taught what chicken pox is like. Next time, we will already be prepared with antibodies, and the disease will be attacked before it can get a hold. We are immune. It is the short delay, while the immune system learns how to make a particular antibody, that allows the disease to get us. And it is that short delay that is overcome by vaccination, where we teach the immune system how to recognize an invader in advance of the attack. Vaccination provides a sample of the foreign protein without the attendant dangers of an infection, and gets the immune system geared up and ready to fight. Forewarned is, literally, fore-armed.

The immune system, dependent as it is on the manufacture by cells of proteins, is obviously a prime candidate for genetic engineering. Better vaccines, vaccines against hitherto untreatable diseases – all have been engineered. There is also the spectre of better diseases with which to wage war. But before getting on to those topics there is another side to the imune system that has attracted a great deal of interest, from genetic engineers, investors and the public: interferon.

Interferon, the wonder drug

Interferon today is seen as something of a wonder drug. It attacks viruses, and holds out hope of a quick cure for the common cold. It can conquer some forms of cancer. It even seems to help against some of the most intractable diseases, such as multiple sclerosis. But when Alick Isaacs discovered interferon in the 1950s, many of his colleagues laughed at him. They couldn't duplicate his results, and thought that interferon was a figment of his imagination. Indeed, some went so far as to call the mystery substance 'misinterpreton'. But Isaacs had been correct all along. The reason his colleagues could not obtain the same result was that they didn't follow the same procedures, but neither they nor Isaacs knew it. Isaacs obtained interferon by injecting cells with RNA. What he didn't know was that it was double-stranded RNA that triggered interferon production. His colleagues, whose RNA was perhaps purer, didn't get the same result because they weren't using double-stranded RNA, and nobody at the time suspected that anything as exotic as double-stranded RNA even existed. Now, of course, we know not only that it exists, but that one of the major groups of viruses uses double-stranded RNA to store its genetic message. The connection is surely more than mere coincidence. Isaacs, alas, did not live to see his work so triumphantly vindicated, or to see the massive industry that has grown up around interferon.

Human cells produce at least three distinct types of interferon, and there are believed to be 12 or more distinct interferon genes. Alpha interferon, previously called type I interferon, comes from leukocytes (white blood cells) and is manufactured in response to a viral attack. Beta interferon is similar and is made under similar circumstances by almost all cells. Gamma interferon, also known as immune interferon, is made largely by the T cells of the immune system, and seems to be the one most potent against cancer. The three sorts of interferon have slightly different powers, but essentially they seem to work against cancers and against viruses. To combat cancer, they seem to ginger up the body's own killer cells and get them to destroy the rampaging tumour cells. This is particularly valuable because, unlike other treatments, interferon is not itself toxic. It acts safely through the immune system rather than directly on the cancer. Against viruses, interferon has two actions:

it destroys viral RNA, and it somehow makes cells resistant to viral attack.

Scientists would dearly love to know more about interferon, but they are hampered because it is incredibly difficult to obtain in useful quantities. Gallons of blood have to be sifted for white cells, which are then induced to make tiny amounts of the precious substance. There just hasn't been enough of it to make a thorough study of its effects. But interferon is, at one level, just another protein, and genetic engineering is all about manufacturing proteins, so naturally interferon has been a prime target of recombinant DNA research.

Three major teams took part, and the finish was very close. David Goeddel and the Genentech team (with a couple of helpers from pharmaceuticals giant Hoffman-La Roche) announced on 12 August 1980 that they had cloned *E. coli*, making one sort of interferon.[1] Tadatsugu Taniguchi and Mark Ptashne's team at Harvard were a little earlier with their clones of the same interferon.[2] But the winners were the people at Biogen, led by Charles Weissmann and Shigekazu Nagata.[3] (Weissmann's team is actually based at Zurich University's Institute for Molecular Biology, but he has very close links with Biogen. He also had the help of Kari Cantell, the Finn who leads the world at producing interferon from human cells.) The paper announcing their triumph arrived at the offices of *Nature* on 24 January 1980.

The teams adopted slightly different approaches, but the aim of each was the same: to get a bacterial clone to manufacture interferon. Genentech's method is perhaps the most straightforward of the three, and it contains one or two neat twists to established methods. The scheme was simple; make cDNA from mRNA, put that cDNA into plasmids, transform cells with the plasmids and select those making interferon.

The mRNA came from human cells growing in culture, which had been exposed to a special 'induction medium' consisting largely of double-stranded RNA. The induction medium switches on the interferon machinery of the cell, so that after induction the cell contains mRNA for interferon. The cDNA was to be inserted into the *Pst* I site of plasmid pBR322, so a string of cytosines was added to the cDNA and a string of guanines to the cut pBR322. The two sorts of DNA were mixed and, without further treatment, used to transform *E. coli*. The *Pst* I site is in the middle of the ampicillin resistance gene, so cells that had taken up the plasmid would be sensitive to ampicillin but resistant to tetracycline. There were 30 000 of them. Finding the ones that coded for interferon would be a major problem. No antibody to interferon was available at the time, and the engineers didn't have any pure interferon DNA or RNA to use as a probe. What they did have was the published sequence of the first few amino acids of the mature interferon protein. They used this, and the universal genetic code for translating nucleic acids into proteins, to construct small stretches of synthetic DNA that would be complementary to the first 12 bases of the interferon gene. Because they didn't know the correct sequence, they had to use all possible codes that would provide the first four amino acids of the protein, but they could be confident that the gene would be one of those, and that the correct primer would hybridize with the gene. To make the probes, they incubated the synthetic primers with mRNA from induced cells and DNA synthesis enzymes. The primer would latch on to the sequence at the beginning of the interferon gene and then the synthesis enzymes would continue to build the complementary strand. This complementary strand could be used to screen for clones containing the interferon gene.

The Genentech scientists incorporated a very clever step here to make sure that the probe was very likely to contain the correct sequence for the interferon gene. They mixed the cDNA with RNA from cells that had not been induced for interferon. Since the cells had not been induced, they would not contain interferon mRNA. Any cDNA copies that were not relevant to interferon would hybridize to the mRNA that was present and could be removed, leaving a fraction of probe that was present in induced cells but not in cells that had not been induced. Very likely this fraction would be largely mRNA for interferon. When all this was done, Goeddel and his colleagues did a preliminary screening of 600 of their 30 000 clones. One – pF526 – gave a strong response with the interferon gene probe.

It looked as if their clever method had worked, but there was disappointment ahead. Cutting pF526 with *Pst* I to release the insert showed that the insert was only 550 base-pairs long, not long enough to code for the whole of interferon. Nevertheless, pF526 provided a much longer stretch of DNA that could be used as a probe, and was indeed used to screen a further 2000 clones. Sixteen gave a positive result and one of those, pFIF3, contained a stretch of DNA that carried a sequence identical to the sequences already published for interferon. Their troubles were almost over. From there it was a relatively simple matter to clean up the gene, removing various untranscribed and unwanted bits, and insert it into a plasmid where it would be translated into RNA and made into mature interferon. One plasmid, pFIF*lac*9, brought the interferon gene under the control of the well-known lactose system, while the other, pFIF*trp*69, put it into the tryptophan system. Either way, Genentech now had bacteria manufacturing interferon. And the interferon, when tested against the natural product, had more or less the same potency.

Genentech was not content to let things rest there. Goeddel tested the bacterial interferon not in a test-tube against specific cells, but in real animals against a killer virus.[4] Encephalomyocarditis virus is lethal, destroying the brain and heart muscles. Squirrel monkeys deliberately infected with it died within a matter of days. Monkeys given a protective shot of bacterially made interferon before the virus did not succumb. Indeed, they showed little sign of having been infected. The cloned interferon was, potentially, every bit as good as the natural protein and a great deal easier to obtain. Under the best circumstances, 2 litres of blood will provide about one-millionth of a gram of interferon; 2 litres of bacterial culture can provide more than 50 times as much, and 2 litres of bacteria are a lot simpler to come by than 2 litres of blood.

Nagata and Weissmann had a similar story to tell. They too cloned an interferon gene into *E. coli* and then tested the product exhaustively against the real thing. In all the tests, the engineered product was all but identical to the real thing. Engineered interferon stimulated natural killer cells to attack other cells that were resistant to unstimulated killer cells. It enhanced the ability of killer cells to detect, and kill, invaders covered with antibody. It blocked the ability of white blood cells to prevent cell movement, just like human interferon. It even prevented the growth of tumour cells. Their comparison of natural and engineered interferon had shown, the team concluded, that 'the activities of the two preparations . . . is indistinguishable'.[5] The tests went further than that. They removed any last lingering doubts that the activity of natural preparations of interferon was due to some impurity. The bacterial interferon did not contain the same impurities as the interferon

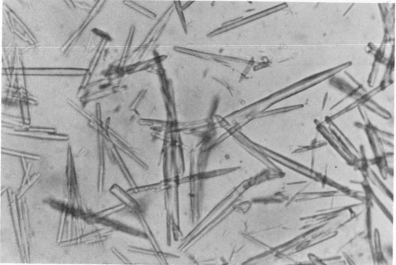

Plate 8.1
Interferon crystals, made by bacteria. Hitherto interferon has been too impure and too scarce to be crystallilzed. (*From Miller, David L., Kung, Hsiang-fu and Pestka, Sidney. Crystallization of recombinant human leukocyte interferon A*, Science 215: 689–90, 1982. *Copyright 1982 by the American Association for the Advancement of Science*)

isolated from white blood cells, but it had the same effects, so those effects were almost certainly due to the interferon and not to any impurity. The tests also raised hopes for artificial interferons: 'the results obtained so far,' wrote Weissmann's team, 'are promising in regard to the possible replacement of natural IFN [interferon] by products made in *E. coli*.'[6]

Some of the engineered interferons have now gone into clinical trials. Side-effects have again proved a bit of a nuisance; Genentech's product apparently causes the same side-effects as natural interferon – headache and fever, mostly – while Biogen's does not, and no one is sure whether those side-effects are a genuine expression of interferon activity or the result of impurities. The Medical Research Council's Common Cold Unit in Salisbury proved ten years ago that interferon was a very effective treatment of rhinovirus infection, better known as the common cold. But it abandoned further work because interferon was so expensive. Now it has started up again, in the belief that engineered interferon will eventually prove cheap enough for widespread use. That means being as cheap as aspirin – a tall order, especially given the involvement of companies like Hoffman-La Roche, but not impossible if the will is there.

It is hard to say just what the benefits of unlimited interferon will be. Simply abolishing the common cold would be an astounding good, as would halting cancers. The effects on multiple sclerosis are promising, and it would be a brave man who ventured a guess at what interferon might not be able to do. So far, as with so many other genetically engineered products, it is not yet in full production, and the limited clinical trials, while encouraging, are not overwhelmingly successful. A writer in *Nature* has described interferon as 'no wonder drug'.[7] I think he is mistaken. Interferon may not be a panacea, but it is likely to prove every bit as much a wonder drug as, say, penicillin.

Because it is there: synthetic interferon

We now know far more about interferon than we ever did. We know, for example, a little about the mechanics of its action. Cells treated with interferon will destroy added RNA much more quickly than cells that have not been so treated. This ability depends on a special enzyme that seems to be switched on by interferon. We also know that some bits of the molecule are more important than others. A single nucleotide mutation, changing G to A and cysteine to tyrosine at position 141, completely abolishes the antiviral activity of interferon, presumably by preventing a sulphur bridge between two cysteines and so altering the shape of the molecule. But there is still a great deal to be done, and the effort goes on, the ready availability of cloned interferons making that effort a little easier.

The work on interferon shows two very clear trends. One is towards ever-larger teams of scientists, all chasing the same hare. Goeddel assembled 18 people to show that his cloned interferon was biologically active, and thanked another 17 in that paper's acknowledgements. In many ways this is simply a reflection of growing specializations within the overall field of genetic engineering – some to synthesize bits of DNA, others to pick out the correct clones, yet others to ensure that the genes are expressed efficiently. And there is no doubt that the team approach pays dividends. Nowell Stebbing, one of the Genentech scientists, explains: 'The time from when we first expressed a human interferon until the time it was tested in a monkey, in a lethal monkey virus infection, that was one month.'[8] Stebbing is clear that having all the components of the team under one roof, as they are at Genentech, is a definite advantage, for the speed and flexibility it offers.

The other change, less noticeable perhaps, is that the genetic engineers themselves seem less awed by what they are doing. They report calmly of bringing a gene under the control of the *lac* operon as if it were an everyday matter, when in fact they are manipulating the very stuff of life. They can, and do, snip out bits of inconvenient DNA, put in stretches they need, move things about so as to make them work better, and all with very little surface emotion. Perhaps that is inevitable, as science becomes technology. Perhaps if they didn't simply take these things for granted they would be too busy wondering about them to get on with the job at hand. But it is a little odd to find them treating the whole business in such a matter-of-fact way. Arthur Clarke once said that any sufficiently advanced technology would seem like magic to us. I have always thought that genetic engineering might seem to have that magical aspect to it. But Professor Brian Hartley, one of England's few entrepreneurial genetic engineers, pricks even that balloon. 'It's amazing,' he says, 'how little magic there is in it and how much of it is intelligent thought.'[9] He's right, of course, but it is still a little disconcerting to find that the literature is becoming increasingly pedestrian, with everything carried out 'as described', or 'by the method of such and such'. The glamour seems to have gone, and nowhere more so than in a final piece of interferon work, the synthesis of the interferon gene.

Admittedly, *Nature* marked the occasion with one of its famous prolix editorials, but the announcement by Michael Edge and his colleagues at ICI that they had made, from scratch, the entire gene for human interferon did not cause a great deal of comment elsewhere.[10] After all, others had synthesized genes before, and interferon had been cloned, so why synthesize? The ICI team joined more than 1000 nucleotides together in the right order, first into 67 short bits about 15 bases long, then those 67 into 11 longer stretches, then those 11 into four even longer bits; and finally all four came together to create the entire synthetic gene, complete with *Bam* HI site at one end and *Sal* I at the other. The synthetic gene was planned around the sequence that Weissmann had published, but was by no means the same as that sequence. Edge took advantage of the genetic code to make the sequence easier to construct, getting rid wherever possible of repeated and complementary sequences that might interfere with the joining-up process and shifting the codons subtly to those that *E. coli* prefers to use. The completed gene was inserted into a plasmid called pPM50, where it came under the control of the *lac* operon, and the clones were screened with a specially made and radioactively labelled probe 60 bases long. Fourteen of them came up positive, and all yielded a fragment of the correct size when broken up with *Bam* HI and *Sal* I. Edge chose one – pIFS1 – for detailed investigation and sequenced the whole thing by the Maxam and Gilbert method. He found it to be 'in complete agreement' with the sequence he had intended to produce.[11] Magical or not, the method had without question worked, leading *Nature* to state: 'The importance of this development is not the gene itself, but the demonstration of the technique. It is a little like climbing Everest, known to be easier the second time.'[12] Quite.

But there is more to the ICI work than a mere technical *tour de force*. In particular, it holds out the hope of tinkering with the interferons in the same way that an earlier generation of biochemists tinkered with antibiotics. The first primitive penicillins, for example, were weak and ineffectual compared with present versions. Fiddling with some of the atoms in the compound enabled the biochemists to construct more efficient, longer-lasting and deadlier versions of the antibiotic. The hope is that the same will prove possible with interferons, that tinkering with them will result in better products; and the synthetic gene offers a good place to begin. The different species of interferon have different activities, some more potent than others, some more specific to a particular target and so on. By combining these features it may be possible to create interferons that are even more efficient than the natural product. Edge admits that 'it will be interesting to determine whether the natural interferons can be improved upon'.[13] Interesting, and important.

Immunization: education for protection

Dr Edward Jenner, in the plentiful spare time offered by his quiet country practice, discovered that the ungrateful cuckoo nestling turfs its foster parents' own nestlings out of their home. That is not why he is remembered today. He also coined the word 'virus', and although that too is not the basis of his fame it is a part of it. Jenner is remembered as the man who invented vaccination, who had the courage to put to scientific test an old piece of rural lore. Milkmaids often had fair unblemished skins, and in an age when people were very lucky to escape the ravages of smallpox this was indeed unusual. Folk said it was because the cowpox that they contracted from their charges protected them from the similar, but much deadlier, smallpox. On 14 May 1796 Jenner inoculated James Phipps, an eight-year-old boy, with pus from a cowpox pustule on a young milkmaid. Later, he deliberately infected the boy with virulent smallpox. Phipps emerged unscathed, and the age of vaccination, named for the cowpox virus *Vaccinia*, had begun.

Jenner's success was quickly accepted, after a great deal of initial public apprehension, because of the obvious benefit it conferred, but there was precious little understanding of the way vaccination worked. Then, as Pasteur developed the germ theory of disease, and specific illnesses came to be linked to specific micro-organisms, it became clear that what was going on was a sort of teaching

session. Exposure to a closely related but less virulent microbe, or
to the dead virulent microbe, taught the body how to deal with that
particular invader. Pasteur succeeded in developing a vaccine for
anthrax, which periodically laid waste to sheep and their
shepherds, using a tamed, or attentuated, form of the anthrax
organism. And of course he developed his life-saving treatment
for rabies.

Pasteur had many ways of emasculating pathogens, growing
them sometimes at higher-than-normal temperatures, sometimes
without enough oxygen. The intention was always the same; to
produce an organism that would be sufficiently like the pathogen to
teach the body to defend itself, but sufficiently weakened to cause
no harm. It was very much a hit-and-miss process, with new
vaccines becoming available as the attenuated organisms came to
light. Protection against tuberculosis, which has so changed our
health, came about entirely by accident. In 1908 Albert Calmette,
director of the Institut Pasteur in Lille, and Camille Guérin were
trying to grow better cultures of the tuberculosis bacterium. They
added bile salts, a natural detergent from the digestive system, in
an attempt to get the bacilli to spread out in the culture dishes.
What they got instead was an attenuated strain of the tuberculosis
organism that, as BCG vaccine (Bacille Calmette–Guérin) has
almost eradicated TB. Other vaccines that depend on attenuated
organisms include the Sabin polio vaccine and the vaccine against
German measles (rubella).

A different approach to vaccination involves not attenuated but
dead organisms. Typhoid, cholera and the Salk polio vaccine all
use dead micro-organisms. The dead organisms still carry the
surface proteins that prod the immune system into action, but they
obviously cannot cause any disease. Yet another technique is to
prepare the body not for the disease organism itself but for the
poison it secretes. Diphtheria and tetanus, for example, cause their
damage by manufacturing a toxin that harms the body. The toxins
themselves are proteins and therefore antigens; treating them with
the preservative formaldehyde destroys the harmful toxic site but
leaves enough other sites for the antibodies to recognize.

Immunization, in all its forms, has undoubtedly been a massive
benefit to mankind. Smallpox, which started it all, has been completely eradicated, and many other diseases that were once major
killers have been brought under control. But still there are risks.

Killed organisms may not confer sufficient immunity, both because they are often given by injection and because they don't multiply and prolong the challenge. Cholera, for example, attacks through the gut wall. That is where the first line of defence ought to be, but when immunized against cholera it is the blood and spleen that hold most of the defenders. Attenuated vaccines are better from that point of view, but they have other drawbacks. There is always the danger that the harmless organism will revert to its virulent form, with the awful result that the vaccine will actually cause the disease. Very occasionally, for reasons that are little understood, immunization itself can cause an inflammation of nerve tissue, and even brain damage. Pathogens are often grown on monkey cells in culture, and there is the fear that they could pick up tumour viruses, like SV40, and transmit them to people. Then there is the final point that many diseases do not, at the moment, lend themselves to vaccination at all, sometimes because there is no suitable attenuated or killed preparation, but more often because the organisms change too quickly. Influenza is the classic example, changing its outward identity very swiftly indeed. Each time a new epidemic – be it Asian flu, Hong Kong flu, Australian flu or whatever – spreads, the influenza virus has developed a new combination of coat proteins. The immunity you may have against last year's flu is not much good against the new variety, and down you go again. So fresh approaches to immunization and vaccination would be more than welcome. Recall that antigens are often proteins, manufactured by the pathogen itself, and that genetic engineering is all about manufacturing specific proteins to order, and you'll appreciate that this is another field in which recombinant DNA research is certain to pay large dividends.

Foot and mouth

In March 1981 farmers on Jersey and the Isle of Wight were dismayed to see that their cattle had developed tell-tale sores on their hooves and around their mouths. It was foot and mouth disease, the first outbreak since 1974, and all the cattle in the affected herds were slaughtered and burned. Across the Channel in Normandy and Brittany there had also been herds afflicted with the disease a little earlier. Here in the UK we do not routinely vaccinate farm animals against foot and mouth, preferring to contain the disease when it does crop up and rely on the moat around our islands; but on mainland Europe vaccination is the norm. Suspicion fell on the vaccines used in France, and samples of the virus from all the 1981 outbreaks were sent to the World Reference Laboratory at the Animal Virus Research Institute in Surrey. The scientists there quickly confirmed that the virus was identical to one that had been isolated near Lausanne in 1965. Foot and mouth virus, like flu, changes swiftly, and it is unthinkable that the outbreaks in France, Jersey and the Isle of Wight were caused by natural spread of that Lausanne virus; in 16 years it would have altered quite perceptibly. But the Lausanne strain had been taken into the laboratories, for study and to manufacture vaccine, and that was where the outbreak had come from. The virus might have escaped from a laboratory, but this was not very likely. More probably, either cows in France had been inoculated with vaccine that was contaminated by the Lausanne strain, or else the vaccine itself was made from Lausanne-strain foot and mouth virus that had not been properly inactivated. Regardless of which possibility is correct, one thing is clear: the outbreaks of foot and mouth, and subsequent slaughter of infected and uninfected cattle alike, were caused, inadvertently perhaps, by man, a flawless example of the two sides to vaccination. It isn't uncommon, either. J. B. Brooksby, a former director of the Animal Virus Research Institute, reckons that 'most recent outbreaks [of foot and mouth] have been linked, at least circumstantially, to vaccine containing residual live virus'.[14] Had the vaccines been made from bioengineered viral antigens, this sort of outbreak could not happen.

More foot and mouth disease vaccine is produced than any other vaccine, and strictly enforced use on some 600 million cattle over the past 25 years has reduced the disease almost to vanishing point, at least in Western Europe. South America produces more than 500 million vaccine doses every year. Each year we slaughter our cattle, and raise a new herd susceptible to the disease, so the market forces have long been there to develop a safer, more effective, cheaper vaccine. Now the science is there too. Foot and mouth disease was the first animal disease to be laid at the doorstep of a virus; it is fitting that a vaccine against foot and mouth disease should be the first genetically engineered vaccine.

There are many threads woven together in the search for a

cloned vaccine, and they all come together, not unnaturally, in the virus's coat proteins. Foot and mouth disease virus carries its genetic message as a single strand of RNA. This is transcribed into a single protein, which is broken up into four chunks by enzymes in the host cell. One of those four chunks is further broken down into the four proteins – labelled VP1 to VP4 – that make up the virus's protective coat. Some of the coat proteins, VP2 and VP4, are remarkably similar from one strain to another. (There are seven strains, or serotypes, and more than 65 subtypes.) The strains differ antigenically, so proteins that are common to all the strains are unlikely to be particularly important as antigens in a vaccine. Most attention therefore focused on VP1. This coat protein varies enormously between strains, with only four out of every ten amino acids the same even in the most similar strains. What is more, a chemical preparation of VP1 does protect pigs from foot and mouth disease, so VP1 looked like the one to go for.

A joint team from the Wellcome Research Laboratories and the Animal Virus Research Institute tackled the problem of cloning VP1 and succeeded admirably. They created a library of coat protein genes from foot and mouth disease virus and sequenced a large part of VP1, but they didn't get expression of the gene.[15] At the same time a large German team was pursuing the same goal, using a different serotype of the virus. The Germans, under Hans Küpper (who quickly moved to Biogen), got further than the English, and got there first. Not only did they create a library of the foot and mouth disease virus protein genes; they also got some of their clones to produce the VP1 protein. They noted, as had others, including the English, that these methods could 'provide a new way of producing a vaccine without the risk of accidental infection by incompletely inactivated virus'.[16]

Küpper's results, while not exactly unexpected, were a pleasant surprise. J. B. Brooksby commented that most conventional virologists had not expected genetic engineering of foot and mouth to come up with anything useful for 'perhaps ten or fifteen years'.[17] Yet here, after less than ten years of genetic engineering, and only a couple of years' work on foot and mouth, was a major antigen being manufactured in *E. coli*. Of course there would be problems in scaling up, and it is noteworthy that within six months Küpper and two colleagues at Biogen had transferred the VP1 gene into *Bacillus subtilis*, which is coming up fast as a more tractable microbial factory than *E. coli*; but they were on their way.[18] Most important among the problems, the engineered coat protein, although it had been gratuitously dubbed the major antigen, had still to be shown able to confer immunity to foot and mouth disease on animals. But that was a minor step, and Brooksby opined that 'the prospects for new foot and mouth disease vaccines are indeed bright'.[19]

Just six months later *Science* received a report detailing the successful use of engineered antigen to confer immunity to foot and mouth disease. The scientists at Genentech had again beaten all contenders, and they had done it not with the favoured VP1 protein but with VP3, which other groups had dismissed as of minor importance. 'We believe,' the Genentech team wrote, 'that this is the first report of an effective protein vaccine derived from the microbial expression of recombinant DNA.'[20] (To be fair, only four of the ten scientists were at Genentech. The rest were staff at the US Department of Agriculture's Plum Island Animal Disease Center in New York. But without the Genentech vaccine, the Animal Disease people would have had nothing to test.)

David Kleid and his colleagues decided, for reasons that aren't entirely clear, to focus on VP3 when everyone else was looking at VP1. They constructed a plasmid library and recovered 'nearly all' of the VP3 gene from plasmid pT465. They then inserted the VP3 gene into another plasmid where it could be brought under the control of the tryptophan system. When cells containing pFM1 grew in a medium that did not contain the amino acid tryptophan they started producing the enzymes needed to manufacture tryptophan from other sources. As they did so, they automatically also produced the VP3 protein, each bacterium constructing between 1 and 2 million molecules of the foreign protein. Indeed, the VP3 protein constituted almost half of the insoluble protein in each cell. So the coat protein was expressed, and in quite acceptable quantities.

Before trying it out on animals, Kleid and his colleagues tested the protein against the real thing. On antibody-binding tests, and in other assays, the engineered protein behaved almost exactly like genuine foot and mouth disease virus VP3, so off it went to the Animal Disease Center to be properly tested. Using well established procedures, the veterinarians inoculated six cattle and two pigs with a preparation of the engineered VP3 protein. A few weeks later the test animals were, in the jargon, 'challenged'. They were confined with an animal that had been deliberately infected with enough foot and mouth disease virus to kill 5000 mice. (That is how they measure these things.) Expectantly, the vets waited to see how their charges would fare. Not one of the immunized animals developed any generalized symptoms of the disease. One cow, it is true, formed a single small lesion on her foot, but neither she nor any of the other test animals that had been inoculated with the engineered vaccine showed any sign of having had foot and mouth disease. Genetic engineers had manufactured a vaccine that worked.

Hepatitis and other problems

So foot and mouth disease is likely to be the first to be fought by genetically engineered vaccines. And the fact that it is predominantly an animal disease should not blind us to the importance of such a vaccine; indeed, the economic importance of livestock probably played a major part in making foot and mouth the first disease to be so threatened. Closer to home, gene cloning is being brought to bear on diseases that are more directly relevant to us.

Take hepatitis B. The virus of hepatitis B attacks the liver, causing a debilitating and often fatal failure of this most important organ. It is also associated with some forms of liver cancer. It afflicts more than 500 million people, and 200 million are so-called carriers, long-term reservoirs of the virus who do not necessarily show any symptoms. Hepatitis is a particular risk for people who work with blood – surgeons, nurses, people in kidney units and so on – and a vaccine would be very useful. Unfortunately, until November 1981 there wasn't one. The prime reason for this failure was that hepatitis just will not grow in laboratory cultures, at least not well enough, and without a supply of the virus any vaccine was more or less out of the question. Now the US Food and Drug Administration has approved a vaccine manufactured by Merck Sharp and Dohme, and recommended that it be used especially on the high-risk groups.

The new vaccine is not genetically engineered. It is made from antigenic particles isolated from the blood of people who carry the disease, and although it works, its source creates a number of problems. There is the problem of general hygiene; hepatitis sufferers who are willing to sell their blood for profit may also carry other diseases; one of these, or live hepatitis, could find its way into a batch of the vaccine. Then there's the cost, estimated to be about $150 for a course of three injections that should offer protection for five years or so. But the biggest drawback is an exquisite catch-22: the vaccine comes from people with hepatitis; it prevents hepatitis; so, as the vaccination programme proceeds, it will, if it is success-ful, pull the rug from under its own feet. With fewer hepatitis carriers, vaccine supply will dry up. No wonder, then, that Merck is also looking to the future and supporting research into a genetically engineered vaccine; and that research is beginning to pay off.

A group under Howard Goodman and William Rutter (who cloned insulin first) has successfully put two hepatitis genes into *E. coli* and got them to manufacture hepatitis proteins.[21] The two genes code for proteins, one of which – the surface antigen – is an important part of the protective envelope around the virus while the other – the core antigen – dwells deeper within the infectious particle. Rutter and his colleagues had already cloned these hepa-titis genes into plasmids, but the bacteria weren't making much of the proteins, so they decided to move the genes and put them under the control of a different system, the tryptophan system. There followed much snipping and joining of DNA, which in essence proceeded as follows. The starting point was a plasmid called p*trp*E2–1, which contains a goodly section of the genes controlling tryptophan synthesis. They cut this plasmid with two restriction enzymes, *Hpa* I and *Taq* I, to release a small fragment, just 32 base-pairs long, that contained part of the tryptophan on-switch and the recognition site that binds to a ribosome and is essential to protein synthesis. A fresh batch of p*trp*E2–1 was digested with *Hpa* I and *Cla* I. These remove a considerably larger fragment on the other side of the *Hpa* I site. Now they inserted the 32-base fragment into that site (*Taq* I and *Cla* I leave the same sticky end). After growing up the transformants and selecting the ones that were ampicillin-resistant, they analysed the plasmids by restriction mapping and direct sequencing. One, which they designated p*trp*L1, was right; it had the beginnings of the tryp-tophan system neatly turned around and ready to accept any fragment that could be inserted into the *Cla* I site.

Phase two required putting the hepatitis gene behind the tryp-tophan switch. Out of the previous hepatitis clones they snipped, with *Hha* I, a 1005 base-pair fragment that carried the gene and a bit more. A later stage called for *Hpa* II linkers, so this fragment was treated with the *Hpa* II methylase enzyme to modify the bases and protect them against *Hpa* II. The start codon of the hepatitis gene is about 15 bases from one end of the gene, so to remove the waste they incubated the fragment with a selection of nucleases that nibbled back the extra matter. That done, synthetic *Bam* HI linkers (which also contain the *Hpa* II site) were joined to either end, and the whole lot digested with *Hpa* II to create the sticky ends. Now the prepared fragment could be joined to the *Cla* I cut p*trp*L1 plasmid – *Hpa* II and *Cla* I produce the same CG sticky end. Into *E. coli*, selection by means of radioactive hepatitis antibody, and Rutter had no less than 17 clones busy producing the core antigen of hepatitis B virus. The busiest of these, called pCA246, manufactured vast quantities of the antigen, up to 10 per cent of the protein it was making. Similar techniques put the other antigen, the surface antigen, into a clone right enough, but no hepatitis antigen could be detected, probably because the bacterial enzymes were breaking it down.

The point of going, very superficially, through all the steps in the construction of pCA246 is to say not what a complicated business genetic engineering is, but what a simple one. For the fact is that every stage is relatively straightforward, resting on all the prior work and putting it to good use. Sequencing provides the order of nucleic acids, which reveals the restriction enzyme recognition sites. Clever thought before reaching for the test-tubes suggests neat short-cuts, and the whole proceeds more smoothly than imaginable. It really has become more like engineering and less like science, in the sense that scientific knowledge is being applied to practical problems.

Still, the problems are not all solved. The engineered antigen hasn't yet been proven as a prophylactic against hepatitis, but that is just a matter of time. The surface antigen, which proved so intractable in *E. coli*, might yet reach production. Not satisfied with its performance in the bacterium, Rutter and his colleagues snipped the gene out once again and put it into a plasmid that will grow in yeast. Yeast, being a eukaryote, albeit a lowly one, does things that *E. coli* cannot, and one of the things it does is to make hepatitis surface antigen beautifully. More than that, the yeast cells also add some of the extra components that seem necessary to make an effective antigen out of the simple hepatitis coat protein, and the engineered product as it emerges from the yeast is a lot more effective. Yeast is good too because man has been growing it in quantity for centuries and knows well how to cope with it, and it produces none of the toxins that bacteria do. The hepatitis–yeast combination looks like a winner.

It isn't the only one, either. All around the world genetic engineers are bringing their talents to bear on the problems of disease. In London, at the Imperial Cancer Research Fund, Mary-Jane Gething is taking the influenza virus apart.[22] She has the complete sequence and structure of the so-called haemagglutinin glycoprotein, a spike of a molecule that carries most of the major influenza antigens. Gething has put the haemagglutinin gene under the control of virus SV40 and used the recombinant chimera to infect monkey cells in culture; three days later each of those cells was covered with more than half a billion haemagglutinin molecules, a potent source of potential vaccine. In New York, a large team under Eckard Wimmer is getting to grips with the polio virus.[23] They have the complete nucleotide sequence of the virus's RNA genome, 7433 bases long. With it they can begin to fathom how polio does its dreadful job, and how to prevent it. In Paris, a group has successfully protected guinea-pigs against diphtheria using a completely synthetic antigen.[24] And in Philadelphia rabies virus is under scrutiny, its major antigen cloned and awaiting development as a vaccine.[25]

Those are just a selection. As the new technology works its wonders it offers the possibility of fulfilling twin hopes. One is for pluripotent vaccines that are simple, stable and cheap enough to get to the rural masses of the developing world; already the six or seven shots, spread over two years, needed to protect a child against the six major childhood diseases have been reduced to just two injections six months apart, and that without recourse to recombinant DNA. With it, who knows what is possible? The second hope is for vaccines against diseases that have so far proved refractory. To spur these hopes a whole new technology, every bit as exciting and powerful as recombinant DNA, is growing up: monoclonal antibodies.

Cesar's glory: monoclonal antibodies

The average foreign invader, be it virus, bacterium or even transplanted cell, is a complex thing. There may be several antigens present on even a simple virus, each capable of generating its own antibody. So a bigger particle, a malaria parasite for example, could be covered with a multitude of different antigens. All will raise antibodies, some more powerfully than others, so that the immune system's response is essentially dirty, a confusion of lots of different antibodies all directed at different antigens on the one invader. That's fine as far as it goes, and one can learn a great deal about the immune system by studying the dirty response. One can also put the isolated antibody collection to work, in radioimmuno-assay or whatever. But to investigate the immune system thoroughly and put its exquisite sensitivity to work, one would like to be able to obtain large quantities of single, pure antibodies, directed against a single known antigen. That is exactly what monoclonal antibodies are.

A single cell manufactures but a single antibody. If one could locate that cell, and grow it endlessly in culture, one would have a source of pure antibody. But finding the cell you are after in the entire spleen (where much of the antibody production goes on) would be akin to finding a cell with a plasmid in a vat of culture, without the selectable properties of the plasmid. And in any case, ordinary cells would not grow endlessly; they seem to have a finite life-time of eight or nine reproductions. The man who overcame these obstacles was Cesar Milstein, often called the father of the monoclonal. Milstein hit on the idea of fusing a single spleen cell to a cancer cell. The spleen cell would spew out a single antibody, and the cancer cell would multiply for ever. The resultant colony of cells would be descended from a single founder, identical clones; hence monoclonal (see figure 8.1). It was a brilliant idea, and it worked; Milstein and Georges Köhler joined myeloma (bone marrow) cancer cells to spleen cells, using a monkey virus to accomplish the fusion, and got clones that secreted single pure antibodies.[26] The problem of selection remains, but if you know what antigen you want the antibody to bind to it it is not such an onerous task to screen the cultured hybridoma cells.

Because they offer the potential of unlimited sources of super-pure single antibodies, monoclonals have had heaped upon them almost as many future benefits as genetic engineering was encumbered with in the early days. They might be the basis for kits to diagnose cancer cells, which probably carry surface antigens that distinguish them from normal cells. The same monoclonals might also allow cancer cells to be traced as they spread around the body.

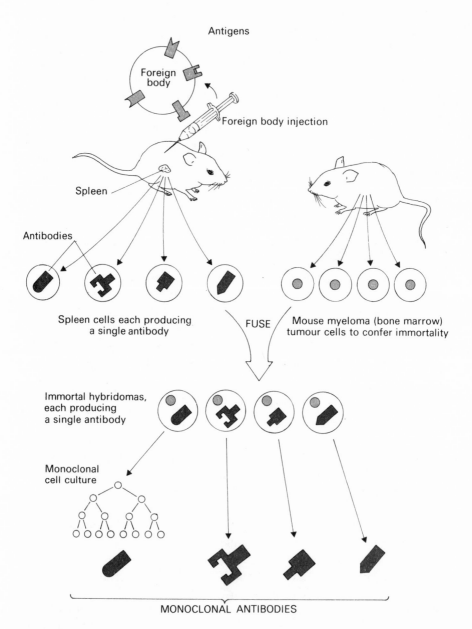

Figure 8.1
Monoclonal antibody manufacture.

Some breast cancers need oestrogen to grow. One way to treat them would be to remove the supply of oestrogen, but this does no good, and indeed positive harm, if the cancer is not dependant on oestrogen. There are tests to tell the two sorts of tumour apart, but they are expensive and time-consuming. Oestrogen-dependent tumours have special receptors on their surface, and a kit based on antibodies to these receptors should make diagnosis, and hence treatment, considerably better. Cancer cells spread at least partly because the body fails to recognize them as deranged. Another monoclonal approach to cancer therapy is to produce antibodies that will stick to the cancer and mask certain portions of the cell surface. This should drastically alter the way the body responds to those cells, and might give the immune system a chance to attack the cancerous cells.

Monoclonal antibodies also offer a method to extract and purify the antigens they recognize, and with pure antibodies one necessarily gets a very pure protein. It is simply a matter of finding the right antibody and growing a lot of it in a monoclonal culture. Then you extract the antibody and attach it to small beads in a column. In at the top you pour a mixture that contains the protein you seek, the antigen the antibody recognizes. If conditions are right, that protein, and that protein alone, will stick to the antibody, and everything else in the brew, which might be a crude extract of bacterial proteins, washes straight through. Then, when you've washed the beads, you change the conditions, probably the acidity, slightly and the antibodies give up their precious cargo. The protein, pure as you could want, drips out of the bottom of the tube. There is already great interest in this separation technique – not surprisingly really, for its application to genetic engineering could make extracting the bacterially produced proteins a snap. A monoclonal against interferon, produced by Derek Burke at the University of Warwick and David Secher who works in Milstein's Cambridge laboratory, has already proved itself in small-scale trials and should revolutionize the production of interferon. The same technique has provided a vaccine against malaria.

Malaria, caused by a small parasite, has been judged the most important infectious disease of man. In Africa alone it is said to be responsible each year for the death of 1 million children under the age of 14. And there has been no vaccine against it. The reason is the complicated life cycle of the parasite, which breeds inside the malaria mosquito and multiplies asexually inside the human body. Each of the stages has different antigens, and if just one infective sporozoite, injected into the blood by a mosquito, should make it past the defences to the liver, all the protection is in vain. Now hybridoma cells have been used to manufacture antibodies to the many malarial antigens and then the antibodies used to extract and purify the proteins themselves. Each protein has been tested as a vaccine, and two of them were very effective, stimulating the body to destroy the invading malaria parasites. Coming full circle, the scientists at Wellcome Laboratories who developed the experimental malaria vaccine now plan to find the genes that code for those proteins, remove them from the malaria parasite, and transplant them into *E. coli*. The *E. coli* will uncomplainingly churn out malarial proteins, which will be purified using the monoclonal antibodies, and a vaccine against this scourge will be possible. Together, monoclonal antibodies and recombinant DNA might bring disease under control not just for the wealthy citizens of the developed world, but also for those of the developing world.

9

EXPLOITATION

*Business, biotechnology and academe achieve a precarious
understanding*

On 7 June 1972 lawyers for the General Electric Company in
America asked the patent office to grant the company protection
for a rather valuable invention. It was a new method for cleaning up
oil spills, one that depended on a strain of the bacterium called
Pseudomonas. The company got the protection it sought for the
process to manufacture the bacterium, and for the technique of
inoculating an oil spill with straw loaded with the bacterium. But it
failed to get a patent on the strain itself. The strain was
undoubtedly new and useful, two prime requirements for patent
protection, and General Electric argued that it had also been
invented, a third requirement.

   Dr Ananda Chakrabarty had invented the new and useful strain
by allowing various strains, each able to gobble up one component
of crude oil, to cross-breed and thus combine their abilities, each of
which was on a separate plasmid (recombinant techniques were not
involved). Chakrabarty laboriously selected a strain of superbugs
that could singlehandedly deal with a spill. The US government
argued that, despite Chakrabarty's obvious part in creating the
superbug, the bacterium could not be patented. General Electric
eventually took the matter right up to the Supreme Court, which
was asked to decide. Stephen Crespi, Patents Controller for the
UK National Research Development Corporation, summarized
the question facing the justices very well: 'Is a living organism
which otherwise complies with legal requirements for patentability
nevertheless disqualified because it is alive?'[1] The answer is 'no'.
On 16 June 1980, by a majority of five to four, the Supreme Court
granted General Electric its patent in the superbug. Chief Justice
Warren Burger, on behalf of the majority, agreed with the lower
court, whose decision the government had challenged. 'We think,'

the Court of Customs and Patents Appeals had said back in 1978, 'the fact that micro-organisms, as distinguished from chemical compounds, are alive, is a distinction without legal significance.'[2]

The Stanford patent

The Chakrabarty decision opened the way to genetic engineers, whose patent applications had been held up pending the Supreme Court's decision. Stephen Crespi, commenting on the case while the decision was awaited, had pointed out 'it is difficult to see why recombinant DNA plasmids should be treated any differently from other chemical substances.'[3] On 2 December 1980 his view was confirmed, in United States patent number 4 237 224. This covered a Process for Producing Biologically Functional Molecular Chimeras, and credited Stanley Cohen and Herbert Boyer as the inventors. Cohen and Boyer assigned all their rights in the patent to Cohen's university, Stanford, which in turn had set up a special 50–50 partnership with Boyer's University of California at San Francisco. The patent is exceptionally broad, covering no less than 14 specific claims, and it is safe to say that very little genetic engineering can be done outside the protection of patent 4 237 224. Transforming cells with recombinant plasmids, using antibiotic markers on the plasmid, blunt-end and staggered-end ligation, with or without splicing enzymes, with or without restriction enzymes – all these and more are covered by the patent.

The Cohen–Boyer patent brought to the surface a lot of ill-will that had been festering beneath the skin of molecular biology. One of the original papers in the *Proceedings of the National Academy of Sciences* had included Annie Chang and Robert Helling as co-authors with Boyer and Cohen. Patent law assumes that co-authors are co-inventors, but Cohen and Boyer claimed that they had provided the major creative input that had resulted in the various successful procedures. Helling, naturally, saw things differently. Asked by university patent lawyers to sign a disclaimer, he said: 'I felt that we were all equal in this, and do not want to sign a letter saying that I was just another laboratory worker. I was part and parcel of the whole thing; I don't feel that I should sign something that I do not believe is true.'[4] Helling wasn't the only objector. John Morrow, who had been important in showing that the *Xenopus* ribosomal genes could be inserted into Cohen's plasmid and thence into *E. coli*, also refused to sign a disclaimer.

In the end, of course, Cohen and Boyer got their patent, but the scientific community is still worried about the issues that the patent has raised. One is the question of individuals benefiting from government-funded research. Neither Boyer nor Cohen will personally get any of the royalties earned by the patent, but there will be other cases that are not so clear-cut. Another is the problem of authorship; accusations that the Stanford and UCSF lawyers had rewritten scientific history to obtain their patent are common, and there is a worry that publication in the scientific literature is being organized with an eye on exploitation rather than communication.

Boyer and Cohen have deflected much of the criticism by their handling of the income from the patent. All of it will go to their universities, where it will be used to support many kinds of research. And the universities will not restrict licences at all. Academics can continue to use the gene-splicing processes as before, with no charge, and commercial companies can obtain a non-exclusive licence for $10 000, with a further annual payment of $10 000. When products that depend on the patented processes come on to the market the companies will have to pay Stanford a royalty of between 1 and 0.5 per cent of the net annual sales. As an incentive to induce companies to take out licences, Stanford and UCSF agreed that companies who signed up before 15 December 1981 would be allowed to offset their annual payments against future royalties; many of the 200 or more gene-exploitation companies in the USA apparently took advantage of this generous offer.

In general, the requirements of Stanford and UCSF, who hold what is clearly a very valuable property, are quite reasonable, and defused much of the explosive power of the patent. As *Nature's* editorialist commented, 'neither university seems out to make a quick buck, or an unseemly number of bucks'.[5] Still, there remains some uncertainty. Some of the pharmaceutical giants who stand to make most from the successful exploitation of recombinant DNA techniques have been closeted with their lawyers, looking for loopholes that will allow them to wriggle out of the Stanford patent. No challenge has yet materialized, but then, neither has any marketable product. When the time comes, the challenge could take either of two forms. One of the companies, or a consortium, could seek to overthrow the patent itself; or someone may try marketing a genetically engineered product without paying the royalties, putting the onus on Stanford and UCSF to defend their rights. It could be an interesting time.

Billion-dollar battle

Whatever becomes of the Stanford patent, there has already been quite a skirmish between the University of California and Hoffmann-La Roche, which perhaps presages the battles to come. When Genentech went public, one of the reasons it created such a stir was that it had a potential goldmine: not insulin, a relatively small market, but interferon, which according to one estimate could be worth $3 billion a year in five years' time. Genentech had cloned the interferon genes under contract to Hoffman-La Roche. The University of California claimed that Roche had, effectively, stolen the genes.

The story goes back to 1977, when a 59-year-old patient lay dying of leukaemia in a Los Angeles hospital. For the sake of science, the patient agreed to the painful procedure whereby cells from the bone marrow were sucked out for investigation. The patient died, but under the tender care of Phillip Koeffler and David Golde, research haematologists at the School of Medicine of the University of California at Los Angeles, those cells thrived. They eventually formed a line that Koeffler and Golde christened, with stark simplicity, KG-1. Golde sent a sample of the cells to his friend Robert Gallo at the National Institute of Cancer. Gallo wanted to see whether the cancerous cells contained viruses; they didn't, but in the process of the investigation Gallo discovered that KG-1 cells produced interferon. Gallo passed the cells on to a colleague of his, Sidney Pestka at the Roche Institute of Molecular Biology ('an institute wholly funded by, but generally regarded as scientifically independent from, the drug firm of Hoffmann-La Roche'[6]). Pestka, by judiciously tinkering with the conditions in which KG-1 grew, turned the line into a superabundant producer of interferon. Now the story becomes tangled because, as science writer Nicholas Wade notes, 'up to this point the handling of KG-1 differed scarcely from any other exchange of materials among academic scientists. But the instant that Pestka made the cells the top interferon producer in his laboratory, they became a very hot property.'[7]

Biogen, in partnership with Schering-Plough, had just announced the cloning of interferon at a splashy press conference; the announcement added $50 million to Biogen's paper value and $426 million to its backer's. The rival partnership between Genentech and Roche was, at this stage, a secret, but they had conceived a method for cloning interferon that would enable them to leapfrog Biogen and Schering. The key was the selection process, in which they would pick out the clones containing interferon from the hundreds of thousands of duds. They had the amino acid sequence of part of the molecule, and from it synthesized the full set of DNAs that could code for that sequence. The set could be used as a probe for the interferon gene, but to give themselves an even better chance of finding it, they needed an enriched source of interferon DNA. KG-1 cells, overproducing interferon as they were, provided that source.

Pestka sent some dead KG-1 cells to the West Coast, where the Genentech scientists isolated the messenger RNA, made their complementary DNA, and shot the whole lot into a bacterial library. The library did contain the interferon gene, the synthetic probe did pick it out, and the rest, as they say, is history (see p. 176). But the University of California is unhappy about all this. Its attorney, Bertram Rowland, is adamant about what he sees as Roche's breaches of conduct: 'The academic relationship is now being subverted by industry. I don't mind if Roche enjoys the benefits of this relationship, as long as they pay for it.'[8] The University is claiming a royalty on the grounds that Koeffler and Golde created the gene that Roche used. 'Is it fair,' asks Rowland, 'that this property, created in a university environment, should be taken by industry and utilized without making some reasonable compensation to the university?'[9]

The University of California may have a case; that is for the courts, brought in by Hoffmann-La Roche in September 1980, to decide. But there are other factors to take into account. Koeffler and Golde certainly had no interest in interferon, and did not establish the KG-1 line to study it. Indeed, it was Robert Gallo who told them that KG-1 produced interferon; they had no idea that it did. Sidney Pestka turned KG-1 from an interesting culture into 'hot property'; there is no harm in that, but why didn't he, or someone from Roche, observe the usual courtesies and ask Koeffler and Golde for permission to clone the cells' DNA and apply for patents on the results? What about the patient? The

University and Roche seem to have decided that neither the patient (now dead) nor his (or her) kin have any interest in the genes, though they 'belonged' to the patient before they ever came into even the University's hands. The issue is complicated, and the courts have not yet made a final ruling. And however the conflict is eventually resolved, the battle between Hoffmann-La Roche and the University of California is most surely a portent of things to come. As Nicholas Wade observes, 'the powerful forces of the profit motive clearly have the capacity to strain and rupture the informal traditions of scientific exchange'.[10]

A conflict of interests

The powerful forces of the profit motive are nothing new in academe; physicists, chemists, engineers and many others have long been involved with industry and exploitation. But they are new to molecular biology, which until ten years ago spent more time in justifying its existence in the absence of any tangible benefits that in dealing with the problems raised by commercialization. At issue are said to be questions of morality and ethics, but it usually comes down to pragmatics. Is there, for example, a difference between the researcher employed by a university and funded by government and the researcher who works for a corporation? How should universities benefit from the application of work that they have nurtured? What of the conflict of interest between the commercial company anxious to protect its discoveries and the scientist committed to the ideal of free exchange of information? Is that conflict made better or worse when the company director and research scientist are one and the same person? The questions keep being asked, and so far no easy answers have emerged, but that hasn't prevented many scientists going ahead and muddying themselves in the polluted stream of commerce.

Genentech and Biogen are the models in the field. Each began as an alliance between capitalists and scientists, both in search of profits and knowledge. The knowledge continues to accumulate, but the profits are more elusive. That has not stopped a horde of more than 200 imitators, some based on a single scientist and one bright idea, others more broadly founded. And the big boys are also taking increasing notice of the field. Chemical giants such as

Monsanto and Du Pont, oil companies like Atlantic-Richfield and Exxon, are joining the pharmaceutical industry in support for molecular biology. In the UK there is Celltech, partly owned by government, with a brief to conduct its own research and exploit commercially the results obtained in government-funded research. Even big institutional investors are getting into biotechnology; the Prudential Assurance Company spearheads one consortium of backers, and brokers N. M. Rothschild have floated a company specifically to invest in biotechnology. The commercial interest has undoubtedly had a good effect on some aspects of the science, but it raises many problems.

In these days of ever-shrinking budgets, the temptation for research organizations to profit from the results they obtain must be great indeed. Past exemplars include the Wisconsin Alumni Research Fund, set up to protect the university from the 'tainted money' that John D. Rockefeller had offered it. WARF was greatly enhanced by the university's patents in vitamin D, and stands as an example of what can be achieved. The Fund has ploughed hundreds of millions of dollars back into basic research. But there are good and bad ways of going about the business of commerce. Stanford and Harvard each recently decided not to accept shares in exploitation companies. The fights were bitter, and split the campus and faculty on both coasts, but it is hard to see any fault in the final decision.

Mark Ptashne, professor of biochemistry at Harvard (and a rival of Gilbert's since the two were involved in the chase for the elusive repressor molecules that can switch off bacterial genes), suggested that the university accept a package of shares in a company that would be set up to exploit research from his laboratory. The university would then share directly in any profits made by the company. Harvard president Derek Bok was at first eager to participate in the venture; but in the end, and after much debate that was at times rather acrimonious, the university decided to back off. The arguments against were straightforward. If the university had an interest, even a minority interest, in a successful business that was dependent on faculty members, it might find it very difficult to avoid favouring staff involved with the business. In an environment where all are supposed to be equal, even the potential for favouritism would be very divisive. And what if the business were not successful? Could the university resist entreaties for special treatment? Considerations such as these helped to sway Harvard against Ptashne's proposal. He went ahead anyway and now sits, with Tom Maniatis, on the board of a new company called, somewhat pretentiously, The Genetics Institute.

Stanford came to very similar conclusions, without the goad of a proposal like Ptashne's but with the precedent of Harvard. Stanford University has agreed not to take an equity position in companies that have faculty members as shareholders. And every faculty member will be required to reveal to any more senior member the extent of his or her connections with industry. Dr Donald Kennedy, Stanford's president, obviously favours the new agreement, which allows academics to benefit financially from their own research but keeps the university in the clear, but he also feels that the problem is by no means solved. 'Perhaps it is time for another Asilomar,' he suggests, 'but it ought to come from the people who are doing the science.'[11] At least one university, however, is not so reticent. The Michigan State University Foundation announced, shortly after the Stanford decision, that it was providing financial support for academics who wanted to exploit their research. Michigan State put up $100 000 to help start a company called Neogen, which will probably specialize in the genetic engineering of plants.

Simply allowing academics to get on with it and invest their expertise in industry solves very few problems. In particular, it does nothing about the conflicts of interest that must inevitably exist. Jonathan King, the MIT molecular biologist who has long been an opponent of unregulated recombinant DNA research, is very worried about this. People who wear two hats – corporate animal and research scientist – are a major concern of his. The scientific community thrives on free exchange of information. The corporation must have a product that is protected, eventually by a patent, perhaps, but initially by secrecy. What, King asks, is the Janus scientist who has just made an important discovery to do? 'If you're planning to use this information for your corporation you just don't pass the information on to the guy in the next lab, because he may do the same thing,' is his answer.[12] In the past the scientific community ostensibly ostracized those who withheld information, although of course there was always some secrecy in competition. 'What's happening now,' says King, 'is the institutionalization of secrecy.' He recounted for participants at the 1982 meeting of the American Association for the Advancement of Science in Washington the story of how, at the last meeting of the American Society of Microbiology, a vice-president of the Exxon Corporation advised scientists to have their presentations notarized before coming to a meeting, and urged them not to speak to anyone on the way there. The laughter that this story provoked conceals a matter of grave concern.

Nor is it simply free exchange of information that worries King. He pointed out to me that MIT's David Baltimore has 300 000 shares in an exploitation company called Collaborative Research. That company went public in December 1981 and the shares were valued at $19 each. Baltimore is on record as the formal proposer of the moves to relax the NIH guidelines on recombinant DNA research; his 300 000 shares give him a $5.7 million stake in a company that would stand to benefit directly from more relaxed guidelines. 'He [Baltimore] is an extraordinary person,' King admits, 'but even he could get influenced by six million dollars.'[13]

A different concern of King's is the direction that research will take if it is guided by profits rather than the public good. 'Genetic engineering technology and commercialization will generate many things that are saleable; many other products that are useful but have a very very small market will not be commercially developed,' King says.[14] He alleges that several pharmaceutical companies have already abandoned human vaccines, 'because if they work you give one shot and there's no more market'. What they have done, says King, it to move into the livestock vaccine market, 'because cattle you slaughter, and there's a new market every year'. (Monsanto has Genentech working on cattle and pig growth hormones, 'looking at ways of producing more meat with less feed'.)[15]

King's point – that there is little percentage in getting to the root cause of a disease when you can produce a profitable palliative – is well taken. Insulin, after all, is a treatment and not a cure for diabetes. The basic research needed to effect a genuine cure will still have to be funded from public coffers. It was a public commitment to basic biomedical research that led to the present understanding of genes and molecular biology, an understanding that in turn allows scientists to exploit genetic engineering. The knowledge was fostered by public commitment, King says, and it is being snatched away into private hands. This is perhaps his most overriding worry, and he is particularly outspoken about the way industry has stolen government's investment. He argues that public health is far too important to be handed over to 'narrow short-term goals like the return on investment'. When we talked about this, King drew an analogy which he admitted many people regard as over the top. But he stands by it.

[Genetic engineering] is like nuclear weapons. We do not allow private corporations to sell them, even though it would be a very profitable market. An assessment has been made that this is not in the public interest to allow corporations to market or build bombs. My own feeling is that the technology of genetic engineering should stay publicly controlled.[16]

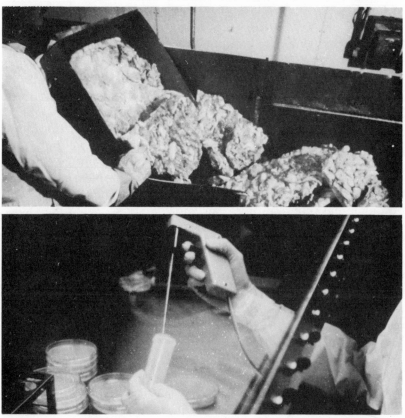

Plate 9.1
Above: pancreata used in the conventional production of insulin from animal sources.
Below: preparation of *Escherichia coli* cultures used in production of biosynthetic human insulin. (*Courtesy Eli Lilly and Company; supplied by Daniel C. Williams*)

Unabated enthusiasm

Jonathan King's is something of a lone voice. Most other people do not accept his view of the exploitation of genetic engineering. Biogen, for example, is not exactly being reticent about its growth. It opened an American laboratory, appointed Wally Gilbert as chairman of the board, and secured $20 million of extra financial backing, all within the space of a few days in October 1981. The lab, just a couple of blocks away from MIT, will be headed by Richard Flavell, one of Britain's gene-cloning experts. Flavell was leader of the gene-cloning group at the National Institute of Medical Research, and he will be spiriting some of that team away with him to Cambridge, Massachusetts. The people he is taking are those who work on the so called histocompatibility complex, a region of the genome vital to immunity and transplant rejection; not surprisingly, commentators have speculated that Biogen may be planning to move into the supply of the tissue-typing reagents that make transplants feasible.

Flavell's departure is a severe blow to the UK's Medical Research Council; quite what Harvard will make of Professor Walter Gilbert's appointment is anybody's guess. Gilbert started life as a physicist, switched to molecular biology, and in 1980 won the Nobel Prize in chemistry for the rapid sequencing technique he invented with Allan Maxam. The move to chief executive officer is one that 'he says he finds "fascinating", because of the chance to "create a structure in the external world"'.[17] Harvard has granted Gilbert a year's leave of absence to go to Biogen, which he helped to found, but he may not return. The department of biochemistry, presently chaired by Mark Ptashne, has a rule that only full-time faculty may be members, so when Gilbert's year is up he will have to either return to the department or resign from it. He has already resigned his American Cancer Society research professorship because the ACS requires its fellows to be full-time researchers, but is sanguine about preserving his links with Harvard. 'If the biochemistry department doesn't want me I will be somewhere else,' he told one reporter.[18] Biogen begins to look increasingly like so many other exploitative companies, with Biogen SA in Geneva, Biogen Inc. in the USA, and a holding company, Biogen NZ, registered in Curacao. Except, of course, that Biogen still doesn't have a penny of sales to its name. It is making interferon for

Schering-Plough, and hepatitis B vaccine for a Japanese phar-maceutical company called Green Cross, but much remains to be done. Biogen also, perhaps wisely, remains a private company. Gilbert will not be drawn on when his board will float some stock, but he does admit that he hopes to see products on sale before the end of 1983. If he is correct and the company goes public *after* initial sales, response from investors could make Genentech's spectacular launch look tame.

Just down the road from Harvard, MIT, after a great deal of anguish, agreed in late 1981 to accept $120 million from millionaire Edwin Whitehead to set up the Whitehead Institute for Biomedical Research. (Duke University had, in 1974 and for reasons that aren't clear, turned down a similar offer.) David Baltimore will head the institute, which will own all patents that might emerge from its work and will benefit directly from licensing of those patents. Critics noted that Whitehead is the single largest share-holder in Revlon, the cosmetics firm, which is moving into bioengineering, and that he also has a venture capital company that has invested in biotechnology. They fear he intends to profit from the institute, but they don't know how. Whitehead himself is angry at these suggestions. 'I am getting awfully tired of having my motives questioned, especially when I think they are pure,' he says. 'If my intentions were to profit from biotechnology I wouldn't give away $120 million to a basic research institute. [The White-head Institute] has no link with any commercial venture; it is purely a philanthropic exercise.'[19]

Du Pont gave Harvard Medical School $6 million to fund research into molecular genetics, the company getting exclusive rights to market products that arise. And the company has also set aside $85 million for its own life sciences complex, to include a 250 000 square foot facility for basic biomedical research. Du Pont intends to spend over $100 million, more than a fifth of its total research budget, on the life sciences in 1982, part of a plan to double the amount of revenue that the company earns from phar-maceutical, agricultural and biomedical products.

Cetus Corporation followed Genentech and let the public in on its stock in March 1981. The company is no Johnny-come-lately, having been started ten years previously in 1971. Nor is it depen-dent on genetic engineering, which is just one string to its bow. The shares went on sale at $23 each and, unlike Genentech's record-breaking ascent, that is roughly where they stayed. But that shouldn't be taken as too gloomy an omen, for the Cetus offering broke a different sort of record. The company raised $120 million with its offering, more than any company in US corporate history had done before.

The floatings of the various companies established to take advantage of recombination continues to provide excitement, not least for the people who have invested time and effort in those companies against the promise of more material rewards. James Watson sees another aspect to it. 'The fact that the speculation today is over recombinant DNA stocks rather than its imaginary biohazard is the best evidence that an unparalleled episode in the history of science has ended.'[20] It may not be true, but like so many of Watson's utterances it has a characteristically fine ring to it.

All over the world there is great interest in biotechnology and genetic engineering, not only from private investors but also from governments. Canada's venture capitalists and mining companies were quick to support genetic engineering research, and in France, Germany, Switzerland, Holland and Belgium there is growing state interest. The Soviet Union is keen not to get left behind, and molecular biology has had 'priority status' since May 1974. One recent report claims that, after what seems to have been an infight between two academicians, the victor, biotechnologist Ovchinnikov, told the annual general meeting of the Soviet Academy of Sciences in December 1981 that Soviet scientists 'were now leading the world in "a number of very important branches of biology"'.[21] (Their published research work shows no evidence of this.) The Soviets have even gone so far as to refuse an exit visa to Professor David Goldfarb, claiming that his work on bacterial plasmids is secret. It recently emerged, however, that Goldfarb was never given security clearance for access to genuinely secret material, which puts the official story in some doubt. Other countries are a little further behind, although India has announced plans to develop a biotechnology capability. Perhaps the most surprising development has come from the government in Rome; the company it intends to launch may bear the name Genitalia.

Celltech is the UK's chosen instrument for exploiting academic research. It is a partnership of several shareholders; largest, with 44 per cent, is the National Enterprise Board, but the Prudential Assurance Company, Midland Bank, and British and Commonwealth Shipping and Technical Development Capital are also involved. The sum at stake is not large – £12 million initially – but Celltech has at least begun to market its first product, a monoclonal antibody to interferon that can purify the protein by 5000 times. This should prove a money-spinner with those working on, and eventually manufacturing, interferons, provided that Biogen's similar products don't capture the market. The company has a special arrangement with the Medical Research Council whereby it has first refusals on any work from the Council. The MRC will inform Celltech about developments before publication, which may necessitate a delay in publication while patents are investigated. In return, Celltech will pass 'a substantial proportion' of any royalties that accrue on to the MRC, which will keep the money separate and eventually invite applications for support from the Celltech Fund.

All is not roses, though. A deal between Massachusetts General Hospital and the West German chemical giant Hoechst AG has raised money for research and a lot of difficulties. Hoechst promised the hospital $50 million over the next ten years in exchange for exclusive patent rights of any research that comes out of the hospital. The US government's General Accounting Office said that the deal might be illegal because Hoechst would be gaining title to federally funded research, but the hospital has assured everyone that the Hoechst money would be kept completely separate from government funds. A politician described the deal as offensive because, although taxpayers contribute £25 million a year to Massachusetts General, Hoechst provides only $5 million a year and yet the company might get exclusive rights to enjoy the fruits of profitable research. But the deal went ahead anyway. The variety of arrangements between academics and business is so great that one can only sit back and watch, hoping for the best. Some will work. One has already failed dramatically.

Man-made tax shelters

E. F. Hutton is one of Wall Street's most respected brokerage firms. In February 1981 it announced a very strong entrant into the biotechnology derby. DNA Science would have $40 million of backing, a Nobel Prize winner on the staff, and an ingenious new scheme to capitalize on academic excellence. Six months later, as 28 July, the due date on the prospectus, came and went without all the capital having been raised, Hutton scratched their horse. The investors got their money back on 4 August. It had nevertheless been a pretty good idea. The company, DNA Science, was to have been an umbrella over a host of smaller subsidiary companies that would be set up near specific researchers' campus laboratories. The scientists would thus be able to retain their links with academe while running a commercial enterprise in which they had a stake. The investors would be financial backers, rather than companies with a direct interest in biotechnology, and they would supply money but otherwise leave the company to its board to run. E. F. Hutton had been developing the concept of DNA Science for a couple of years, and the closing of the deal on one of the subsidiary companies was used as a platform to launch it. Taglit – the word is Hebrew for discovery – was to be an Israeli biotechnology venture utilizing the undoubted expertise of scientists at the Weizmann Institute in Rehovot. Nobel Prize winner Christian Anfinsen gave up a very good position with the National Institutes of Health to head Taglit for DNA Science, and the new company was poised to exploit interferons, monoclonal antibodies for diagnosis, and a project to increase the protein in wheat. E. F. Hutton then went looking for the $40 million it needed.

Some came easily enough, but the firm's original intention to eschew drug companies and chemical manufacturers had to be abandoned. DNA Science agreed to take money from, among others, Allied Chemical and Johnson & Johnson. Allied was promised rights to certain industrial processes, and Johnson & Johnson likewise got rights to the company's pharmaceutical developments. This created a discrepancy between the institutional investors, who would simply reap a dividend, and these corporations, who would benefit doubly (or more) from their investment. The $40 million did not, in the end, materialize, and E. F. Hutton decided to abandon the original idea. Anfinsen was left high and dry in Israel, where he now has a visiting professorship at the Weizmann Institute and is considering ways of revitalizing Taglit. Hutton too has not entirely forsaken DNA Science. Changes in tax law could make research and development a haven for those who would like to diminish their tax liabilities, and Hutton is said to be restructuring DNA Science to take advantage of this. The end result could put basic biomedical research into the same category as movies, real estate, and racehorses; tax shelters for the wealthy.

The failure of DNA Science represents perhaps a hint of realism creeping into the genetic engineering saga. The United Nations' plan for an International Centre for Genetic Engineering, which would 'attempt to promote technology transfer between developed and developing nations in a non-commercial setting', is surely the exact reverse.[22] On past form, such an enterprise would seem doomed to failure. But then, so too would most of the genuinely commercial attempts to exploit recombinant DNA. Products have been an unconscionably long time coming, as the would-be industrialists discover that there are difficult obstacles to surmount in moving up from laboratory bench to stainless steel fermenter. The very thing that makes genetic engineering so powerful – the replicating micro-organisms – creates those problems, for living things need very special care. And crippled organisms, carrying the added baggage of engineered genes, quickly lose out to any mutant that manages to shed its load. Ensuring that a fermenter grows engineered bacteria and not revertant mutants is going to be a painful headache. Dr Gilbert Omenn, Science and Public Policy Fellow at the Brookings Institution, a think tank in Washington, has made a thorough study of the subject, and he is not optimistic. 'I firmly predict,' he told me,

that within a few years many of these ventures will fail, that many of the young scientists who found these opportunities irresistable will be seeking re-entry into the universities. Lawyers and taxmen and marketing experts are going to dominate these companies and the scientists and engineers will have done their piece and be left behind.[23]

Even the much-heralded cheap pharmaceuticals could be just a dream. Jonathan King has no illusions:

The public is going to have to buy back what it itself financed. I will be very surprised if insulin comes out on the market – human insulin – at a price much lower than bovine or porcine insulin. And I'm willing to predict that it will come on the market at a higher price with the notion that it is something special: It's human; human insulin.[24]

Which will be fine for Eli Lilly and Genentech, but no real good for the rest of us.

10

RETHINKING

Recombinant DNA provides molecular biologists with some intellectual surprises

Towards the close of the 1960s, molecular biologists had a good deal to be pleased about. They had made enormous strides in understanding the complex processes that are the foundations of life, and they had a very clear picture of many parts of the subject. They knew the structure of DNA, how the helices coiled about one another and how that enabled them to reproduce. They knew how DNA is translated into RNA, and how the genetic message is taken from DNA to the ribosomes to direct the manufacture of the all-important proteins. They even knew the details of the code, the words that stored, as nucleotide triplets, the details of the amino acids along a protein. A big morale booster was discovering that the code appeared to be the same in all the forms of life looked at. Such a code, which seemed to be randomly organized in that there was no obvious logical connection between the nucleotide triplet and the specific amino acid, must have arisen by a lucky chance. That it was the same in all forms of life was powerful proof that all life had evolved by descent from a single origin, a single filament of life, as Charles Darwin's grandfather Erasmus called it.

But despite these accomplishments, and they were undeniably major ones, the molecular biologists were beginning to get restive. There was so much that they still did not understand, especially when it came to genes in organisms other than very simple pro-karyotes. How are genes controlled, switched on and off in an orderly sequence? What were the so-called tumour viruses about? Could their ability to alter the growth of a cell offer any clues to the way the cell normally controlled its own growth? How did the body manage to contain such vast flexibility of response in its immune system? These were, and remain, fascinating questions, and we are now a little closer to answers, but in the 1960s it seemed that such questions might prove intractable for a long time. Ways to handle the DNA with sufficient precision, to probe its workings and introduce the little perturbations that reveal so much about a smoothly working system, simply did not exist. The advent of restriction enzymes, with their exquisite ability to make just the cut you ask for in a piece of DNA, changed all that. Soon it was possible to manipulate DNA with an easy familiarity, reading genes, building new ones from scratch, shifting bits of genetic material around, and so on. And once those methods were commonplace, they could be used to attack some of the more unusual problems.

Some of the results we have already examined; the technology that has been applied in pursuit of the material goals we as a society set ourselves. These applications of science – rightly characterized as engineering rather than science – are valuable in the extreme, and as the engineers develop their craft the applications will become even more desirable. But in the first instance it was the science of molecular biology that benefited most from the skills of the genetic engineer. The techniques of recombinant DNA opened up whole new realms of molecular biology; for, unlike so many fields, the engineer in recombinant DNA is often also the basic research scientist, as pleased to push back the frontiers of knowledge for its own sake as to improve the human lot materially. The fruits of those endeavours will make the engineering easier in the future, just as they have in the past.

DNA from A to Z

James Watson and Francis Crick proposed their model for the structure of DNA as much because it was so simple and elegant as because they had the data to support it. The data they did have, so-called X-ray crystallographs, were the best available, but even they didn't permit the pair to deduce the position of the individual atoms that go to make up DNA. Instead, they had to be content with knowing the larger elements – the sugar, bases and phosphates – and putting these together in a way that satisfied the X-ray data but was even more satisfactory biologically. The double helix made sense. That is why it was so readily accepted.

Over the years, however, as the techniques to picture atomic structure improved, people turned again to DNA. They discovered that the Watson and Crick model didn't quite fit the data as well as it might. There were little inconsistencies here and there that were a trifle disconcerting. Three separate forms of DNA had been described, each stable under different conditions and each essentially a version of the same basic structure. The B form is the one Watson and Crick worked with. It is the form that DNA takes up when it is wettest, and the double helix is said to be relaxed. The helix is right-handed – looked at from one end, the chains spiral away clockwise, to the right – and the two helices run in opposite directions. The other forms, A and C, appear as the molecule dries out, and represent a sort of shrinking, with less space between the bases and a tighter pitch to the helix. The structures themselves seemed all right, but part of the problem was that DNA is not an easy molecule to crystallize, and hence it is very difficult to get good pictures of its atomic structure. The techniques developed in recombinant DNA research made it possible to approach the problem from a slightly different angle. Instead of extracting and purifying natural DNA, with all the vagaries that its variable structure introduces into the process of crystallization, why not build DNA to order, ensuring that it will crystallize accurately?

That was what Alexander Rich and his colleagues at Massachusetts Institute of Technology decided to do. Rich got two Dutch organic chemists to build him four-base stretches of deoxyguanine and deoxycytosine. He then crystallized these little segments, which, because they were complementary, would form perfect double-stranded DNA. Because all the bits of DNA were identical, they would form a very regular crystal, one that would allow Rich to see the atomic structure. Growing the crystal and taking the X-ray pictures proved to be the easy bit, and Rich knew at once that he had the information to solve the structure very accurately. Doing it was another matter. 'We were very excited,' he recalled, 'but it was not an easy structure to solve. It took us 1 ½ years to solve it, and when the structure came out it took us a long time to believe what we were seeing.'[1] The reason is that they were seeing a DNA molecule that coiled the wrong way: it was left-handed (see figure 10.1).

The backbone of the molecule, instead of winding smoothly round as it did in normal DNA, zig-zagged back and forth down the helix. Because of this, and because the structure was so unlike the A, B and C forms, Rich called it Z DNA. What was it for? Rich refused to believe that this was a structure without a function, but first he had to convince skeptics that it was indeed a structure that could be found in nature. It could be detected in solution, as well as in the crystal, which was one point in Rich's favour. But the

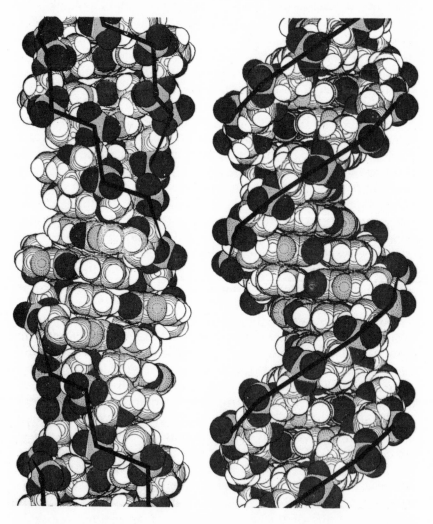

Figure 10.1
Left-handed Z DNA and right-handed DNA. (*From Kolata, G., Z-DNA: from the crystal to the fly,* Science, *214: 1108–10, 1981. Copyright 1981 by the American Association for the Advancement of Science. Courtesy Alexander Rich*)

solutions had to have a very high concentration of salt, and it seemed that, as the amount of salt was increased, the customary B form suddenly flipped and shuffled and rearranged itself into the Z form. An encouraging finding was that the cytosine–guanine polymer would form Z DNA at a normal salt concentration, provided that the bases were methylated. Aside from pointing the way to finding Z DNA in nature, this also hinted at a function. Eukaryotes seem to control genes to some extent by methylating GC pairs. Z DNA seemed to be more stable with methylated bases; 'this suggested,' said Rich, 'that Z DNA is involved in gene regulation. It was not so obvious, however, how to find Z DNA in biological systems.'[2]

The answer was to use antibodies. Normal B DNA doesn't stimulate the immune system at all, probably because there is so much of it around from birth. But, perhaps because it is rarer, Z DNA turned out to be a potent antigen, and with the known antibody Rich could go looking for the same antibodies in nature. He found them in mice suffering from an autoimmune disease called lupus, in which the immune system goes haywire and turns upon its host. There were no antibodies to Z DNA in undiseased mice. Best of all, Rich attached a fluorescent probe to the antibody and then bathed giant chromosomes from the salivary gland of the fruitfly with the probe. The giant chromosomes are composed of thousands of identical strands of DNA lined up together, and the structure of the DNA is mirrored in a pattern of dark and light bands along the length of the giant chromosome. To Rich's delight, the fluorescent probe glowed forth from the light interbands. Geneticists have long speculated that the banding of the giant chromosomes has something to do with the regulation of genes. Rich's discovery strengthens this idea, but there is still a great deal of mystery surrounding DNA and how it works.

Just supposing Z DNA is important in controlling which genes are expressed and which silenced, the question of how exactly it accomplishes this remains unanswered. There are hints, like the fact that Z DNA allows the double helix to become supercoiled a lot more easily than the normal B form, and it seems that supercoiling, which is essential to pack the metres of DNA into a single cell, is vitally important to the business of gene regulation. The bits to be transcribed into messenger RNA must be accessible to the polymerizing enzymes, and so the tight coils must be relaxed.

Perhaps Z DNA permits this access to the bases of the genetic code. There are further hints that, under the right conditions, B DNA can suddenly switch into Z DNA, and vice versa. That too could assist with gene control. All in all, the simple Watson–Crick double helix, with its theoretically elegant mechanism for allowing DNA to fulfil that primary requirement of life – replication – is turning out to contain a lot more secrets yet. The ability to read and synthesize chunks of DNA is vital in revealing those secrets. But revelations of the structure of DNA are as nothing compared with the revelations of the structure of the gene.

Genes in pieces

James Watson opened his account of their discovery of the double helix with the words 'I have never seen Francis Crick in a modest mood.'[3] But Crick himself is indeed modest about a radical change in perception that has swept through molecular biology in the past couple of years: although it has completely overturned everyone's way of thinking about genes, he insists on calling it ' a *mini*-revolution in molecular genetics'.[4] The change was occasioned by the discovery that genes are not the simple long stretches of DNA they were originally thought to be. A single gene may be split into as many as seven or eight pieces, separated by lengths of DNA that apparently carry no genetic message. In the molecular biologists' favoured subject, *E. coli*, this is not the case, but it does seem to be true not only of the eukaryote cells of 'higher' organisms, but also of the lowly viruses that infect those cells. Sensible genetic messages routinely alternate with utter nonsense. And the discovery that this was so Crick describes as 'almost as surprising as if you were reading, say, a novel by Jane Austen and in the middle of a paragraph you found a rather garbled version of an advertisement for deodorant'.[5] The machinery of the cell not only reads this frightful mélange, but accurately snips out the offending deodorant adverts to leave an impeccable copy of Austen. Which bits of that machinery do the editing, and how, are still puzzles, as are the reasons for the existence of these portions of intruding DNA, but the explanations we have so far do a good job of accounting for the facts.

Those facts accumulated slowly, partly because the work with

E. coli had seemed so elegant, so cut and dried, that it seemed pointless to look elsewhere. The transmission of the hereditary messages from gene to mRNA to protein looked like the kind of simple system that one could believe in. And the essential continuity of life tempted people to think that what was true of a bacterium would be equally true of a blue whale. But anomalies began to surface. For one thing, there seems to be vastly too much DNA in the eukaryote genome. Humans, for example, pack about 5000 million base-pairs – 1.7 metres – of DNA into each cell. If the average gene is somewhere between 1000 and 4000 nucleotides long, and if it takes 10 000 genes to run the human body, that is only a hundredth of the DNA present in the cell. Even if there are 100 000 genes, that would still leave more than 90 per cent of the genome unaccounted for. Why would a cell waste its resources copying and taking care of vast amounts of DNA with no obvious function?

Then again, RNA too seems overabundant. Great long strands, longer by far than any messenger RNA, were discovered in the nucleus. What were they? Shorter mRNAs had a head and tail exactly like the long so-called heterogeneous–nuclear RNAs (hnRNAs). Did that mean that the messengers were somehow created from the hnRNA by snipping out bits and splicing the remains, including head and tail, together? Different types of mRNAs had identical heads and tails. Did this signify that each was spliced out of the same long molecule of hnRNA by making the joins at different places?

By early 1977 there were lots of similar questions around, but few answers. Then Phillip Sharp and his group at MIT mixed mRNA for the hexon protein of an adenovirus (which causes a respiratory infection in humans) with restriction fragments of the viral DNA, hoping to locate the genes on the viral genome. Heteroduplexes between RNA and DNA formed and could be clearly seen in electron micrographs, but so could something else: a small tail at the end of the mRNA, which did not hybridize to the DNA. This was very strange. It showed up over and over, so it was not an experimental error, but if the tail was part of the message for hexon, why would it not join to the genetic code for hexon? Richard Roberts's team at Cold Spring Harbor had found the same sort of tail, and both groups decided to see whether the tail might attach to some other portion of the viral genome. It did: the little tail bound nicely to a stretch of DNA far upsteam from the main hexon gene. That meant that the mRNA was not a simple one-for-one copy of the DNA. Genes apparently came in segments, and those segments were somehow brought together into a functioning piece of mRNA.

The two groups, Sharp's and Roberts's, presented their icnoclastic results to one of the renowned Cold Spring Harbor symposia that summer; the audience found its perception of the nature of the gene irrevocably changed. 'Just doing the experiments meant admitting to a brand of heresy,' Sharp confesses. 'Nothing like it had ever been seen in prokaryotes.'[6] And Joe Sambrook, a Cold Spring Harbor researcher, reported in *Nature* that 'the audience was amazed, fascinated, and not a little bewildered' by the revelations.[7] When the messenger was annealed to a longer fragment of DNA the picture became a little clearer. Three loops of single-stranded DNA streamed away from the mRNA–DNA hybrid. Those loops were intervening sequences, inserts of DNA that did not appear in the finished messenger. (They are the reason that Crick's dream, back in the 1950s, of a Rosetta Stone that would enable him to crack the genetic code with ease would have come to nought. Without knowing the code, he could never have become aware that there were indeed intervening sequences on the DNA.) Where had the messenger come from? It *was* an edited version of the heterogeneous–nuclear RNA, now called the 'primary transcript', from which the intervening sequences had been neatly excised.

The anomalies were beginning to seem less anomalous. The superabundant DNA was, at least partially, composed of intervening sequences, and the hnRNA too was superabundant because it, rather than the messenger, was the faithful base-for-base transcript of the genetic code. Split genes began to turn up elsewhere too, first in other mammalian viruses but then in the mammals themselves. Philip Leder at the NIH outside Washington found them in the globin genes of mice, and in the UK Richard Flavell found them in rabbit globin genes. From there, they turned up everywhere. Insulin and other hormones, albumins, immunoglobulins, other globins – the genes for all of them contained their intervening sequences. The gene for α-collagen is the current leader, with 52 separate coding sequences. Only the histone and interferon genes seem to be in a single piece.

A problem of naming arose, as it so often does. Wally Gilbert called the parts that wind up as protein, the expressed minigenes, 'exons'. The inserts, then, were 'introns'. This is in keeping with the old tradition in molecular genetics of calling single words 'codons', single genes 'cistrons' and functional groups of cistrons 'operons'. (There were also mutons (single nucleotides) and recons (adjacent pairs of nucleotides), but these have fallen out of favour.)

Not everyone is happy with Gilbert's neologisms, though, not least because it is hard to remember whether 'ex' stands for 'expressed' or 'excised'; and many prefer to distinguish 'intervening' and 'encoding' sequences, or 'excised' and 'conserved' fragments. The naming of 'introns' and 'exons' becomes particularly hard to defend in the case of certain viral genomes; these masterpieces of tight packing have regions of the DNA that are excised when building one sort of message and conserved when building another. Are they introns, or exons? As a headline writer put it, 'one gene's intron is another gene's exon'.[8] And the same gene can apparently be spliced according to more than one set of signals. One version of human growth hormone mRNA produces a hormone that enhances growth but does not affect the metabolism of carbohydrates. A different version, 10 per cent bigger but spliced out of the same primary transcript, alters growth and carbohydrate metabolism. Presumably the larger mRNA includes an extra exon that is an intron in the smaller. What is one to do? It makes more sense to think in functional rather than misleadingly descriptive terms.

How and why

Two outstanding problems of split genes remain. How is the primary transcript edited and spliced, and what is the evolutionary significance of this bizarre arrangement?

Paul Berg puts the problem very succinctly. 'How,' he asks, 'does a system recognize a nucleotide at point A and another at point B some five or seven thousand bases away, bring the two together, break the chemical links and join the adjacent sequences – all with such high precision that the reading frame is maintained?'[9] The obvious editor would be a set of complementary bases at either end of the intervening sequence. These could then seek one another out, pair up, and form a hairpin loop that could easily be cut out.

Given the rapid sequencing methods that had been developed, it wasn't long before a number of transitions between coding and intervening sequences had been read in detail, but no such complementary sites could be found. But, then, nor were the transition sites totally random. The sequences seemed to be related to two so-called consensus sequences, with a GT doublet at the start of the splice and an AG at the end. These suggested an alternative method for splicing out the intervening sequence: a small RNA molecule attaches to the splicing enzyme and pairs with the bases at either end of the intervening sequence. The RNA would thus bring the two exons together and hold them in position while the splicing enzyme cuts the intron out and joins the two exons together (see figure 10.2). RNAs with the right sequences to match some introns have been discovered, which lends credence to this idea. So far, it has proved very difficult to make a splicing system work reliably in the test-tube. But it will be done, and when it is we may learn how the cell does this astounding trick. Why is another matter.

Theories abound, but few are totally satisfactory. In some genes, such as the globins and the immunoglobulins, the introns mark out functional regions of the protein. That is, the stretches coded by each exon correspond to a part of the molecule that plays some particular function. In globins, the part of the molecule that latches on to the oxygen-bearing haem group is clearly delineated from the other amino acid stretches by introns, and in the genes for antibodies the separation is very precise indeed. The effect of the intervening sequences in the antibody genes is absolutely clear: they allow cells to assemble the parts of an antibody into functional wholes, offering permutations between the existing antibody minigenes that vastly increase the flexibility of the system. And that flexibility has suggested to some people that in general intervening sequences permit more rapid, and more effective, evolution of the genes.

The argument is that the intervening sequences would allow bits of protein to be shuffled around, so that one might make a new enzyme by taking part of one and the rest of another and putting them together. In essence, then, split genes speed evolution along. One champion of this view is Wally Gilbert, who points out that with split genes 'evolution can seek new solutions without destroying the old. . . . Since the gene is spread out over a larger region of DNA, recombination . . . should be enhanced.'[10] Philip Leder

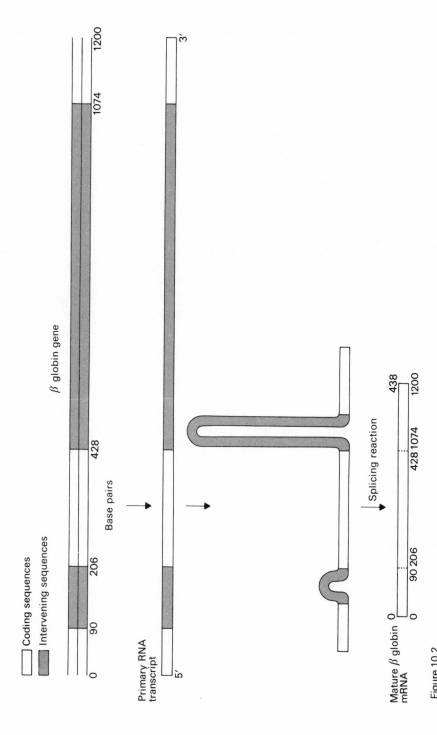

Figure 10.2
RNA processing. The primary transcript must be accurately spliced to remove the intervening sequences before the mature messenger RNA can direct protein synthesis.

takes an almost diametrically opposed view. He sees intervening sequences as biological brakes that retard recombination and act as stabilizers to prevent change. In Leder's scheme of things, because there are long nonsense stretches between the important bits of genes, crossing over between the two chromosomes during sexual reproduction is less likely to break into the middle of a gene and destroy it. Changes are more likely to be dumped into the nonsense zones, where they will do less harm. The fact that recombination is more likely to occur in an intervening sequence than in a coding sequence means that the functional gene is likely to be preserved. But he isn't sure that the argument will ever be resolved. 'Chances are it may never be, since evolutionary arguments can't be proven conclusively one way or the other,' says Leder. 'Intervening sequences may have arisen for reasons that will forever remain obscure.'[11] And to make matters worse, some of the intervening sequences act as special signals, which allow bits of the genome to be bodily snipped out and moved to another location entirely. Antibody genes are rearranged in this fashion before they are even transcribed into RNA, yet another source of flexibility in the immune system.

Split genes could have other uses too. One very appealling idea is that the snipped-out intervening sequence acts as a signal to another part of the genome. It would then be, in effect, a message that gene A has been transcribed and processed so now it is time to transcribe gene B. Globin proteins are ideal candidates for this sort of system. Paul Berg is very keen on this idea for split genes, and has apparently bet Francis Crick a case of wine on the outcome of experiments Berg is doing to test it.

There are, as Gilbert and Leder and Berg possibly realize, two entirely separate problems in thinking about split genes. One is how they began; what evolutionary benefit allowed the first split gene, the first intervening sequence, to spread. The second is why they continue; what benefit they confer now that they have spread. Origins and maintenance may be related, but as Leder notes they need not be.

Some of the 'explanations' of all that excess DNA are woolly-minded in the extreme. It is 'selfish', the ultimate parasite actively copying itself at the expense of the rest of the genome. It is 'ignorant', being copied willy-nilly even though it confers no benefit on the genome, but not actively promoting its own replication. It speeds evolution. It slows evolution down. It provides for future evolution. It is a remnant of past evolution. Different aspects of the question will obviously call for different answers, and more than one account may be appropriate; but it is a shame that in their search for solutions molecular biologists are so often hampered by their ignorance of evolution and natural selection. This is all the more ironic because they are exceedingly familiar with the base substance of evolution. A gathering of molecular biologists, convened to discuss evolutionary aspects of genome organization at a conference in Cambridge in the summer of 1981, looked a little sheepish as one of the top thinkers in evolution, John Maynard Smith, told them what he thought of their theorizing. Very gently, he intimated that much of it was not up to scratch, that they might be going astray. Peering through his pebble-thick spectacles, he reminded the molecular biologists that 'people have been thinking about evolution for a long time, and some of their conclusions may be worthy of attention'.[12] As the science continues to illuminate split genes, genuine evolutionary answers may become more apparent. But there is another – not the last, I'm sure – conundrum that split genes have set us.

Mitochondria are the little sausage-shaped bodies inside every eukaryote cell and they provide the cell with energy. Plants have similar bodies called chloroplasts, which trap the energy of sunlight and store it as chemical bonds in food. Mitochondria and chloroplasts both have their own independent supply of DNA that codes for some of the proteins they need. Partly because of this, and the fact that they divide in two like simple bacteria, it has been suggested that they are indeed the descendants of bacteria that took up a sort of shared life inside other cells, offering a supply of energy in exchange for a safe place to live. The evidence in favour is quite impressive, but gene structure poses a problem. No present-day bacteria have split genes, but some mitochondria do. Does this mean that the little organelles have not evolved from a bacterial ancestor? In truth we don't know. It could be that some bacteria long ago did have split genes, and they are the primitive mitochondria. Or, indeed, there may be bacteria around today whose genes are split. We haven't looked at very many. Some viruses have split genes, and take advantage of the host cell's splicing apparatus; perhaps the primitive mitochondria developed split genes because it made them more efficient in a cell that was already using split genes. And while the DNA of yeast mitochondria is very split indeed, the human mitochondrial genome seems to contain no intervening sequences at all. The yeast mitochondrial DNA is five times longer than the human, but seems to contain no more genetic information. Why is this so? Questions, more questions, as the science behind genetic engineering probes the very basis of life.

Not so universal a code

Left-handed DNA and bits of genes scattered through the genome. Genes that jump from place to place. Is nothing sacred? The answer is no; for other studies of mitochondria have revealed that not even that most holy dogma, the universal genetic code, is entirely correct. There are nucleotide triplets that code for a different amino acid when they are in a mitochondrial gene than when they are in a nuclear gene. The differences are not huge, it is true, and seem to be restricted to the top codons and just a few others. The most common stop signal in nuclear mRNA is UAA; mitochondria save a few bases by using a single U as a stop signal, relying on the fact that RNA always has a small chain of A's, the poly-A tail, added to the end of the molecule. They also have different stop signs; AGA and AGG mean 'stop' in the mitochondria but 'arginine' in the nuclear DNA. The triplet AUA codes for isoleucine in nuclear DNA and methionine in the mitochondria. The small differences in the code we can, perhaps with difficulty, accept; mitochondria manufacture their own transfer RNAs to bring the correct amino acids along to the growing protein chain, and these simply interpret some codons differently from conventional tRNAs. But it seems that the code in human mitochondria differs not only from the human nuclear genetic code but also from the yeast mitochondrial code. For example, AUA codes for isoleucine in nuclear DNA, and in the yeast mitochondria, but in the human mitochondria it specifies, as mentioned, methionine; this is proving altogether more difficult to understand.

A final enigma concerns the tRNAs themselves. The nuclear genetic code requires a minimum of 32 different sorts of tRNA to recognize every possible codon. The reason it is not 64 is that the third position of the tRNA anticodon can, in the words of Francis Crick's celebrated theory, 'wobble'. It can pair with a non-complementary base, according to specified rules. But the mitochondrial genome seems to use only 22 different tRNAs, just two more than are needed for the 20 amino acids, and more or less to ignore the third letter of the codon. There are other tRNAs that apparently recognize a four-letter codon; they would be extremely valuable in undoing the harmful effects of some mutations. 'Mitochondriacs', as they sometimes call themselves, have many a mystery still to solve.

11

OUTLOOK

What does the future hold?

Looking back over this historical development of molecular biology, one thing is clear; the future of the subject has always been unpredictable. Some advances, it is true, have been the result of a long, well-planned and sustained campaign, but right from the very beginning happenstance has played its part. That makes it extremely difficult to predict future developments with any degree of certainty. One can make a vague generalization – say, that biologists will gain a deeper understanding of the fundamental process of gene regulation and control – and be confident that the prediction will come true. But when it comes to specific forecasts, and especially when one attachs time to those predictions, one is liable to go very awry.

Medicine

The speed of advance within genetic engineering bears this out. Back at the start, in the early 1970s, people confidently predicted unlimited supplies of human insulin. Even the most optimistic were probably surprised by the speed with which this came partly true, not just for insulin but for the other hormones too. When the laboratory results burst upon a waiting world, further predictions had to be made of when those products would become available on a wide scale. They proved themselves wildly optimistic. At present, no genetically engineered therapeutic product for people is available on the open market anywhere. There are services and products to assist the genetic engineer, but nothing for the man in the street. So, with the pitfalls of soothsaying firmly in mind, what can we expect of recombinant DNA in the future?

I suspect that medical advances are what most people would like to see, and those there will undoubtedly be. The products already engineered will find their way on to the market before too long, and in the near future we will see all manner of extensions to this work. Other hormones will join the list of those already cloned, making it possible to treat the entire spectrum of disease due to hormonal imbalance. These are, of course, still treatments rather than cures, but they would nevertheless be an enormous benefit. How much better, though, to provide genuine replacement therapy. Diabetes, to take a simple example, may well be due in some cases to a mutated insulin gene; if that gene could somehow be replaced with the correct version it would make the diabetic's life entirely normal. Replacement needn't even be in the pancreas. It might be possible to create a new 'pancreas' elsewhere in the body, by taking out some of the patient's cells, giving them a good copy of all the genes needed to control insulin secretion, growing them up into a small organ, and then implanting this new organ where it can go to work. And in those cases where the insulin genes seem to be all right but the control mechanism is wrong, genetic engineers might be able to tinker with the DNA so as to fix the control mechanism and bring insulin production back to normal. Bearing in mind that every cell contains every gene, the engineers might find it more convenient to work somewhere else, say in a bit of abdominal muscle, switching on the insulin genes that are present there and creating a new sugar-controlling organ completely independent of the faulty pancreas.

This sort of replacement therapy – replacing the gene itself rather than its product – has already been tried; Martin Cline would be a hero now if his experiments with thalassaemia had succeeded. But the obstacles are formidable. You have not only to insert the correct gene, but also to make sure that all the controlling sequences that regulate the expression of that gene are there too, and you have to get the package into enough cells to make a difference. Cline has shown that it can be done, and teams of scientists all over the world are exerting themselves in an effort to improve the technology of gene replacement. Already they have pushed Cline's results further, obtaining transfer between rabbit and mouse, for example, and good expression of the foreign gene in its new host. Some, by transferring the genes into the developing eggs, have managed to get the new genes into every cell in the mouse, including the sex cells; those mice have fathered offspring who also contain the foreign gene. Now that really would provide a cure! Normally the sex cells are kept strictly distinct from the cells of the body. One could treat someone with a genetic defect, say sickle cell anaemia, by giving a new globin gene to the bone marrow cells, but the sex cells would still carry the defective sickle cell gene. One day it might be possible to replace the gene even in the sex cells, so that the disease would not be passed on to unborn generations of children.

With advanced gene replacement therapy, all manner of diseases might come under beneficial control. Down's Syndrome is caused by an extra chromosome, a third copy of chromosome number 21. Might it be possible in the future to switch that extra copy off without affecting the other two, so that the Down's child is effectively restored to normal? Would this need to be done before birth? Or might it be better to find out exactly why the third chromosome causes the changes it does and then seek to neutralize those changes, rather than switching off the whole chromosome? The possibilities are enormous, not just for Down's Syndrome but for a whole host of what were once called inborn errors of metabolism. Genetic engineering should also make it possible to discover more about diseases that seem to have a hereditary component, but one that is not quite as simple as we would like.

Doctors in California recently discovered an unusual protein in the brain of certain people. It was similar, but not identical, to one of the proteins used to carry messages between brain cells. It looks, on the surface, like a mutant version of the normal transmitter protein. Those patients suffered a wide spectrum of diseases, including multiple sclerosis, alcoholism, acute depression and schizophrenia, and the only unifying factor linking these disparate groups was that abnormal brain protein. Nobody has yet discovered whether the gene for that protein is defective, but it is a safe bet to assume that it is. And there are strong hints from other studies that severe depression, or melancholia as some people call it, also has a genetic component. That could mean that these intractable diseases would be amenable to genetic therapy, a replacement of the defective gene. Such therapy will probably mean tampering with the brain: do we really want to do that? Nor are these the only diseases that might succumb to advanced genetic engineering. Heart disease, stroke, high blood pressure, even susceptibility to cancer – all seem to have a genetic component, but it will surely be a very long time indeed before we can engineer genes to remove these scourges.

What about the plethora of other factors under genetic control? They may not be diseases, but we would be able to tamper with them just the same. Coupled with the explosive increase in test-tube baby know-how, genetic engineering has the potential to create a vast army of identical clones, each produced to some preset specification. Cannon fodder, scientists, opera singers – all could be manufactured to order if the effort that went into putting men on the moon were directed to this new form of exploration, and if we knew which, if any, genes, were involved – a much greater obstacle. The spectre of swarming hordes of clones, built to the whim of a deranged dictator, frightens; but actually it needn't. I doubt that it would ever be worthwhile as an exercise, even if it were possible, which is also in doubt. We are so profoundly ignorant of the ways in which the genome finally gets expressed in a working body that we couldn't even begin to alter the genome to order in any major way. Single genes, yes; but rewriting the blueprint to get a different sort of machine is likely to remain beyond us. We could grow a race of giants, say, by tinkering with growth hormones. This has already been done with sheep, who have been induced to manufacture antibodies to their own anti-growth hormone and thereby end up twice the size of their unaltered siblings. So we could engineer human giants tomorrow, and perhaps even clone them; but the prospect of genetically engineered mindless zombies, eager to do their master's bidding, doesn't worry me at all. The existing methods of brain-washing and mind control already do that and more, as the devastating effects of the new cults testify. With simple technologies like those at your disposal, why bother with genetic engineering? And, as Sir Peter Medawar pointed out, good old classical artificial selection could easily have done the job by now if anyone had wanted it done.

Cloning might have its place, though, in spare part surgery. The problem with transplants is that the immune system of the recipient tends to recognize the transplant as foreign and reject it. In extreme cases the healthy transplant can even turn on the host. The proteins that label cells as self or foreign are under the control of a special set of genes, and molecular biologists are working very hard on the immune system and its genes. They may in the future be able to overcome some of the problems of rejection by tailoring the transplant so that it produces the same antigens as the host and so is completely disguised. Another route would be to create a clone for everyone, remove its brain, and keep it in suspended animation as a source of spare parts. A transplant from a donor of this sort would be like a graft between identical twins, with no fear of rejection. But the expense of keeping a vegetable clone alive just in case you might need its parts one day would almost certainly be prohibitive.

Limitless organ transplants call up another spectre, that of immortality. Nobody knows exactly why cells, and ultimately the bodies they constitute, die, but it seems that there is an accumulation of genetic errors such that the biochemical machinery progressively becomes more and more inefficient. Eventually part of it packs up – death. Different creatures have different lifespans – the mouse lives at most three years, while the bat can survive for twenty or more – and it seems that the longer-lived bat has much more efficient DNA repair enzymes than the more ephemeral mouse. Man is already pretty long-lived, compared with other animals of our size, but as the repair enzymes must be under genetic control, there is the possibility of engineering those genes to provide even more efficient repair and even longer life.

At the other end of our allotted span is the astounding process of embryonic growth, from a single fertilized cell to a perfectly formed human baby in nine months. Alas, sometimes it isn't so perfect. The question then is, what to do? There are a number of interrelated problems here. One is the question of diagnosis. The sooner parents and doctors know that there is something wrong with a developing embryo, the sooner they can do something about it. That something might be therapy of a sort, though that possibility seems now to be pretty remote for most problems; or it might be an abortion. Either way, the quicker the information is available, the better. Genetic engineering is already helping here, with improved diagnostic tests for detecting genetic diseases. Some are based on monoclonal antibodies to specific products associated only with the disease. Others might involve making a hybrid between the embryo's DNA and a specific probe that would seek out a particular gene. Already probes for abnormal haemoglobin genes, such as thalassaemia, are well advanced. An important point here is that prenatal diagnosis is not a step on the path to unlimited abortion. There are of course cases in which the sensible decision is indeed a therapeutic abortion – therapeutic for the mother. But at present some 95 per cent of tests conducted on an embryo have a favourable outcome. The baby is perfectly normal and the parents can be reassured. The more efficient this process can be made, the more likely people are to avail themselves of it and the fewer unwanted babies will be born.

Diseases caused, directly or indirectly, by faulty genes are thus an obvious target for genetic engineers. Another is in the fight against other more conventional diseases, those caused by pathogens. There are already genetically engineered vaccines undergoing trials, and these should provide vastly increased protection against a whole range of diseases in the future. Evidence that some cancers are caused by viral attack is growing; might we one day be vaccinated against cancer? Monoclonal antibodies will almost certainly make it possible to create vaccines against diseases that were previously recalcitrant in the extreme, and if the economic savings that can be obtained from biotechnology are passed on to the customers, there could be a substantial increase in public health even for the poorest countries. The feedback then might stagger even the most optimistic demographer; for if people knew that their children were not likely to be stolen from them by disease they might be much more willing to limit family size. Genetically engineered protection against disease could thus solve a multitude of problems. Genetically engineered approaches to contraception – whether monoclonal antibodies to the sex hormones, a vaccine against foetal proteins or some other interference – will play their part too.

New drugs, too, might come out of genetic engineering – not just new versions of old drugs, but entirely new products quite unseen in nature. Biogen has already tinkered with the various interferon molecules, each with its own properties, to produce new hybrid interferons, 'some of which,' according to one report, 'were significantly more effective in biological tests than the natural antiviral proteins'.[11] Doctors in Cambridge are growing monoclonal antibodies that recognize tumour cells. These may one day be useful to diagnose cancers, but for the immediate present the doctors intend to use them as delivery vehicles for very toxic drugs. The drug will be attached to the antibody, which will carry it to cancer cells and only cancer cells. Because the drug is targetted on the cancer cells, the doctors can use a lower dose over all and so reduce the risk of harming perfectly normal cells while still killing the tumour. These hybrids, between a molecule that will carry a payload to a particular organ and a payload that will do a specific job on that organ, are likely to be a very promising avenue to explore.

Drugs will also be engineered in a slightly different way. The original penicillin was pretty puny compared with the versions available today. Not only has the mould that produces the raw material been selected to manufacture thousands of times more penicillin, but the chemists have learned how to alter the molecule to make it more effective against bacteria. Tacking on different chemical groups to make so-called analogues can affect, for example, the speed at which the drug is broken down by enzymes. If it lasts longer, it will work better, and all manner of drugs have been tailored by chemists in this way to make them more efficient. With genetic engineering, the possibility arises of tampering not with the molecule but with the blueprint for that molecule, so that the cell synthesizes an analogue and no further treatment is needed.

One can even imagine the ultimate in analogue production, a system that builds unnatural amino acids into a protein. The 20 amino acids used in life are all very well, but sometimes changing a couple of amino acids in a protein will enhance the efficiency of, say, a hormone. At the moment this has to be done chemically, because living systems can use only the words in the genetic code, and that means the 20 vital amino acids. But it might in future be possible to rewrite the genetic code, create transfer RNAs that will carry unnatural amino acids, and slot them into the correct place on an engineered RNA message, transcribed from an engineered gene. The cell itself would then be building a totally novel protein with tools you have supplied, to instructions you have written. What sorts of things might be made this way I have no idea, but I'm sure the organic chemists have a few ideas they would like to try.

As far as meddling with vital processes goes, the potential for genetic engineering is limitless. Diseases, whether caused by faulty genes or pathogens, will be brought under better control, and a whole spectrum of life-enhancing procedures will probably become commonplace. But there is more to life than health. All the health in the world is no good unless one also has food to eat.

Woolly jumpers

Medical advances notwithstanding, nowhere is the impact of genetic engineering likely to be more keenly felt than in agriculture. We have already used artificial selection to alter crops and livestock so that they give us more of what we want – pigs that are long and lean for bacon, bulls that turn feed into meat at a rate that is hard to believe, chickens that lay more eggs in a lifetime than their ancestors could ever have imagined. Maize and other cereals could never have evolved in the wild, because one of their most important properties from our point of view is that the seeds stay attached to the ear. In nature, this would be a recipe for disaster, with no seeds being spread to new areas. All these, and the other living things we have modified to suit our needs, have been achieved through artifical selection of the varieties we want. We still rely on nature, occasionally abetted by X-rays and the like, to throw up the varieties, and while we may try to encourage certain traits we cannot tailor crops or plants to order. At least we couldn't, until now.

Dr Ronald Wetzel, a senior scientist at Genentech, has this to say on the subject:

Experiments in which two organisms from *different* species are interbred to generate an unusual juxtaposition of properties have until now been confined to the eugenic riddles popular with children. What do you get when you cross eugenics with recombinant DNA technology? Answer: the ability to generate new organisms by transferring genetic traits without regard to species barriers to reproduction.[2]

That means taking the properties you want from wherever they may be, and putting them where you want them. Insulin shifted from a human pancreas to a gut bacterium is one example, but in agriculture and the chemical industry there are many more opportunities.

Already there are attempts to give plants new abilities, although the difficulties are formidable. The cellulose wall that surrounds every plant cell makes it very difficult to insert plain DNA as you can with bacteria. Techniques to use naked plant cells, called protoplasts, have been developed, but then there is the problem of reconstituting a mature adult plant from the naked cell. It can be done, but at the moment it is still a tricky business.

Selection is another problem. With bacterial plasmids it is quite easy to ensure that there are markers that will enable you to find those cells that have taken up the recombinant molecules. With plant cells this is much more difficult, though again, it can and is being done.

Vectors are a bit of a problem too; plants suffer their fair share of viruses, and some are being exploited to carry new genes into the cells. Most fascinating, there is a set of bacteria that cause plant tumours. Crown gall is one, and another is hair root disease. The bacteria that cause these diseases harbour so-called tumour-inducing, or Ti, plasmids, which have the very useful property of inserting their DNA into the plant's chromosomal DNA. Genes can be put into the Ti plasmid of one of these bacteria and the engineered bacterium used to infect a plant. The bacterium does all the hard work, of penetrating the cell wall and ensuring that its Ti plasmid is inserted into the plant's DNA; all that remains for the engineer is to ensure that the DNA he has given the plant will do what he wants it to. Techniques for plant genetic engineering may still be in their infancy, but much has already been achieved.

Plants need nitrogen to make proteins, but they cannot use the most abundant source of nitrogen, the air. They have to get nitrogen in other forms from the soil. Legumes, however, have a special association with certain bacteria: the bacteria *can* incorporate atmospheric nitrogen into compounds that the plant can use, and because of the nitrogen-fixing bacteria legumes need less nitrogen fertilizer. The green revolution, with its new high-yield strains of wheat, was a dismal failure because the high yield could be achieved only if the plants were fed copious quantities of fertilizer; in poor lands the soil too is often poor, and fertilizer is expensive. If the wheats had been able to harbour nitrogen-fixing bacteria, the story might have been different, and I am sure we will see this sort of development in the not too distant future. Legumes are not perfect, either. Even with its bacterial friends, soya often does not put as much protein as it could into its beans. Given extra nitrogen, it can make extra protein. But rather than adding external nitrogen, it might be possible to engineer the bacteria so that they become even more efficient at what they are already doing so well.

Another tack might be to alter the photosynthetic pathway, by which the energy in sunlight becomes trapped in the chemical energy of foods. Some plants, sugar cane for example, are much more efficient than others. How fine it would be if the genetic engineers could extract the efficient genes from sugar cane and insert them into crops such as wheat and rice. The combination of nitrogen-fixing bacteria and a more efficient photosynthetic apparatus could solve many of the world's food problems.

The most exciting agricultural application of genetic engineering, to my mind, is the work on seed storage proteins. These are the compounds that the thrifty parent plant is laying aside to give its offspring a better chance in the world. We have subverted them for our own use, but there is a problem in that. As human beings, we can make some amino acids from other raw materials, but there remains a group of amino acids that we cannot manufacture and that we must eat in our food. Lysine is one of these essential amino acids. Unfortunately for us, cereals don't seem all that keen on lysine, and the seed storage proteins of cereals, notably one called zein, are, from the human point of view, deficient in lysine. Ordinarily this doesn't matter much. Nutritionist and cook Colin Tudge explain why: 'One of nature's many serendipities, which almost tempts me to believe in her beneficence, [is that] the pulses, including the beans, are rich in lysine, and if pulse and cereal are eaten together, then the surplus in the former largely makes good the deficiency in the latter.' Tudge goes on to point out that 'pulses and cereals commonly occur together in all the world's great cuisines: beans and tortillas in Mexico; rice or chapatis and dhal in India; rice and bean curd in China; and beans on toast in Britain.'[3] Far be it for me to suggest that they might in so doing diminish the world's cuisines, but the genetic engineers could rectify the basic problem by adjusting the gene for zein so that it puts a few more lysines into the storage protein. The resultant food might be boring, but it would keep people alive.

On the animal side, it is hard to see what further improvements could be made on the already distorted animals we husband. Disease control is important, and is already succumbing to recombinant DNA. The first commercially available vaccine from genetic engineering protects pigs and cattle against scour, an intestinal disease caused, appropriately, by *Escherichia coli*. Food conversion too could be made more efficient, again by adjusting the enzymes involved, so that it took less feed to make the same amount of meat. Perhaps one could think about engineering entirely new forms of meat, a vast organ culture of immortal muscle cells supplied with a steady stream of crude nutrients (perhaps from other engineered cells) and harvested by hacking off a slab. Would the effort be worthwhile, though, or might we do better to improve our existing methods of husbandry so that they are more efficient and more humane? Would it be acceptable to engineer further docility into livestock? What about cutting out the middle man entirely, and engineering cattle or sheep with chloroplasts in their skin cells instead of mitochondria? That way we could simply leave the animals out in the sun with a supply of water and a few other nutrients. The chloroplasts would harness sunlight and the animal cells would convert that energy into meat. It sounds far-fetched, and it is, but it is not impossible that we will one day see green sheep dotted about a barren landscape. Or should we forget genetic engineering entirely and re-educate people away from the meat they regard as the *sine qua non* of the civilized material life? With better plant proteins, that might be more feasible.

Yet another alternative is that, instead of engineering the foodstuffs, we could engineer the people who eat them. If we can make plants and pigs more efficient, why not humans? We too have those enzyme systems, and if they are open to fixing in other creatures they are open to fixing in ourselves. The prospect may not be very appealing, but it could have its uses. A colony of space explorers, out to find new worlds to inhabit, would surely be more successful if the people were more efficient and needed less food. A combination of efficient foods and efficient eaters would stand a much better chance of survival.

All these suggestions may sound incredible. But already people have succeeded in some very fundamental manipulations of this sort. Bio-engineers at ICI have taken a gene from *E. coli* and given it to a different bug, *Methylophilus methylotrophus*. *M. methylotrophus* has the extremely useful property of being able to live on methanol, but it is not terribly efficient at it. With a gene from *E. coli* that helps it to make better use of ammonia as a source of nitrogen, *M. methylotrophus* becomes better at converting methanol into carbon, and hence a much better source of single-cell protein, which is what the endeavour is all about. The ICI engineers are quite clear about what they have achieved. 'The alteration we have made in *M. methylotrophus* could not have been achieved either by selection . . . or by a conventional mutagenic approach. It represents the planned adaptation of a microorganism to a man-made environment.'[4] *M. methylotrophus* already had the capability to use methanol; giving it the enzyme from *E. coli* only made it better. One could extend the abilities of microorganisms to do things we want them to but which they are not capable of.

Yeast is a potent source of alcohol, which it can make from almost any sugar or starch. The cellulose that makes up the bulk of plants is very similar to starch, but few animals possess the enzymes needed to break cellulose down into its sugar components. (That is why herbivores have to rely on other organisms – usually bacteria of some sort – to do the job for them, renting out stomach space as a living fermenter vessel.) If you could give yeasts cellulases to break down plant cell walls, you could feed them entire plants, rather than just the sugars. And with alcohol rapidly proving itself as a substitute for petrol in internal combustion engines, that would be a profound benefit.

For better and for worse

So far I have discussed largely the potential benefits of genetic engineering; like all science, however, recombinant DNA can be applied for good or evil. Without dwelling on the blacker side, it is clear that genetic engineering could be put to very bad uses indeed.

The one that springs to mind is biological warfare. This has the advantage that, because one is dealing with a living, reproducing system, one needs very little material to begin with. It would take tonnes of cyanide, for example, to poison even a small reservoir, but a litre of virulent *Salmonella* culture would do the job very nicely. Genetic engineering could be used in many ways to make weapons. Bugs more lethal than the ones we have already got would not be difficult to design. Professor Donald Louria, a senior executive at New Jersey Medical School, offers one suggestion, what he calls a two-pronged attack. He can foresee a bacterium with two mechanisms that would kill, and the unsuspecting use of antibiotics against one would enhance the potency of the other. He also predicts bacteria engineered to carry one of the poisons for which no antidote is known (and there are several) and being further designed to stick to the gut walls, delivering their poison to a very sensitive area. One remarkable poison that the professor mentions is a Russian fungus called *Fusarium sporotrichoides*; without any engineering, the toxin of this fungus remains lethal for six years and is not rendered harmless, as are so many poisons, by boiling. That, in a bacterium, would be a very powerful weapon indeed. Professor Louria thinks that without too much effort a terrorist group could manufacture a lethal biological weapon and introduce it into the drinking supply of a capital city. As the epidemic spread, suspicion that it was the work of a foreign power might lead to nuclear retaliation. 'I believe,' says Professor Louria, 'there are those among us on this planet who are so venal, so committed to achieving power, or simply so mentally warped that they would do exactly as I have outlined.'[5]

There are other routes too. Biological warfare against crops, rather than people, becomes a distinct possibility, with strains of pathogen tailored to the strains of food crop that the enemy is growing. Alternatively, one could use an organism that would never be suspected of being a weapon. Influenza periodically goes on the rampage when its antigenic coat proteins mutate to a new form that most people's immune system does not recognize. Imagine the consequences of deliberately changing the coat proteins of some other disease. This would have the added advantage that you would know what you had done, and could vaccinate your population accordingly, while the enemy would be slain. By a similar effort you could develop a new antibiotic and engineer a common bacterium to be resistant to it. Then, with a stockpile of the antibiotic, you would be safe in releasing the weapon over an enemy.

The potential for killing on an unprecedented scale undeniably exists in genetic engineering. How is that potential to be kept under control? Certainly not by agreements, pacts, treaties and so on; although these devices may do a little good, they certainly will not deter the determined biological warmonger, and the beauty of genetic engineering is that, compared with other forms of mass destruction, the capital costs are very low. One hopeful sign is that biological warfare has long been possible, but has remained unused. Genetic engineering may make it easier to employ, but the inherent horror may still prevent its use. Or has the reticence been due to fear of uncontrollability, a fear that properly engineered biological weapons could allay? Control must rest with the scientists, who have shown they are capable of policing themselves. They have also shown that they are human, open to the same pressures and temptations as other humans. MIT's Jonathan King points out that molecular biology is one of the few areas of research science that has not seen the fruits of its labours turned against humanity. We can only hope that it stays that way.

I began by saying that before the mushrooming of the new molecular biology scientists in the field were becoming restive. I portrayed them as frustrated by their inability to progress. But there was another side to it too, a boredom that sprang from what appeared to be entirely routine work. It was valuable, no doubt, but it was not exciting. James Watson captured the essence of this feeling when, in 1970, he wrote: 'There are times in every science when the outline of future progress seems predictable, straightforward and a little boring. Inevitably this leads many to wonder whether they are in the right field.'[6] I don't suppose anyone in molecular biology will feel that way again for quite a few years to come.

NOTES

1 Beginnings

1 Judson, H. F., *The Eighth Day of Creation*, Simon & Schuster, New York, 1979, p. 28.
2 Ibid., p. 29.
3 Ibid., p. 36.
4 See Watson, J. D., *The Double Helix*, Atheneum Publishers, New York, 1968. Judson (note 1) gives Crick's account.
5 Watson, J. D. and Crick, F. H. C., Molecular structure of nucleic acids: A structure for deoxyribose nucleic acid, *Nature*, 171: 737–8, 1953.
6 DuPraw, E. J., *DNA and Chromosomes*, Holt, Rinehart & Winston, New York, 1970.
7 As note 5, p. 738.
8 As note 1, p. 188.
9 Crick, F. H. C., Nucleic acids, in *Recombinant DNA*, ed. David Freifelder. W. H. Freeman, San Francisco, 1978, p. 8.
10 Fruton, J. S., *Molecules and Life: Historical Essays on the Interplay of Chemistry and Biology*, John Wiley-Interscience, New York, 1972, p. 170.
11 Sanger, F., letter to author, 19 October 1981.
12 Crick, F. H. C., The genetic code: III, in *Recombinant DNA*, ed. David Freifelder. W. H. Freeman, San Francisco, 1978, p. 22.

2 Restriction

1 Roberts, R. J., Restriction and modification enzymes and their recognition sequences, *Nucleic Acids Research*, 8: r63–r80, 1980.
2 Luria, Salvador E., The recognition of DNA in bacteria, in *Recombinant DNA*, ed. David Freifelder. W. H. Freeman, San Francisco, 1978.

3 Anderson, E. S. and Felix, A., Variation in Vi-phage II of *Salmonella typhi, Nature*, 170: 492–4, 1952.

4 Arber, W. and Dussoix, D., Host specificity of DNA produced by *Escherichia coli*. I. Host controlled modification of bacteriophage λ, *Journal of Molecular Biology*, 5: 18–36, 1962; Dussoix, D. and Arber, W., Host specificity of DNA produced by *Escherichia coli*. II. Control over acceptance of DNA from infecting phage λ̄, *Journal of Molecular Biology*, 5: 37–45, 1962.

5 Arber, W., Promotion and limitation of genetic exchange, *Science*, 205: 361–5, 1979, p. 363.

6 Meselson, M. and Yuan, R., DNA restriction enzyme from *E. coli. Nature*, 217: 1110–14, 1968.

7 Yuan, R., letter to author, 23 October 1981.

8 Yuan, R., The reaction mechanism of type I restriction endonucleases, in *Gene Amplification and Analysis*, vol. 1, ed. J. G. Chirikjian. Elsevier-North Holland, Amsterdam, 1981, p. 46.

9 As note 6, p. 1114.

10 Old, R. W. and Primrose, S. B., *Principles of Gene Manipulation*, University of California Press, Berkeley, 1980. p. 9.

11 Rosamond, J., Endlich, B. and Linn, S., Electron microscopic studies of the mechanism of action of the restriction endonuclease of *Escherichia coli* B, *Journal of Molecular Biology*, 129: 619–35, 1979.

12 Smith, H. O., Nucleotide sequence specificity of restriction endonucleases, *Science*, 205: 455–62, 1979, p. 456.

13 Smith, H. O. and Wilcox, K. W., A restriction enzyme from *Hemophilus influenzae*. I. Purification and general properties, *Journal of Molecular Biology*, 51: 379–91, 1970, p. 390.

14 Kelly, T. J. Jr and Smith, H. O., A restriction enzyme from *Hemophilus influenzae*. II. Base sequence of the recognition site, *Journal of Molecular Biology*, 51: 393–409, 1970, p. 399.

15 Ibid., p. 405.

16 As note 12, p. 455.

17 Danna, K. and Nathans, D., Specific cleavage of simian virus 40 DNA by restriction endonuclease of *Hemophilus influenzae*, *Proceedings of the National Academy of Sciences*, 68: 2913–17, 1971, p. 2916.

18 Sharp, P. A., Sugden, B. and Sambrook, J., Detection of two restriction endonuclease activities in *Haemophilus parainfluenzae* using analytical agarose-ethidium bromide electrophoresis, *Biochemistry*, 12: 3055–63, 1973, p. 3062.

19 Sharp, P. A., letter to author, 14 October 1981.

20 Sharp, P. A., This week's citation classic, *Current Contents Life Sciences*, 25 (3): 11, 1982.

21 Fuchs, C., Rosenvold, E. C., Honigman, A. and Szybalski, W.,

A simple method for identifying the palindromic sequences recognized by restriction endonucleases: the nucleotide sequence of the *Ava* II site, *Gene*, 4: 1–23, 1978.

22 As note 8, p. 4.
23 Roberts, R. J., letter to author, 8 October 1981.
24 Roberts, R. J., Restriction endonucleases, *CRC Critical Reviews in Biochemistry*, 4: 123–64, 1976.
25 As note 1, p. r75.
26 Old, R. W., letter to author, 8 October 1981.
27 As note 12, p. 458.
28 Burton, W. G., Grabowy, C. T. and Sager, R., Role of methylation in the modification and restriction of chloroplast DNA in *Chlamydomonas, Proceedings of the National Academy of Sciences*, 76: 1390–4, 1979.
29 As note 2, p. 58.

3 Tools

1 Quoted in Fruton, J. S., *Molecules and Life: Historical Essays on the Interplay of Chemistry and Biology*, John Wiley-Interscience, New York, 1972, p. 74.
2 Singer, M. F., Introduction and historical background, in *Genetic Engineering, volume 1: Principles and Methods*, ed. J. K. Setlow and A. Hollaender. Plenum, New York, 1979, pp. 2–3.
3 Ibid., pp. 7–8.
4 Quoted in Fruton (note 1), p. 259.
5 Temin, H. M., RNA-directed DNA synthesis, in *Recombinant DNA*, ed. David Freifelder. W. H. Freeman, San Francisco, 1978.
6 As note 2, p. 7.

4 Manipulation

1 Cohen, S. N., The manipulation of genes, in *Recombinant DNA*, ed. David Freifelder. W. H. Freeman, San Francisco, 1978, p. 113.
2 Press release, 14 October 1980, p. 2.
3 Quoted in Kolata, G. B., The 1980 Nobel prize in chemistry, *Science*, 210: 887–9, 1980, p. 887.
4 Berg, P., Dissections and reconstructions of genes and chromosomes, *Science*, 213: 296–303, 1981, p. 299.

5 Jackson, D. A., Symons, R. H. and Berg, P., Biochemical method for inserting new genetic information in DNA of simian virus 40: Circular SV40 DNA molecules containing lambda phage genes and the galactose operon of *Escherichia coli, Proceedings of the National Academy of Sciences*, 69: 2904–9, 1972, p. 2908.

6 The debate is covered in chapter 6, and in the form of what they call a documentary history in Watson, J. D. and Tooze, J., *The DNA Story*, Freeman, San Francisco, 1981.

7 Lobban, P. E. and Kaiser, A. D., Enzymatic end-to-end joining of DNA molecules, *Journal of Molecular Biology*, 78: 453–71, 1973.

8 Mertz, J. E. and Davis, R. W., Cleavage of DNA by RI restriction endonuclease generates cohesive ends, *Proceedings of the National Academy of Sciences*, 69: 3370–4, 1972, p. 3374.

9 Sgaramella, V., Enzymatic oligomerization of bacteriophage P22 DNA and of linear simian virus 40 DNA, *Proceedings of the National Academy of Sciences*, 69: 3389–93, 1972.

10 Scheller, R. H., Dickerson, R. E., Boyer, H. W., Riggs, A. D. and Itakura, K., Chemical synthesis of restriction enzyme recognition sites useful for cloning, *Science*, 196: 177–80, 1977.

11 Mandel, M. and Higa, A., Calcium-dependent bacteriophage DNA infection, *Journal of Molecular Biology*, 53: 159–62, 1970.

12 Cohen, S. N., Chang, A. C. Y. and Hsu, L., Nonchromosomal antibiotic resistance in bacteria: Genetic transformation of *Escherichia coli* by R-Factor DNA, *Proceedings of the National Academy of Sciences*, 69: 2110–14, 1972.

13 As note 1, p. 116.

14 Cohen, S. N., Chang, A. C. Y., Boyer, H. W. and Helling, R. B., Construction of biologically functional bacterial plasmids in vitro, *Proceedings of the National Academy of Sciences*, 70: 3240–4, 1973.

15 As note 1, p. 119.

16 Chang, A. C. Y. and Cohen, S. N., Genome construction between bacterial species in vitro: Replication and expression of *Staphylococcus* plasmid genes in *Escherichia coli, Proceedings of the National Academy of Sciences*, 71: 1030–4, 1974, p. 1033.

17 As note 1, p. 119.

18 Morrow, J. F., Cohen, S. N., Chang, A. C. Y., Boyer, H. W., Goodman, H. M. and Helling, R. B., Replication and transcription of eukaryotic DNA in *Escherichia coli, Proceedings of the National Academy of Sciences*, 71: 1743–7, 1974.

19 Bolivar, F., Rodriguez, R. L., Greene, P. J., Betlach, M. C., Heyneker, H. L., Boyer, H. W., Crosa, J. and Falkow, S., Construction and characterization of new cloning vehicles: II. A multi-purpose cloning system, *Gene*, 2: 95–113, 1977.

20 Thomas, M., Cameron, J. R. and Davis, R. W., Viable molecular hybrids of bacteriophage lambda and eukaryotic DNA, *Proceedings of the National Academy of Sciences*, 71: 4579–83, 1974.

21 Blattner, F. R., Williams, B. G., Blechl, A. E., Denniston-Thompson, K., Faber, H. E., Furlong, L.-A., Grunwald, D. J., Keifer, D. O., Moore, D. D., Schumm, J. W., Sheldon, E. L. and Smithies, O., Charon phages: Safer derivatives of bacteriophage lambda for DNA cloning, *Science*, 196: 161–9, 1977.

22 Hohn, B. and Murray, K., Packaging recombinant molecules in bacteriophage particles in vitro, *Proceedings of the National Academy of Sciences*, 74: 3259–63, 1977.

23 Collins, J. and Hohn. B., Cosmids: A type of plasmid gene-cloning vector that is packageable in vitro in bacteriophage λ heads, *Proceedings of the National Academy of Sciences*, 75: 4242–6, 1978.

24 Broome, S. and Gilbert, W., Immunological screening method to detect specific translation products, *Proceedings of the National Academy of Sciences*, 75: 2746–9, 1978.

25 Grunstein, M. and Hogness, D. S., Colony hybridization: A method for the isolation of cloned DNAs that contain a specific gene, *Proceedings of the National Academy of Sciences*, 72: 3961–5, 1975.

26 Paterson, B. M., Roberts, B. E. and Kuff, E. L., Structural gene identification and mapping by DNA.mRNA hybrid-arrested cell-free translation, *Proceedings of the National Academy of Sciences*, 74: 4370–4, 1977.

5 Unravelling

1 Wensink, P. C., Finnegan, D. J., Donelson, J. E. and Hogness, D. S., A system for mapping DNA sequences in the chromosomes of *Drosophila melanogaster, Cell*, 3: 315–25, 1974.

2 Clarke, L. and Carbon, J., Biochemical construction and selection of hybrid plasmids containing specific segments of the *Escherichia coli* genome, *Proceedings of the National Academy of Sciences,* 72: 4361–5, 1975.

3 Clarke, L. and Carbon, J., A colony bank containing synthetic Col E1 hybrid plasmids representative of the entire *E. coli* genome, *Cell*, 9: 91–9, 1976.

4 Maniatis, T., Hardison, R. C., Lacy, E., Lauer, J., O'Connell, C., Quon, D., Sim, G. K. and Efstratiadis A., The isolation of structural genes from libraries of eukaryotic DNA, *Cell*, 15: 687–701, 1978, p. 689.

5 Lawn, R. M., Fritsch, E. F., Parker, R. C., Blake, G. and Maniatis,

T., The isolation and characterization of linked δ- and β-globin genes from a cloned library of human DNA, *Cell*, 15: 1157–74, 1978.

6 Lewin, R., Evolutionary history written in globin genes, *Science*, 214: 426–9, 1981.

7 (Anon.), Banking DNA sequences, *Nature*, 285: 59, 1980.

8 (Anon.), letter to author, April 1982.

9 Wozney, J., Hanahan, D., Tate, V., Boedtker, H., and Doty, P., Structure of the pro α2(I) collagen gene, *Nature*, 294: 129–35, 1981.

10 Smith, A. J. H., DNA sequence analysis by primed synthesis, *Methods in Enzymology*, 65: 560–80, 1980.

11 Maxam, A. M., and Gilbert W., Sequencing end-labelled DNA with specific chemical cleavages, *Methods in Enzymology*, 65: 499–560, 1980.

12 Sanger, F., Determination of nucleotide sequences in DNA, *Science*, 214: 1205–10, 1981.

13 Gilbert, W., DNA sequencing and gene structure, *Science*, 214: 1305–12, 1981, p. 1310.

6 Regulation

1 Watson, J. D. and Tooze, J., *The DNA Story*, Freeman, San Francisco, 1981.

2 Sinsheimer, R., Troubled dawn for genetic engineering, *New Scientist*, 68: 148–51, 1975, p. 150.

3 Ibid., p. 151.

4 Singer, M. F. and Soll, D., DNA hybrid molecules, *Science*, 181: 1114, 1973.

5 Berg, P., Baltimore, D., Boyer, H. W., Cohen, S. N., Davis, R. W., Hogness, D. S., Nathans, D., Roblin, R., Watson, J. D., Weissmann, S. and Zinder, N. D., Potential biohazards of recombinant DNA molecules, *Science*, 185: 303, 1974.

6 Quoted in note 1, p. 38.

7 Jahoda, M., Once a jackass . . ., *Nature*, 295: 173–4, 1982, p. 173.

8 Brenner, S., Six months in category four, *Nature*, 276: 2–4, 1978, p. 2.

9 Quoted in Grobstein, C., *A Double Image of the Double Helix: The Recombinant-DNA Debate*, Freeman, San Francisco, 1979, p. 90.

10 Ibid.

11 As note 8.

12 Quoted in Dickson, D., DNA guidelines for further attenuation, *Nature*, 290: 281–2, 1981, p. 281.

13 (Anon.), Goodbye to guidelines, *Nature*, 295: 356, 1982.

14 As note 1, p. 262.
15 King, J., New diseases in new niches, *Nature*, 276: 4–7, 1978, pp. 6–7.

7 Applications

1 Panasenko, S., Cameron, J. R., Davis, R. W. and Lehman, I. R., Five hundredfold overproduction of DNA ligase after induction of a hybrid lambda lysogen constructed *in vitro, Science*, 196: 188–9, 1977.
2 Itakura, K., Hirose, T., Crea, R., Riggs, A. D., Heyneker, H. L., Bolivar, F. and Boyer, H. W., Expression in *Escherichia coli* of a chemically synthesized gene for the hormone somatostatin, *Science*, 198: 1056–63, 1977.
3 Ibid., p. 1059.
4 Newmark, P., Human growth hormone shortage persists, *Nature*, 294: 200–1, 1981.
5 Goeddel, D. V., Heyneker, H. L., Hozumi, T., Arentzen, R., Itakura, K., Yansura, D. G., Ross, M. J., Miozzari, G., Crea, R. and Seeburg, P., Direct expression in *Escherichia coli* of a DNA sequence coding for human growth hormone, *Nature*, 281: 544–8, 1979.
6 Ibid., p. 548.
7 Olson, K. C., Fenno, F., Lin, N., Harkins, R. N., Snider, C., Kohr, W. H., Ross, M. J., Fodge, D., Prender, G. and Stebbing, N., Purified human growth hormone from *E. coli* is biologically active, *Nature*, 293: 408–11, 1981.
8 Ibid., p. 410.
9 As note 4, pp. 200–1.
10 As note 5, p. 544.
11 Quoted in (anon.), Gene jugglers prepare foundations for insulin factory, *New Scientist*, 74: 515, 1977.
12 Villa-Komaroff, L., Efstratiadis, A., Broome, S., Lomedico, P., Tizard, R., Naber, S. P., Chick. W. L., and Gilbert, W., A bacterial clone synthesizing proinsulin, *Proceedings of the National Academy of Sciences*, 75: 3727–31, 1978.
13 Ibid., p. 3730.
14 Talmadge, K., Stahl, S. and Gilbert, W., Eukaryotic signal sequence transports insulin antigen in *Escherichia coli, Proceedings of the National Academy of Sciences*, 77: 3369–73, 1980, p. 3372.
15 Talmadge, K., Kaufman, J. and Gilbert, W., Bacteria mature preproinsulin to proinsulin, *Proceedings of the National Academy of Sciences*, 77: 3988–92, 1980.
16 Quoted in Lewin, R., How Genentech made human insulin, *New Scientist*, 79: 926, 1978.

17 Quoted in (anon.), Genetic engineers make human insulin, *New Scientist*, 79: 747, 1978.

18 Sures, I., Goeddel, D. V., Gray, A. and Ullrich, A., Nucleotide sequence of human preproinsulin complementary DNA, *Science*, 208: 57–9, 1980, p. 59.

19 Yanchinski, S., Genetic engineers battle over insulin, *New Scientist*, 88: 760, 1980.

20 Keen, H., Pickup, J. C., Bilous, R. W., Glynne, A., Viberti, G. C., Jarrett, R. J. and Marsden, R., Human insulin produced by recombinant DNA technology. Safety and hypoglycaemic potency in healthy men, *The Lancet*, II: 398–401, 1980, p. 398.

21 Le Roith, D., Shiloach, J., Roth, J., and Lesniak, M. A., Evolutionary origins of vertebrate hormones: substances similar to mammalian insulins are native to unicellular eukaryotes, *Proceedings of the National Academy of Sciences*, 77: 6184–8, 1980.

22 Cline, M. J., Stang, H., Mercola, K., Morse, L., Ruprecht, R., Browne, J. and Salser, W., Gene transfer in intact animals, *Nature*, 284: 422–5, 1980, p. 422.

23 Ibid., p. 425.

24 Quoted in Marx, J. L., Gene transfer given a new twist, *Science*, 208: 386–7, 1980, p. 387.

25 Mercola, K., Stang, H. D., Browne, W. and Cline, M., Insertion of a new gene of viral origin into bone marrow cells of mice, *Science*, 208: 1033–5, 1981.

26 As note 22, p. 425.

27 Wade, N., Gene therapy caught in more entanglements, *Science*, 212: 24–5, 1981.

28 Quoted in (anon.), Genetic engineer who broke the rules is punished – a little, *New Scientist*, 90: 605, 1981.

29 Quoted in Wade, N., UCLA gene therapy racked by friendly fire, *Science*, 210: 509–11, 1980, p. 510.

30 Ibid., p. 511.

31 Sun, M., Cline loses two NIH Grants, *Science*, 214: 1220, 1981.

8 Vaccines

1 Goeddel, D. V., Shepard H. M., Yelverton, E., Leung, D., Crea, R., Sloma, A. and Pestka, S., Synthesis of human fibroblast interferon by *E. coli*, *Nucleic Acids Research*, 8: 4057–74, 1980.

2 Taniguchi, T., Guarente, L., Roberts, T. M., Kimelman, D., Douhan, J. III, and Ptashne, M., Expression of the human fibroblast interferon gene in *Escherichia coli*, *Proceedings of the National Academy of Sciences*, 77: 5230–3, 1980.

3 Nagata, S., Taira, H., Hall, A., Johnsrud, L., Streuli, M., Ecsodi, J., Boll, W., Cantell, K. and Weissmann, C., Synthesis in *E. coli* of a polypeptide with human leukocyte interferon activity, *Nature*, 284: 316–20, 1980.

4 Goeddel, D. V., Yelverton, E., Ullrich, A., Heyneker, H. L., Miozzari. G., Holmes, W., Seeburg, P. H., Dull, T., May, L., Stebbing, N., Crea, R., Maeda, S., McCandliss, R., Sloma, A., Tabor, J. M., Gross, M., Familletti, P. C. and Pestka, S., Human leucocyte interferon produced by *E. coli* is biologically active, *Nature*, 287: 411–16, 1980.

5 Masucci, M. G., Szigeti, R., Klein, E., Klein, G., Gruest, J., Montagnier, L., Taira, H., Hall, A., Nagata, S. and Weissmann, C., Effect of interferon-α1 from *E. coli* on some cell functions, *Science*, 209: 1431–5, 1980, p. 1434.

6 Ibid., p. 1435.

7 Newmark, P., Interferon: decline and stall, *Nature*, 291: 105–6, 1981, p. 105.

8 Stebbing, N., quoted in a BBC World Service broadcast, Genes for Sale.

9 Hartley, B., quoted in a BBC World Service broadcast, Genes for Sale.

10 Edge, M. D., Greene, A. R., Heathcliffe, G. R., Meacock, P. A., Schuch, W., Scanlon, D. B., Atkinson, T. C., Newton, C. R. and Markham, A. F., Total synthesis of a human leucocyte interferon gene, *Nature*, 292: 756–62, 1981.

11 Ibid., p. 761.

12 (Anon.), The longest synthetic gene . . . so far, *Nature*, 292: 667. 1981.

13 As note 10, p. 761.

14 Brooksby, J. B., Genetic engineering and foot and mouth disease vaccines, *Nature* 289: 535, 1981.

15 Boothroyd, J. C., Highfield, P. E., Cross, G. A. M., Rowlands, D. J., Lowe, P. A., Brown, F. and Harris, T. J. R., Molecular cloning of foot and mouth disease virus genome and nucleotide sequences in the structural protein genes, *Nature*, 290: 800–2, 1981.

16 Küpper, H., Keller, W., Kurz, C., Forss, S., Schaller, H., Franze, R., Strohmaier, K., Marquardt, O., Zaslavsky, V. G. and Hofschneider, P. H., Cloning of cDNA of major antigen of foot and mouth disease virus and expression in *E. coli, Nature*: 289: 555–9, 1981, p. 559.

17 As note 14.

18 Hardy, K., Stahl, S. and Küpper H., Production in *B. subtilis* of hepatitis B core antigen and of major antigen of foot and mouth disease virus, *Nature*, 293: 481–3, 1981.

19 As note 14.

20 Kleid, D. G., Yansura, D., Small, B., Dowbenko, D., Moore, D. M., Grubman, M. H., McKercher, P. D., Morgan, D. O., Robertson, B. H. and Bachrach, H. L., Cloned viral protein vaccine for foot-and-mouth disease: responses in cattle and swine, *Science*, 214: 1125–9, 1981, p. 1128.

21 Edman, J. C., Hallewell, R. A., Valenzuela, P., Goodman, H. and Rutter, W. J., Synthesis of hepatitis B surface and core antigens in *E. coli, Nature*, 291: 503–6, 1981.

22 Gething, M.-J. and Sambrook, J., Cell-surface expression of influenza haemagglutinin from a cloned DNA copy of the RNA gene, *Nature*, 293: 620–5, 1981.

23 Kitamura, N., Semler, B. L., Rothberg, P. G., Larsen, G., Adler, C. J., Dorner, A. J., Emini, E. A., Hanecak, R., Lee, J. J., van der Werf, S., Anderson, C. W. and Wimmer, E., Primary structure, gene organization and polypeptide expression of poliovirus RNA, *Nature*, 291: 547–53, 1981.

24 Audibert, F., Jolivet, M., Chedid, L., Alouf, J. E., Boquet, P., Rivaille, P. and Siffert, O., Active antitoxic immunization by a diphtheria toxin synthetic oligopeptide, *Nature*, 289: 593–4, 1981.

25 Anilionis, A., Wunner, W. H. and Curtis, P. J., Structure of the glycoprotein gene in rabies virus, *Nature*, 294: 275–8, 1981.

26 Köhler, G. and Milstein, C., Continuous cultures of fused cells secreting antibody of predefined specificity, *Nature*, 256: 495–7, 1975. Milstein, C., Monoclonal antibodies, *Scientific American*, October 1980, 56–65.

9 Exploitation

1 Crespi, S., Patenting nature's secrets and protecting microbiologists' interests, *Nature*, 284: 590–1, 1980, p. 590.

2 Quoted in Wade, N., Court says lab-made life can be patented, *Science*, 208: 1445, 1980.

3 As note 1, p. 590.

4 Quoted in Dickson, D., Inventorship dispute stalls DNA patent application, *Nature*, 284: 388, 1980.

5 (Anon.), Stanford's patent prize, *Nature*, 292: 571–2, 1981, p. 572.

6 Wade, N., University and drug firm battle over billion-dollar gene, *Science*, 209: 1492–4, 1980, p. 1492.

7 Ibid., p. 1492.

8 Quoted in note 6, p. 1492.

9 Ibid., p. 1493.

10 As note 6, p. 1494.

11 Quoted in Dickson, D., Backlash against DNA ventures?, *Nature*, 288: 203, 1981.

12 King, J., press conference at the annual meeting of the American Association for the Advancement of Science, Washington DC, 5 January 1982.

13 King, J., conversation with author, Washington DC, 6 January 1982.

14 As note 12.

15 Dickson, D., US industry moves into biotechnology, *Nature*, 292: 397, 1981.

16 As note 13.

17 Wade, N., Gilbert may leave Harvard for Biogen, *Science*, 214: 526–7, 1981, p. 527.

18 Quoted in ibid., p. 527.

19 Quoted in Norman, C., MIT agonizes over links with research unit, *Science*, 214: 416–17, 1981, p. 417.

20 Watson, J. D. and Tooze, J., *The DNA Story*, Freeman, San Francisco, 1981, p. 490.

21 Rich, V., Keeping a secret, *Nature*, 295: 275, 1982.

22 Stein, M. D., UN plans centre, *Nature*, 293: 600, 1981.

23 Omenn, G., conversation with author, Washington DC, 5 January 1982.

24 As note 13.

10 Rethinking

1 Quoted in Kolata, G., Z-DNA: from the crystal to the fly, *Science*, 214, 1108–10, p. 1108.

2 Ibid., p. 1109.

3 Watson, J. D., *The Double Helix*, Atheneum, New York, 1968, p. 7.

4 Patrusky, B., Split genes: more questions than answers, *Mosaic*, 10(5): 38–44, 1979, p. 39.

5 Ibid.

6 Ibid., p. 42.

7 Sambrook, J., Adenovirus amazes at Cold Spring Harbor, *Nature*, 268: 101–4, 1977, p. 102.

8 Borst, P. and Grivell, L. A., One gene's intron is another gene's exon, *Nature*, 289: 439–40, 1981.

9 Quoted in Lewin, R., How conversational are genes?, *Science*, 212: 313–15, 1981, p. 314.

10 Gilbert, W., Why genes in pieces?, *Nature*, 271: 501, 1978.
11 As note 4, p. 44.
12 Quoted in Robertson, M., Gene families, hopeful monsters and the selfish genetics of DNA, *Nature*, 293: 333–4, 1981, p. 334.

11 Outlook

1 Lewin, R., Biggest challenge since the double helix, *Science*, 212: 28–32, 1981, p. 29.
2 Wetzel, R., Applications of recombinant DNA technology, *American Scientist*, 68: 664–75, 1980, p. 674.
3 Tudge, C., *Future Cook: Politics, Philosophy and Recipes for the 21st Century*, Harmony Books, New York, 1980, p. 21.
4 Windass, J. D., Worsey, M. J., Pioli, E. M., Pioli, D., Barth, P. T., Atherton, K. T., Dart, E. C., Byrom, D., Powell, K. and Senior, P. J., Improved conversion of methanol to single-cell protein by *M. methylotrophus*, *Nature*, 287: 369–401, 1980, p. 401.
5 Quoted in Berry, A., Genetic weapons 'pose threat that rivals plague', *Daily Telegraph*, 16 October 1981.
6 Patrusky, B., Split genes: more questions than answers, *Mosaic*, 10(5): 38–44, 1979, p. 44.

GLOSSARY

Adenine A purine nucleic acid base. It pairs with thymine in DNA and uracil in RNA.

Amber A class of mutations that causes protein manufacture to stop prematurely. It is caused by a change in the genetic code which puts a 'stop' sign in the wrong place.

Amino acids The basic building blocks of proteins. There are many types, but only 20 are found commonly in living organisms.

Antibody A protein manufactured by the immune system in response to the presence of an antigen. Each antibody is shaped to fit precisely to its antigen and help destroy it.

Anticodon The region by which a tRNA molecule recognizes a codon on mRNA.

Antigen A substance, usually foreign in origin, that causes the immune system to manufacture antibodies.

Bacteria A major class of prokaryotes, the simplest organisms that can reproduce unaided.

Bacteriophages Viruses that infect bacteria.

Base Part of the building blocks of nucleic acids. There are two types, purines, and pyrimidines.

Biocontainment A method for preventing bacteria and other similar organisms from escaping. As well as being confined by physical barriers, the bacteria are chosen so that they need certain substances, which are not found in nature, to grow.

Biopolymers Long chain-like molecules made by living things. Proteins are polymers of amino acid monomers, while cellulose and starch are biopolymers made from sugar monomers.

Chimera An organism, or a piece of DNA, constructed from two different species.

Chromatography A technique for separating a mixture of substances. A solution of the mixture is poured on to a special medium and carried through it by solvents. Each component travels at a characteristic speed that depends on its identity.

Chromosomes Strictly speaking, structures in the nucleus that contain the hereditary message. They are made of DNA in association with proteins. The naked DNA of prokaryotes is, however, often called a chromosome.

Clones The genetically identical (that is, asexual) decendants of a single organism.

Cloning vectors Used to put DNA into a cell.

Coding sequence The region of a gene that is expressed, that is, translated into protein. Also called an exon.

Codon The three-letter words of the genetic code. Each codon (not counting the punctuation marks) specifies a particular amino acid.

Complementation A genetic technique in which the scientist provides a working copy of a gene to enable cells with a defective copy of that gene to grow.

Cosmid A cloning vehicle that attaches foreign DNA to the packaging sites of a virus and thus packages the foreign DNA into an infective viral particle.

Crystallograph A picture produced by bombarding crystals with X-rays. It can be interpreted to show the internal arrangement of the molecules of the crystal.

Cytosine A pyrimidine nucleic acid base. It pairs with guanine.

Deoxyribose The sugar of DNA.

Dimer Two monomers linked together; the smallest possible polymer.

DNA Deoxyribonucleic acid, which carries the hereditary message in most forms of life.

Double helix The usual structure of DNA molecules, with complementary strands twined around one another.

Electrophoresis A technique for separating a mixture of substances. It uses an electric current to move the substances, each of which travels at a characteristic speed that depends on its identity.

Enzymes Biological catalysts. They are proteins that enable chemical reactions to take place at lower temperatures, and they are responsible for the biochemistry of the cell.

Eukaryotes A major class of living things, often considered to be more highly organized than prokaryotes. They possess a well-defined nucleus which contains the DNA.

Exon The region of a gene that is expressed, that is, translated into protein. A better term is 'coding sequence'.

Genes Stretches of nucleic acid that code for a specific protein. (This applies to molecular biology; one can also speak of genes for particular traits, which may not correspond to single stretches of nucleic acid.)

Genetic code The relationship between the triplet codons on the nucleic acids and the amino acids in proteins.

Genome The entire hereditary message of an organism.

Guanine A purine nucleic acid base. It pairs with cytosine.

Hormones Chemical messengers of the body, carried in the bloodstream from a gland to a target organ.

Induction The process that causes a provirus earlier inserted into the host cell's DNA to break free and start to multiply.

Intervening sequence The region of a gene that is not expressed as protein, being spliced out of the primary transcript before the protein is made. Also called an intron.

Intron The region of a gene that is not expressed as protein, being spliced out of the primary transcript before the protein is made. A better term is 'intervening sequence'.

Leukocyte A white blood cell.

Library A collection of hosts that between them carry the entire genome of an organism.

Ligase An enzyme that joins DNA strands together.

Lysis The breaking of a cell wall. May be achieved physically, chemically, or by a virus multiplying inside the cell.

Messenger RNA (mRNA) Carries the genetic code for a protein from the DNA to the ribosomes, where the code is read and the protein manufactured.

Mitochondria The powerhouses of the cell. They transfer chemical energy from foods to energy-rich storage compounds that can then be used to power chemical reactions elsewhere in the cell.

Modification enzyme The counterpart to restriction enzyme. It marks the recognition site by chemically modifying some of the bases, so the restriction enzyme can no longer cut the DNA.

Molecule A complex of two or more atoms held together by chemical bonds.

Monoclonal antibody An antibody derived from a single clone of antibody-producing cells. It is therefore extremely pure.

Monomers The units that combine to form a polymer.

mRNA Messenger RNA.

Mutation Any change in the genetic material.

Nucleases Enzymes that destroy nucleic acids.

Nucleic acids The repositories of genetic information. They consist of a chain of alternating sugars and phosphates; attached to each sugar is a base, a letter of the genetic code.

Nucleoside A base attached to a sugar.

Nucleotide The building blocks of nucleic acids. They consist of a sugar which has a base attached to one atom and a phosphate group to another. Bonds between the phosphate group of one nucleotide and the sugar of another link the chain.

Nucleus The region of a eukaryote cell that contains the DNA.

Operon A group of genes that occur together on the DNA, responsible for some aspect of metabolism. The genes are all under the control of a single regulator.

Palindromic Reading the same backwards and forwards (e.g. the word 'level'). In nucleic acid sequences, especially restriction enzyme recognition sites, it means that the two strands of the double helix carry the same sequence of bases.

Pathogen An organism that causes disease.

Phage Short for 'bacteriophage'.

Phosphate group A molecule of phosphorus and oxygen that can store energy. Links the nucleotides of a nucleic acid polymer.

Plaque A small hole formed in a lawn of bacteria by the spread of bacteriophage from a single infected cell.

Plasmid A small circle of DNA that can reproduce independently of the main chromosomes. Can transfer from one cell to another, even across species.

Polymerase An enzyme that catalyses the growth of a nucleic acid chain.

Primary transcript The first transcription of DNA into RNA. It is processed into messenger RNA.

Prokaryotes Living things that do not contain a distinct nucleus.

Prophage A bacteriophage that has become integrated into the host cell's DNA.

Provirus A virus that has become integrated into the host cell's DNA.

Purine A type of base of nucleic acids. Adenine and guanine are purines.

Pyrimidine A type of base of nucleic acids. Uracil, thymine and cytosine are pyrimidines.

Recombinant DNA A single molecule combining DNA from two distinct sources.

Restriction enzyme An enzyme that recognizes a specific base sequence on DNA and cuts the DNA. Some restriction enzymes cut the DNA at a particular point, others at random.

Ribose The sugar of RNA.

Ribosome A small body made of RNA and proteins. The site of protein synthesis.

RNA Ribonucleic acid. Generally acts as an adjunct to DNA helping to carry out the genetic instructions on the DNA; however, some viruses store their genetic information as RNA rather than DNA.

Shotgun A technique for breaking the entire genome of an organism into small pieces and inserting all those pieces into suitable hosts to form a gene library.

Thymine A pyrimidine nucleic acid base. It pairs with adenine.

Transcription The synthesis of RNA from a DNA template.

Transferase An enzyme that attaches new bases to the end of a nucleic acid chain.

Transfer RNA (tRNA) The molecule that ferries amino acids to the ribosomes, where an anticodon on the tRNA reads the codon on the mRNA and inserts the required amino acid into the growing protein chain.

Transformation The process whereby a piece of foreign DNA is taken up by a cell and gives that cell new properties.

Translation The conversion of the genetic code on mRNA into a protein.

tRNA Transfer RNA.

Uracil A pyrimidine base found only in RNA. It pairs with adenine.

Vectors Used to transfer DNA into cells.

Virus The smallest type of organism. Viruses cannot reproduce on their own, but have to infect a cell and usurp its machinery.

FURTHER READING

The field is moving so fast that few books, this one included, can be thought of as up to date. The second edition of *Principles of Gene Manipulation* by R. W. Old and S. B. Primrose (University of California Press, Berkeley, 1980) is an excellent advanced guide. For the latest developments, very little slips past the collective attention of *Nature, New Scientist* and *Science*.

Index

About the Author

Jeremy Cherfas, formerly biology editor at *New Scientist*, now divides his time between teaching in the zoology department at Oxford University and science writing for publication and broadcast. He has written a number of books, the latest of which is *The Monkey Puzzle*, co-authored with John Gribbin.